DEMYSTIFYING SUCCESS

Success Tools and Secrets They Don't Teach You in High School

LARRY M. JACOBSON, MBA, Ed.D

T.I.M.E.
INSTITUTE LLC

Copies of the book are available at special quantity discounts for sales promotions, training, fundraising, or educational use. The author is also available for speaking engagements, keynotes, seminars, and other multimedia presentations.

Published by:
T.I.M.E. Institute, LLC
1107 Fair Oaks Avenue #141
South Pasadena, CA 91030
www.timeinstitutellc.com

Layout and cover design by Susie Ward, SGWDesign.com

Copyedited by Kate Sancer Jacobson, T.I.M.E. Institute, LLC

Printed in the United States of America

Demystifying Success: Success Tools and Secrets They Don't Teach You in High School
Larry M. Jacobson
1. Title 2. Author 3. Personal Development 4. Personal Finance

Library of Congress Control Number: 2013955935

ISBN: 978-0-9910803-0-4

Acknowledgements

I dedicate this book to:

My mother, Susan Jacobson, and my grandmother, Anne Wasserlauf, for all of their love and support. If not for their ultimate courage and sacrifices, this book would never have been possible to share with all of you!

And of course, my beautiful and talented wife, Sharon-Kate Sancer Jacobson, for her long hours of dedication, support, and incredible creativity on this important endeavor!

To my family, friends, and mentors whom I'd also like to thank and recognize for their assistance, guidance, and support throughout the years, and without whom this book would not have been possible: Dr. Donald Jacobson, Leigh Jacobson-Benowitz, Jeffrey Jacobson, Sidney Wasserlauf, Frances Schneider, David Moonitz, Cathy Jacobson, Jay Benowitz, Shari Kellner-Jacobson, Hailey Benowitz, Abby Benowitz, Sam Jacobson, Marli Jacobson, Olivia Jacobson, Eric Mandell, Vinnie Freda, Dr. Ennette Morton, Janet Mroz, Scott R. Miller, Lynne Campion, Adam Isrow, John E. Wakefield, Dr. David N. Baker, Kenny Aronoff, Christy Whitman, Dr. Nikolai Wasilewski, Randy Chaplin, Todd Davis, Dan Manns, Viki Winterton, Annie Mello.

Contents

Introduction 1

    Be the Change You Wish to Be 7

    Structure of This Book 9

    How to Read This Book 10

    A Final Word of Advice 12

Chapter 1: Managing Your Fears 15
What would you do if you weren't afraid?

    Learning to Manage Your Fears 18

Chapter 2: Awareness 25
So, how's that life working for you?

    The Power of Awareness 26

    Give Yourself an Honest Reality Check 29

    Can an Iced Tea Impact Your Overall Success? 34

    Probability versus Possibility 36

    Life Lessons for Success 41

    Call to Action 44

Chapter 3: Who Are You Really? 47
Do you suffer from a bad case of mood-poisoning?

    Healthy Personal Relationships 52

    The Friends Exercise 56

    For Better or For Worse 62

    King or Queen of Your Castle 66

    Mentors and Masterminds 68

    Network, Network, Network 71

    Call to Action 76

Chapter 4: The Business of YOU 79

Be YOU, because everyone else is taken.

Your Actions Speak Louder Than Words 87

Your Health: Nutrition and Exercise 91

Nutrition 94

Exercise 96

Call to Action 101

Chapter 5: Making the Grade? 103

How you choose to use your time determines your quality of life.

Creating Study Plans 107

From the Classroom to the Boardroom 111

Word Associations 114

Utilizing All Available Tools for Success 116

Call to Action 117

Chapter 6: See Your Future, Be Your Future 119

Dreams are for bedtime, goals are for success.

Change Your Thoughts, Change Your Life! 119

Dreams are for Bedtime, Goals are for Success! 123

Operation Three Sixty Five 129

Positivity is a Key Secret for Success 133

Finding Your Right Balance for Success 148

Call to Action 155

Chapter 7: No Nonsense Decision-Making! 157

*Do your decisions dictate your situations, or do your
situations dictate your decisions?*

The Strategy of Decision-Making 158

Your Intentions Drive Your Decisions 163

Can Making Mistakes Enhance Your Success? 166

The Art of the Pause 175

Follow Your Passion for Success 179

Call to Action 186

Chapter 8: The Dollars and Sense for Creating Your Wealth 191

Are you a wealth creator, or do you suffer from "'financial obesity"?

So What IS Personal Finance? 194

Defining Your Own Financial Success 198

Understanding the Value of Money 207

How to Strategically Define and Create Your Future Wealth...216

Lessons to Help You Grow Your Future Wealth 219

Unleash Your Successful Wealth Creator 238

Will You Be Able to Ride Off into the Sunset? 239

Call to Action... 244

Chapter 9: Epilogue 249

Where Do You Begin? 251

Embrace the "Why?" 252

T.I.M.E. for Success 253

Invest in Yourself 255

Appendix.. 257

The Four Quadrants for Life Balance 259

Monthly Expense Model...261

About the Author 263

Introduction

When I set out to write *Demystifying Success*, I wanted to provide young adults (ages 16 to 25) with the needed tools, techniques, and personal/financial guidelines to help them grow success on their own terms. I also wanted to help educate anyone else who never really learned these important lessons from an early age. I knew I wanted to design this book to be practical and straightforward so you could immediately jump in, reach your goals, and achieve success as soon as possible. As such, I chose to candidly share personal stories of my own failures and successes to help you avoid the very same pitfalls which have prevented so many others from achieving their ultimate life-long success.

Sadly, the majority of the information and educational concepts shared in this book are currently not being taught in most U.S. high schools and colleges. Honestly, I find it shocking that for a country that prides itself on its technological and educational advances, most of its population is financially illiterate—and through no fault of their own. How can parents and teachers be expected to educate young adults when they themselves are lacking this very same knowledge? The answer is they can't. And as a result, more and more young adults are now entering the real world financially illiterate and ill-prepared to achieve their future success. To help do my part, I felt inspired to write this book because I am passionate and dedicated toward helping others break the generational cycle of financial illiteracy.

We, as a society, have been negligent in helping to prepare our young adults for their future success. I believe it is now our obligation to begin the long-overdue process of educating future generations, like yourself, with solid personal and financial foundations. These crucial life skills include personal finance, strategic decision-making, goal-setting, plan implementation, and evaluation—tools that are necessary for our society to continue to compete and thrive in our ever-changing global economy. The need for these life skills to be understood and incorporated into daily lives is clearly evident by the financial turmoil experienced by more and more adults between the ages of 40 to 60. This group in particular suffers from a national epidemic that I refer to as, "financial obesity"—one's obsessive and self-sabotaging need to constantly overspend and remain financially unhealthy. In fact, since 2008, one can rarely open up a newspaper, go online, or turn on a TV without reading or hearing about the growing economic concerns regarding the lack of wealth and employment in this country.

In case you get the urge to beat yourself up for something that might not be within your control—stop and realize that you have now chosen to read this book because you *want* to change your path and create the successful life you desire. If you feel bad or ashamed about lacking these skills—don't! When I graduated high school and college, I still didn't know these important tips and secrets either. I had to discover many of these concepts on my own because either no one around me knew them, or they chose not to let me in on their secrets. Whatever the reason, I had to learn my lessons the hard way. Because on top of my basic lack of confidence and insecurities at that time, I was also too naïve to know what questions I should have been asking to help improve my future. So back in 1992, after plenty of personal failures and successes, I took it upon myself to finally figure out, and break down, how successful people earned and cultivated their wealth. And since I wished I was privy to these secrets back when I was your age, I consider it a privilege to be able to share and demystify them with you now.

So, who am I, Larry M. Jacobson, to be a "groundbreaking authority" on success? And why should you bother to listen to what I have to say on the subject? Well, to help give you some perspective, my personal successes include:

- Contributing author for two #1 international best-selling books: *Ready, Aim, Influence! Join Forces, Expand Resources, Transform Your World* and *Ready, Aim, Captivate! Put Magic in Your Message and a Fortune in Your Future*

- 22-year career as a record executive with the world's largest music and publishing company

- Completion of four academic degrees in music and business

- Member of several national honorary academic societies in college such as Omicron Delta Kappa (National Leadership Honor Society), Golden Key Honor Society, Alpha Lambda Delta, and Phi Eta Sigma

- Treasurer/Chief Financial Officer for the University of Maryland School of Music's Board of Visitors and the Los Angeles Leggers Running Club

- Continuing guest speaker and keynote speaker for colleges, universities, and corporations which include Indiana University, University of Maryland, Berklee College of Music, Marriott International, and others

- Online Trading Academy graduate for proactive stock trading and investing, options, foreign exchange (Forex), and e-mini futures

- Finished three full-marathons and nine half-marathons

- Networked at several "meet and greet" events with prominent business people and world leaders such as billionaire investor, Warren Buffett, basketball legend and entrepreneur, Magic Johnson, American Idol judge and musician, Randy Jackson, best-selling author and speaker, Michael E. Gerber, ABC's Secret Millionaire, James Malinchak, and the late President, Ronald Reagan, amongst others

- Worked as a professional on-air radio personality for different FM radio stations

- Attended numerous Grammy Award ceremonies and one Academy Awards (Oscars) event

- And, most importantly, through continually working hard on improving myself, I now enjoy healthy and fulfilling relationships with my family, colleagues, and friends—which creates an overall life balance of wellness, happiness, and success.

But before I begin demystifying secrets for your success in this book, I would like to share a little bit about my story, and how I got to this particular point in my life.

I was fortunate to have grown up during the 1970s in a very competitive suburban Long Island neighborhood, made up of second and third generation European descendants. However, like most immigrants, my grandparents and great-grandparents came to this country with very little money and found themselves having to assimilate with many different types of cultures. Through their hard work ethic and their pursuit of the American dream, they were able to provide my parents with a moderate to middle class background—both of my parents were not too wealthy growing up.

They were both exposed to various aspects of poverty, but eventually became the first in their families to go to college and pursue greater opportunities (thanks to my grandparents).

My parents met as students at City College in Queens, New York. After graduation, they got married and my father went on to attend dental school at Temple University in Philadelphia, Pennsylvania. Upon graduation, he became a successful oral surgeon in Brooklyn, New York. My mother, who had been a teacher during that time, decided to go back to graduate school since my younger brother, sister, and I, were all older and more self-sufficient. She earned a master's degree in Psychology from C.W. Post College on Long Island. Education was important to both of my parents, but especially to my mother. It was always her desire that my brother, sister, and I, all earn master's degrees so that we could always rely on a strong educational background.

During my sophomore year in high school, my parents got divorced. I was 15 years old and it had a profoundly negative effect on me. It became harder and harder to remain focused on my schoolwork, so my grades began to suffer. In fact, I had so many after-school tutors that I used to joke and tell everyone I was homeschooled. I muddled through, eventually graduated high school, and then went off to college. I attended the University of Maryland to pursue a music performance degree in percussion. It wasn't until my first semester at Maryland that I finally taught myself how to study—which became the cornerstone of my life-long time management success. As my grades improved, I even made the dean's list for my academic excellence.

Following my graduation from Maryland, I went on to pursue my master's degree in music for jazz studies and percussion performance at Indiana University. After I became the Indiana University Union Board Concert Director and fostered a network of music industry contacts, I knew that I wanted to pursue a career in the music industry once I graduated. I managed to forge a positive working relationship with Creative Arts Agency (CAA) agent Brett Steinberg, who was kind enough to introduce me to his friend, a "young, up-and-coming record executive" at MCA Records, Vinnie Freda. Vinnie and I hit it off, and he hired me to work with him in the recording administration department just two weeks after I graduated from Indiana University. During my 22-year tenure with MCA Records/Universal Music Group (UMG), I was promoted up the ranks from summer intern to Vice President of Financial Services for North America. While busy climbing the corporate ladder, I realized that I could no longer succeed with only my music degrees, so I decided to go back to school. I completed my master of business administration and doctor of education in organizational leadership degrees at Pepperdine University while working full-time at UMG.

All of these experiences have contributed to helping me formulate my principles and strategies for demystifying personal and financial success. After attending numerous seminars and webinars delivered by prominent speakers and educators, as well as having read countless books by best-selling authors on the subject of personal happiness and success, I have finally written the book that I wish someone had handed to *me* back when I was in high school and college. If I would have had the knowledge that I am now sharing with you in this book, it would have helped me to become one of the fortunate 3% of the population that was exposed, from an early age, to good money management and solid financial and personal habits. It would have given me, like those lucky 3%, the confidence and discipline to create my own personal goals and plans toward achieving my success. This is the same goal I have for you—I want you to rise to the top and accomplish whatever you choose to do.

Over the last several years, I have spoken and shared my life experiences and principles with many of my students, family, and friends. And I have been fortunate to witness them achieve their own breakthrough successes by applying my strategies to their own lives—

positively transforming their careers, relationships, and personal finances. As a young adult, I believe that if you commit and invest in your success today by choosing to adopt and follow the principles and lessons that I have provided in this book, then you will start off with more knowledge and information than the majority of your fellow classmates—and even possibly more than your parents, teachers, and friends—which will enable you to go on and successfully pursue all of your life goals and desires.

Be the Change You Wish to Be

At the age of 32, I was a young man filled with many regrets about missed opportunities. After several failed attempts over the years to shortcut my way to success, I finally asked myself a brutally honest question, "So, how's that life working for you?" The answer wasn't pretty. But it finally helped me to realize why I kept making such poor personal and financial decisions that delayed me from achieving my success earlier. In fact, it was that life-changing revelation that finally got me to take my first action steps toward turning my goals into a reality. While sitting in my two-bedroom apartment in Sherman Oaks, California one night in 1996, I decided to send President Bill Clinton an email at the White House about four core subjects that I believed were either being ignored or omitted from our nation's high school curriculum, and I felt that they should be taught in every high school in this country: personal finance, self-esteem, personal development (planning and goal setting), and time management—the four topics that I now address in great detail throughout this book.

A few weeks after I sent my email, I received a response letter back from the White House, signed by President Clinton. The President thanked me for sharing my ideas, and outlined his administration's agenda to enact their Education 2000 program. Now here we are, approaching nearly 20 years later, and despite my best efforts in reaching out to the President, the near collapse of our entire financial infrastructure in 2008, and the ongoing cycle of generational misinformation surrounding financial illiteracy in our public school systems, I am grateful that I am finally in a position to share this hard-earned knowledge with you today. This information is designed to help educate young adults address the misperceptions surrounding money and spending (as well as many of the underlying emotional reasons why so many adults today struggle with "financial obesity"). The information in this book is timeless. It can be learned and shared amongst students, parents, and teachers in order to ensure that young adults (ages 16 – 25), and adults of all ages, grow to be excellent money managers and wealth creators.

This is not a "dream and feel-good" book. I take real-world knowledge, gleaned from my own personal and financial experiences, and suggest actionable ideas while also providing easy-to-follow, step-by-step examples and exercises so that you can immediately start to apply your newfound understanding and begin building your own future success. To quote an old Chinese proverb, "You can give a man a fish and you can feed him for a day. Teach a man to fish and you feed him for a lifetime." It is always better to invest in your success and teach yourself something new, rather than rely on others to do it for you. By enhancing your own knowledge base, especially when it concerns your financial and personal success, you will be empowering yourself to break and/or avoid bad habits and patterns in the future.

The fact is, anyone who is willing to take the time to read, adopt, and incorporate the principles in this book will have a huge advantage over the majority of Americans who barely survive above the current poverty level. And since you are reading this, it's clear you've decided to really commit to your continued personal improvement! Therefore, that advantage will be yours for the taking provided you also commit the time to complete all of the Calls to Action presented throughout this book. By doing so, you will greatly increase your odds for success as you will truly be investing in yourself to improve your own long-term personal and financial outcomes.

Structure of This Book

I truly do want to help you become one of the advantaged 3% of all young adults who learn how to achieve their desired goals and success from an early age. To do this, I am going to show you how to focus your awareness in order to identify opportunities and evaluate your *probable* outcomes for success by teaching you good financial habits, how to establish concrete personal goals, and how to create action steps to accomplish them. To help you demystify your success, I have organized this book into four sections:

Section I: Self-Awareness

This section focuses on concepts and experiences associated with self-discovery. You will start by distinguishing between *probability* (what will likely be), versus possibility (what could be) to become more aware of when to take advantage of the right opportunities when they arise. Next, I cover how "happiness" is nothing more than a positive state of mind that is primarily influenced by how you feel about yourself (self-esteem). Like the great American industrialist, Henry Ford, once said, "Whether you believe you can or you can't, you are right." Lastly, I cover the power of creating your authentic "personal brand" and the importance of sound mental and physical health. By heightening your self-awareness and improving your self-esteem, your overall confidence and unique personal brand will improve and pave the way for greater future success.

Section II: Developing Your Tools for Success

This section addresses good time management skills and action steps for success. Your quality of life is often determined by how well you utilize your time. I will teach you how to control time rather than allowing time to control you. You will learn why good study habits in school, from an early age, will ultimately lead to a successful work ethic in your professional life. Next, I will share my personal goal-setting techniques and secrets that have allowed me to become president of several organizations, a student/protégé of such musical legends as Dr. David N. Baker and Kenny Aronoff, as well as success models I designed to help empower you to build and enhance your own strengths and goals to succeed.

Section III: Taking Action

Successfully executing your life-long goals is all about aligning yourself (who you are, right now) with all of the knowledge and experiences that you have acquired throughout your life. In this section, you will learn *why* aligning your intentions with your strategic decisions often lead to *probable* outcomes for success when opportunities arise.

Section IV: Wealth Creation

Since money is a key component to both financial security and personal success, in this last section I will show you how to properly manage and budget your money so that you can live a very happy and fulfilling life. I will also share my wealth-creating model that will help you understand how the very wealthy continue to increase their wealth over time, as well as educate you on the importance of saving your income, managing your debt, and monitoring your spending habits so you can avoid the same financial pitfalls (e.g., *financial obesity*) that currently plague so many adults.

How to Read This Book

"Keep away from people who try to belittle your ambitions. Small people always do that, but the really great make you feel that you, too, can become great." ~ Mark Twain

As we all know, there are no guarantees in life. However, if you choose to adopt and follow the basic concepts and lessons I address in this book, you should be able to make more timely and strategic decisions that will positively impact your personal and financial success. It is my intention that this book not only serve as a reference guide for you now, but in the future as well. As you can tell, I cover a lot of important information here. Therefore, so you'll be more prepared to immediately begin creating your personal and financial success, I would like to offer the following suggestions when you're reading this book to make the material more manageable.

My first suggestion is to read through the entire book once so that you grasp how the chapters and sections build upon one another. Hold off on working through the Calls to Action for your second read. The purpose of this book is to take you through a journey of self-discovery by helping you to identify and realign your current self, with your future (more successful) self. As such, each section of this book will provide you with the tools, techniques, and knowledge to accomplish this goal. If you skip around, you may fail to connect the dots. It might then take you longer to accomplish your goals, or even worse, you might develop bad habits that will need to be unlearned before you can realign yourself again with your long-term goals.

After you read this book once, when you go through and read it again, I suggest that you really interact with the material. Make the information your own—highlight the sections that resonate the most with you, pick up a separate notebook to write down your thoughts, and work through all the Calls to Action at the end of the designated chapters. Most importantly, if you come across a term or concept that you are not sure of, look it up! The purpose of this book is to impart knowledge to help YOU, and you do not want to sell yourself short by cutting corners. When reading this book for the second time, you will want to read one chapter at a time while making sure to take the time to complete all of the

Calls to Action provided at the end of each chapter (again, cutting corners may cost you future opportunities). How many people do you know who can simply pick up a musical instrument and start playing, or start off running a marathon without ever having run a mile before, or speak a new language without any instruction? Not many. The only way you will learn any new skill is by committing yourself to the process and then doing the work. The Calls to Action at the end of the chapters are very important to your educational and strategic outcomes for success. So take whatever time you need to carefully write out and complete each exercise in this book. Since repetition is the key to retaining information, I highly recommend that you reread your highlighted sections and review your notes and responses to the Calls to Action on a regular basis: quarterly, semiannually, and annually to reassess your progress and growth. Remember, you are always welcome to modify or add to your prior chapter Calls to Action. The more frequently you review, the more comfortable you will become with executing your plans to achieve your goals.

Finally, you might find it helpful to select a mentor, friend, or family member who can help you accomplish the goals that you set for yourself after reading this book. Remember, true change only occurs when you take the required action to be the change you wish to be.

A Final Word of Advice

"We cannot teach people anything; we can only help them discover it within themselves." ~ *Galileo*

Within this book, I have provided you with both theoretical (the why), and practical (the how) knowledge that I have acquired from my own, and others', past experiences to help you navigate your life around potential obstacles and pitfalls. Despite your enthusiasm to read and master all of the information and material offered in this book, you will need to be patient while you absorb and assimilate it.

Initially, you may feel impatient and anxious, even confused by the information that I am providing, because it is new or it goes against the so-called wisdom or programming that you were led to believe, by less informed people, throughout your life. Like me, you may also feel a little resentful and frustrated that you were never educated about all of this important information earlier; but don't be too angry...unfortunately, many older people don't know about this information either.

And speaking of age, it really doesn't matter if you aren't a young adult when reading this book. While it may be advantageous to be reading this when you're younger (because you are not yet entrenched in the complications and responsibilities inherent in older adults' lives), if you are an older adult, just remember this fact: you are never too old to learn new ways to change, improve, and manifest your desired outcomes to achieve lifelong personal and financial success. Whatever your age, just commit to being extra patient with yourself while going through this information so that you can apply these lessons going forward.

Like I said before, I wish someone would have handed me this book when I was your age. It would have made my life a whole lot easier. I could have avoided some real financial pitfalls and been even more focused to achieve success earlier. However, my loss is your gain! It is always much easier when you get (and take) the opportunity to learn from others' mistakes and successes. Just remember, most people do not become successful overnight. We've all heard it before because it's absolutely true: it takes a lot of hard work, patience, and dedication to attain what you really want. Your commitment to adopt all of the new positive habits outlined in this book—right here, right now—will definitely help empower you to handle and overcome many potential obstacles. Once you incorporate these success tools and secrets into your everyday life, I have all the faith that you, too, can achieve your goals to grow your own personal and financial success.

Now, let's get started!

1

Managing Your Fears

What would you do if you weren't afraid?

As a young adult growing up between the ages of 16 and 25, life must seem a little uncertain and scary to you right now. But just think, you have the advantage of being among the first generation to grow up in the 21st century—with all the perks of being able to carry out the majority of your consumer-related, business, and even social transactions from your smartphone, computer, or tablet devices from virtually anywhere in the world. And while it is true that these technological tools enhance our daily lives, the drawback is that they have taken jobs away from people (including either your, and/or your friends' parents). This downsizing (or outsourcing) has left many adults financially crippled due to prematurely losing their jobs long before they were ready to retire. Consequently, they've been forced to overextend themselves financially by either living off of their credit or savings (if they had any), leaving them unable to afford many of life's expenses—which would include putting their children through college, or even worse, losing their homes. Have I got your attention? Does this make you a little more nervous or concerned about your future? Good! If not, it should.

Following 2008's financial crisis (which set off the Great Recession), as of February 2009 the number of bankruptcy filings in the United States was up 29% (*Automated Access to Court Electronic Records*). By August 2009, the average American's personal savings rate (as a percentage of their spendable income) was only 3%, according to the Bureau of Economic Analysis. "Consumer spending is 70% of the U.S. economy and with the exception of the super-rich, there has been no growth in consumer incomes in the 21st century," stated Paul Craig Roberts (*The Economy Is a Lie Too*, 2009). And as of October 10, 2009, our country's national debt was $11.9 trillion compared to $2.9 trillion on September 30, 1989. So, for a country that prides itself on its educational and technological advances, how did this happen? Why are so many people in such economic turmoil? More significantly, how do YOU plan to avoid these same personal and financial pitfalls that so many middle-aged adults are currently experiencing at this time in their lives? Confused? That's understandable. It took me 22 years to answer these same questions. The main reason why so many young adults today fail to grow up to be successful is that most do not have a clear definition or plan for success.

When I first started writing this book, I spoke to several mentors and friends. I quickly came to the realization that if I were to ask a hundred young adults to define their meaning of success, I would probably get a hundred different answers. Does success mean having a lot of money? Being the president of a big company? Owning a huge house and a fancy car? Being a Hollywood movie star? A famous musician or athlete? A Wall Street billionaire? Which definition is correct? All? Some? Most? Confusing, right? When I thought about the one thing that almost all young adults never really confront, it would be fear—which is probably the most obvious common denominator preventing them from defining their success. Why fear? Because the majority of our parents, high school teachers, and college professors probably never discussed personal and/or financial success with us as kids.

As I reflect back on my own childhood, I am both amazed and miffed as to why nobody ever thought to discuss these important topics with me, and more importantly, why I never thought to ask. Like most first and second-generation children of television (adults between the ages of 40 - 60), all I ever seemed to learn how to do as a kid was to spend money—never how to save, earn, and grow my money by investing it wisely. Basically, I was educated by my favorite Saturday morning cartoon characters and fellow TV kids about how much better off my life would have been if I only ate or drank certain types of foods, wore certain types of clothes, or drove certain types of cars. I never really learned how I was going to afford to pay for these "must have" things, just that I needed them to be happy and feel successful. So I basically started to become "afraid" that I would not be successful without them, "afraid" that I would never be able to afford them, and "afraid" about how I was going to pay for them (if I did, in fact, manage to acquire them). Do you see the consistent pattern here? I'll give you a hint...FEAR.

The great Greek philosopher, Aristotle, once wrote, "We are all the sum total of our experience." To learn from one's experiences is paramount to truly becoming successful. By sharing my, as well as others', personal experiences with you throughout this book, it is my hope that you will learn how to grow your own success. The important success strategies that resulted from these lessons helped me to work my way up from being a summer intern, to the Vice President of Financial Services, North America for one of the world's largest record and publishing companies. These strategies are key success secrets and tools others have utilized to become presidents of companies and create new technologies and thought processes that you are likely using today. How could these strategies help you?

My personal philosophy for success is simple: *Do what you love every day of your life while surrounding yourself with positive people who love and support you.*

Demystifying Success is a book based on four overall concepts or themes: awareness, shifting your beliefs and attitudes, taking action, and creating the proper financial foundation to ensure your future wealth and success. You will also learn why positivity attracts success and the importance of filling your life with people who love and support you.

Life really is too short. Do not be like most people who simply live their lives in fear and only dream about the things they wish they could achieve. Don't live your life with regrets. You can do this. Take the time needed and commit to absorbing and implementing this life-changing information. Like my wife likes to say, "Your future self will thank you."

Learning to Manage Your Fears

According to founding father and inventor, Benjamin Franklin, "All mankind is divided into three classes: those that are immovable, those that are movable, and those that move." I am sure you have come across friends and classmates who have fallen into one of these three categories: The first, *immovable*—those who always sit in the back of the class and never raise their hands or ask questions and, therefore, always wonder what it might be like to succeed, but were always too afraid to try. And the third, *move*—those who always volunteer, lead, and as a result, succeed. And then there are the majority of us, the second, *movable*—those who often sit in the middle, constantly wondering if this will be the day that we find our courage and answer the teacher's questions, ask out that classmate we have been staring at for months but have been too afraid to talk to, or finally decide to take charge of our lives. If this is you, the good news is you are not alone!

Back in high school, I used to dream a lot about being a world-famous musician. I often spent hours practicing and studying drums with my two amazing private drum teachers: Dave Clive and world-renowned drum clinician, Dom Famularo. After graduating high school, I told my parents that I really wanted to study music in college; however, they wanted me to get a liberal arts education because they felt it would be easier for me to earn a living after I graduated.

To my dismay, when I arrived at the University of Maryland and I began registering for my freshman liberal arts classes, I realized I was miserable. I knew all along that my desire was to be a world-famous drummer and the thought of sitting in those liberal arts classes depressed me. After much debate, I finally convinced my parents to let me study music at Maryland. However, after my audition and acceptance to the University of Maryland's Department of Music's Percussion Program, I soon realized that had my parents actually agreed to let me study music sooner, I would have chosen to pursue a college or university that had a bigger music program than Maryland's. That is why I decided to apply in the fall of my freshman year to both Indiana University and the University of Michigan's percussion departments.

Once I made my decision to audition for both Indiana and Michigan, I immediately started to imagine what it would be like to attend one of these prestigious music schools, having the opportunity to perform alongside some of the greatest drummers and percussionists in the country while being in one of their orchestras, jazz bands, etc. I imagined hanging out with old high school friends who were also attending both universities for their undergrad studies. How cool would that be? So while still a freshman, I submitted an audition tape (which I had made at Maryland) to the University of Michigan. Then I flew out to Bloomington, Indiana and auditioned in person for the head of the Indiana University Percussion Department at the time: the legendary George C. Gaber. It turned out to be one of the most intense auditions I had ever had. I can still remember the joy, pride, and relief I felt when I got my acceptance letters from both schools, welcoming me as a potential undergraduate percussion student. Great news, right?

As I imagined, I now had the opportunity to study with some of the best young drummers and percussionists in the country, study music at a prestigious music school, and hang out with my old high school buds. Things were all coming together as I had intended except for one important thing...I was terrified! Yes, fear started to consume me. Within a couple of weeks, I regrettably contacted both Indiana University and the University of Michigan and informed them that I would not be transferring to their prestigious music schools. Regardless of all the positive things that I would have experienced had I simply followed my instincts and transferred to Indiana University or the University of Michigan, I allowed fear to take control. I was devastated. Despite the acknowledgment and confirmation that both schools bestowed upon my musical talents and abilities, I chose to forego my passion and goals. In a matter of moments, everything that I had wished for and manifested was gone because I was afraid. I let insecurity overwhelm me, and fear won. It was in that very moment that I promised myself I would learn how to manage my fears so that I would never again let fear stop me from getting what I wanted.

Because of my resolute decision to face my fears and get them under control, I went on to excel during the remainder of my four years at the University of Maryland. I became the president of two music organizations, ascended from a white belt to a red belt in Tae Kwon Do during my senior year (where four times in the eleven months I studied, I was awarded outstanding student of the month). And beginning in my sophomore year until I graduated, I was the timpanist and percussion section leader for the University's premier performing group, the Symphonic Wind Ensemble. As a result of all my efforts and positive attitude, I was honored with the 1986 Symphonic Wind Ensemble's Musicanship Award (voted upon by the Maryland Band Directors and presented to only one member of the Wind Ensemble annually). When I received it, the University's Director of Bands, Mr. John Wakefield (one of my first mentors), presented it to me for my outstanding musicianship and contributions to the Ensemble.

I did it! I learned how to manage my fears. Best of all, three years later in the winter of my senior year, I flew back to Bloomington, Indiana and once again, I auditioned for George C. Gaber, but this time as a more confident potential graduate student. Yes, you guessed it! In the fall of 1986, I started my graduate studies in music (Percussion Performance) at the prestigious Indiana University School of Music.

I shared my above accomplishments in detail not to brag, but to illustrate what I could do when I set my mind to managing my fears, which then bolstered my confidence, and led me to achieve my desired success. You, too, can decide to manage your fears and pursue your goals. It really is achievable once you figure out what you truly want. You will find that by clearly envisioning what your heart and mind desires, your passion will fuel your determination, and then your determination will carry you through to see your goal to its completion. The question for you to answer is this: Will you face your fears and pursue your goals?

Because I chose at that moment in time to overcome my fears, I went on to attend Indiana University (IU) as a graduate music student, and I met my IU mentors (and legendary musicians) Dr. David N. Baker and Kenny Aronoff. I not only pursued a master's degree in percussion, but also a master's degree in jazz studies. I joined Indiana University's programming board—the Union Board—and became the University's concert director where I promoted such musical talents as Chick Corea, The Pixies, The Violent Femmes, and others. I also pioneered a relatively new philanthropic record project called, "Live from Bloomington," a project that supported the local Hoosier Hills Food Bank (the project celebrated its 25th anniversary in 2011).

All of these achievements ultimately led me to Los Angeles, where I met my first business mentor, Vinnie Freda, who hired me as a summer intern for MCA Records immediately following my graduation from IU in 1990. I went on to enjoy a 22-year career in the music industry at the Universal Music Group as their North American Vice President of Financial Services.

Overall, I've been blessed these past 25 years because I chose to manage my fears and start growing my success from an early age. The good news is, now you can get that head start too, because you chose to read this book at this pivotal time in *your* life.

"You Don't Have to Be Great to Start, But You Have to Start to Be Great." ~ Zig Ziglar

As I explained earlier, the main reason why so many people seem to fail and never achieve their goals and success is that they either lack the necessary information that provides the important ingredients and tools to succeed, or they simply succumb to their fears and never make any real efforts to ever get out of their negative comfort zones. This challenge involves doing the necessary work to improve their current situations, or even better, understanding how to avoid them altogether.

Motivational speaker and salesman, Zig Ziglar, was absolutely correct when he said, "You don't have to be great to start, but you have to start to be great." Take this opportunity to learn how to thrive and achieve anything in life that you set your mind to doing, especially from an early age.

Think about how your parents, teachers, friends, and most importantly, your own early life experiences have impacted your "learned" negative fears and emotions. Who taught you yours? Unless we learn how to manage these challenges from an early age, they will become harder and harder to correct because they become more habit-forming as we get older. Anyone who has ever truly become successful in life has had to overcome and manage their fears so they could take the necessary action steps to accomplish their goals.

Most well-established adults who endured struggles in their child-hood and are driven by their own desire and determination, have managed to overcome any lingering self-defeating fears because they *chose* to shift their unhealthy attitudes and learned perspectives as they manifested their desired outcomes. I am going to outline and walk you through the steps that I had to take, and which I implemented over the past 25 years, in order to help me overcome my fears and allow me to grow my success, both personally and professionally. In fact, I still use these same tools today to help me to continue to achieve my success. By understanding why these tools work for me and so many other successful people, YOU will also acquire the power to change your own outcomes for success.

Remember, I wrote this book to help you get out of your own way so you can start thriving outside of your current comfort zone, which is what may be preventing you from achieving the life you truly desire. If you are not effectively pursuing your personal and financial goals, then now's the time for you to take control of your fears and self-doubt so you can pursue your *probable* outcomes for success.

I am grateful to be your guide on this journey to help you grow your personal and financial success.

2
Awareness

So, how's that life working for you?

At some point in your life you may have heard the expression, "You can't always judge a book by its cover." I want to tell you that this expression, as far as first impressions go, is false. In fact, nine out of ten times you most certainly will judge others based upon your first impression because humans are wired to assess and respond to them. This is why your mother, father, or teachers often told you, "It is always important to make a good first impression." If you choose to dress like a duck, don't be upset if someone calls you a duck. Successful people live based in reality—what they actually *observe*, versus what they *envision it to be* (fantasy). They not only base how they perceive others upon who or what they see in front of them, but they are also well-aware everyone else is perceiving them just as they are too. So they know they must always put their best foot forward in every single situation because one can never undo a first impression.

To be successful, you need to live in the real world because fantasies will only lead you to make unhealthy decisions and life choices.

Therefore, to avoid any unnecessary detours or pitfalls that could possibly delay you from achieving your desired success, begin cultivating a realistic awareness of what you want to achieve in your life by learning (or re-learning) to trust your own instincts and to align yourself with the right people and resources to help you accomplish your goals. That is why your journey must begin right here, right now, with a strong internal and external awareness of your own reality. It is imperative that you train yourself, from an early age, to be sharp and aware of your surroundings to ensure that you always keep your eyes wide open to any potential opportunities that may come your way, while avoiding so-called false realities (or fantasies) others may want you to ultimately settle for. Be wary of those who believe, or try to convince you, that their so-called fairy tales are grounded in some form of reality. Always remember that dreams and fantasies are for those who wander aimlessly through life (unfulfilled), whereas reality serves those who choose to succeed.

The Power of Awareness

Have you ever had that feeling of disappointment when you really set your mind to achieving something and things did not quite turn out the way you envisioned? My father used to refer to this unwelcomed outcome as, *"Man plans, God laughs."* Under those circumstances, despite all your well-intentioned efforts, things still didn't turn out the way you planned...or did they? Did you ever wonder why successful people always seem to come out ahead despite their temporary setbacks? Or why opportunities always seem to knock on their doors? The answer is really quite simple. Unlike most people who have been programmed, from an early age, to negatively respond to disappointing outcomes, successful people often perceive these same setbacks as potential opportunities to pave the way for something even better that they may not have even realized they might have needed or wanted. As a result of their heightened awareness, successful people always try to see the bigger picture (the plan) when they do not always get the immediate responses they are after. Whereas, most people tend to get angry or upset at themselves or others when things don't go their way. Successful people rarely waste their time and energy giving in to their short-term disappointments because they allow themselves the time for things to play out according to their bigger plans.

The power of awareness stems from three independent components of your personality that collectively affect your ability to either enhance, or derail your overall confidence and success. So what are these three awareness components for success?

The Demystifying Success Awareness Diagram

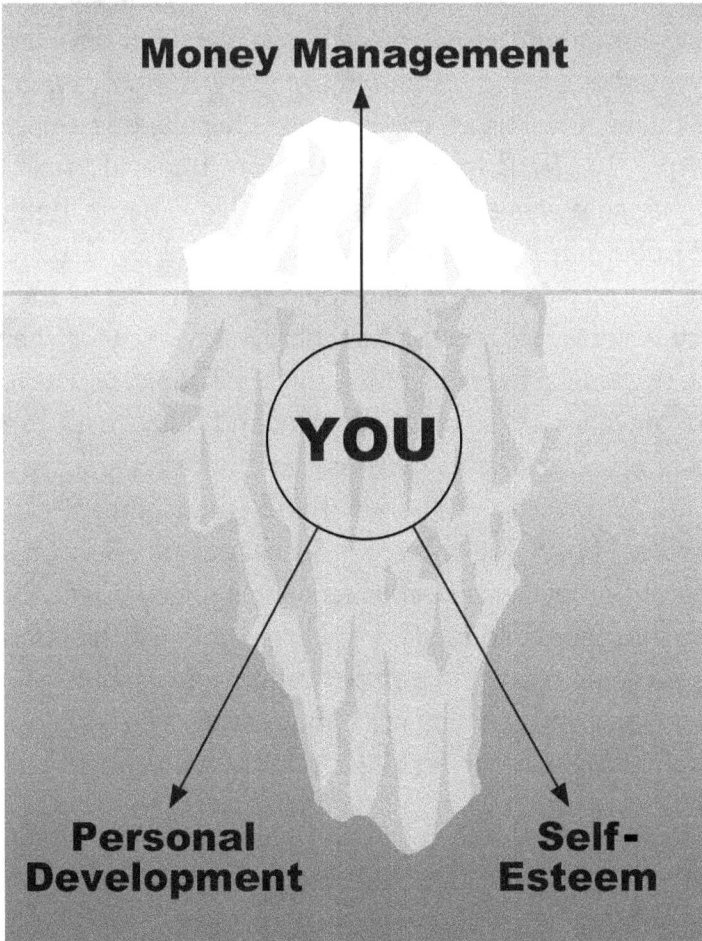

Money Management

YOU

Personal Development

Self-Esteem

1. **Self-Esteem** – Developing one's own confidence, core values, and inner strength ("How I choose to be treated by others.")

2. **Personal Development** – One's goals, values, and study/work ethic ("How others will perceive me.")

3. **Money Management** – Savings, debt risk management, and wealth creation ("How I choose to manifest personal and financial success.")

As shown in the iceberg diagram, most people primarily focus on the "tip" of their own self-worth, or in this analogy, their financial status (e.g., money management) because it is the easiest of all three components for everyone to see and measure. But like the larger chunks of the iceberg that are submerged under the icy water, your other two components—self-esteem and personal development—are also more difficult for others to see at the surface. We all know, or have heard, the tale of the *Titanic*—the majestic ship that set sail on April 10, 1912 from Southampton, England to New York. This mighty ship was supposedly unsinkable. That is, until it hit a massive iceberg in the Atlantic Ocean on April 14, 1912 because the crew miscalculated what they could not "see" below the surface of the icy waters. They focused primarily on only what they *could* see—the tip. Unlike the crew of the mighty *Titanic*, you will need to be aware of what's not so clearly evident and cultivate all three components of your personal awareness, and not simply focus all your energies on improving only your money management—the obviously visible, "tip of the iceberg." Successful people exude confidence because they learned from an early age how to manage their fears and turn them into successes. Unless you find the discipline to start focusing on improving and cultivating your own three components, from an early age, you will continuously sabotage your future outcomes despite all your best efforts to create wealth.

As you begin creating and cultivating one, two, or all three of your personal awareness components, the first thing I want you to do if you feel negative, unsupported, or stuck is to forgive yourself for unconsciously adopting all of the bad or unfounded programming that you might have received or inherited from your parents, teachers, friends, or others in the past. They all probably meant well, but they may have inadvertently projected, or simply passed forward, generational misinformation that was shared with *them* from an early age. My aim is to make you aware of your possible negative programming so that from this moment forward, you can stop making future decisions either by morphing yourself into someone else's view of who you should be, or by acting out the stories you have always been told. Instead, it's time for you to start taking stock of what you really want and why—without anyone else's influence. If you are still unsure about what I am talking about, here is a quick reality check to see how you perceive yourself. Take a moment to look in the mirror and ask yourself, "So, how's that life working for you?" It's a simple question really, that requires no excuses, no blame—just a simple need to be honest with yourself about how you perceive your reality. If you said anything other than "stellar" or "successful," you are probably not in alignment with what you truly want. Do not worry; you are not alone. A lot of good people don't realize that they are unknowingly acting out other people's programming. Unlike many adults, the good news is that you are still young enough to reprogram your awareness to fit within your own desired path for success. Bad habits are much harder to correct or change at an older age. This is why you want to make sure your desired outcomes are always in alignment with your current realities.

Give Yourself an Honest Reality Check

Regardless of your answer to my question, "So, how's that life working for you?" I would still like you to sit down and do the following exercise. This is important because every decision, goal, or purpose throughout your life will begin based on the foundation of your level of awareness.

The first thing I would like you to do is find a very quiet room with no distractions, no smartphones, no music, no computers, no television, etc., and just sit down with a pen and paper—very old school—and give yourself what I like to call an "honest reality check." I truly believe that to start building your power of awareness, you must base it in reality. What that means is that you have to put aside any fears, insecurities, or self-judgment you may have when doing this exercise. Do not overthink things and do not compare yourself to anyone else. Just allow this exercise to resonate with you—without giving any thought to anyone else's influence.

To complete this exercise, there are three things I would like you to focus on:

1. How do you think others perceive you? What do you think other people really think about you? (*Self-esteem*)

> **TIP:** If you would like a real assessment of what others think about you, I would like to suggest something that I asked my friends to do for me when I was in my 20s. Choose five friends who you really trust and respect, and ask them to <u>type</u> (not handwrite) five things that they really like about you, and five things that they wish you would change about yourself, and ask them to return their answers to you anonymously. By requesting anonymous replies, your friends will be more inclined to be honest with you about their responses because they will not feel like they are hurting your feelings. I cannot tell you how beneficial and informative this exercise was for me. It will truly help you understand how others perceive you.

2. How do you want to be perceived by others? What would you like other people to think about you? How do you plan to add value to other peoples' lives? (*Personal development*)

3. How do you intend to manifest wealth in your life? (*Money management*)

By choosing to focus on how others perceive you, how you want to be perceived by others, and how you intend to manifest your wealth in the future, you will begin building and cultivating your awareness, which will continue to grow your confidence and personal development. Do not be frustrated if you have any trouble answering any of these questions. The purpose of this exercise is to help you become more aware of who you really are, and more importantly, who you would like to be. Doing this work from an early age, provides you with a great opportunity to get a jumpstart on taking control and making changes to how you will be perceived by others.

I first created this "reality check" exercise because the old negative programming I had battled as a college undergrad, along with some poor decisions, had conspired to derail me from my original plans. I was no longer pursuing my passions and goals, I was no longer aware, and I lost my perspective. Despite the success I achieved while at Universal Music Group, I felt stagnant working for the same company for 20+ years, primarily doing the same job with the same responsibilities for 8+ years, I was 50 pounds overweight, I was in debt from a previous relationship, and I stalled in terms of completing my dissertation for my doctorate in education. I WAS STUCK! As a result, I found myself making excuses for why my life had gotten off course, and I felt like I had a bad case of mood poisoning. I was enabling my bad decisions rather than dealing with my underlying issues. I was in complete denial about how unhappy I had truly become, and it started to affect my self-esteem, my ability to motivate myself, and even worse, it started to affect my self-identity. I became less and less aware of potential opportunities because I felt so miserable. My self-loathing had gotten so bad that I *had* to get out of my own way and get unstuck. As a result, I forced myself to step back and ask myself how, or more importantly, *why* I had allowed myself to get that way. I knew it was time to start asking myself a lot of difficult questions, and just like I sug-gested you ask yourself, I stood in front of my bathroom mirror and asked myself, "So, how's that life working for you?" Once I began to own the decisions and mistakes that I had made, I became more aware of my own reality. I finally started to reclaim my life. I lost 63 pounds, I completed my dissertation and graduated from Pep-perdine University, I took control of my finances again, and I left my prior job to follow my passion: educating young adults, as well adults of all ages, to define and create success on their own terms.

I won't lie to you. My personal transformation wasn't easy. It took active discipline and serious commitment. Through my determi-nation and awareness, along with a lot of support from mentors, family, and friends, I was able to complete the majority of my goals. To help keep myself accountable throughout this process, I had decided to keep a journal documenting my goals (losing weight, finishing the dissertation, etc.) along with the action steps (a list of things to do, who would I contact, etc.) that I took with me each day, which helped me to reach my desired outcomes.

When I finally achieved my transformational goals and reviewed my journaling, I found I was able to map out my journey. When I stud-ied this so-called road map, I realized that I had designed a powerful transformational model that included the following three phases:

1. The Awakening Phase, or as I also like to call it, *The Realization Phase*. It was that "a-ha" moment when I finally asked myself, "So, how's that life working for you?" As I said earlier, it was a simple question that really required me to just be honest with myself and address those things in my life that were no longer supporting my desired outcomes for success. Once I committed myself to taking complete ownership of my life, I empowered myself to stop making excuses, stop blaming others for my own bad decisions, and I finally owned my personal choices and actions. Through gaining this heightened self-awareness, I started to identify my negative behavior patterns more clearly and saw how my early negative programming was sabotaging my future success. Once I stopped projecting my negative feelings, I became emotionally stronger and more confident, and I began realigning my goals with my desired outcomes. It was both exciting and reinvigorating to reclaim my healthier self as I began to feel things shift. But then, as if I had been running a marathon, I hit a wall. It was the second phase of my transformation.

2. The Tunnel of Transition Phase, or as I also like to call it, *The Uncomfortable Phase* resides somewhere between your awakening and your pending new paradigm shift. Just like traveling through a real tunnel, this phase can at times feel almost claustrophobic. The darkness and uncertainty one experiences during any unknown transition in life usually causes one to feel overwhelmed. However, despite these feelings of anxiety, I can assure you firsthand that it is worth your efforts. As you enter your "tunnel," you will need to remind yourself that you have chosen this new path for yourself for a reason: your old life doesn't work anymore.

3. The Transformation Phase, or as I also like to call it, *The Para-digm Shift* is when you get to experience the success you desire, but only if you have not allowed fear and uncertainty to derail you from your new life. To reach this final phase of awareness, you will need to be persistent until you find the light at the end of your tunnel. Not only will you need to have cleared your tunnel of transition, but you will also need to continuously reevaluate your goals and objectives so that you do not inadvertently veer off course and sabotage yourself from your future success. This will enable you to remain your transformed and best self. It does take a certain level of disciplined vigilance—just like maintaining anything does. Think about the old saying when it comes to staying fit: "No pain, no gain." This sentiment not only applies to your physical well-being, but also to your healthy mental state.

I was very fortunate to be able to figure out how to realign my goals with achieving my desired outcomes by applying my fear-managing techniques that I first implemented as an undergraduate at the University of Maryland, as well as enhancing my awareness through these three phases. Throughout this book, I will continue to openly share the knowledge, tools, and secrets that I have acquired which will enable you to create your own goals and future success.

Can an Iced Tea Impact Your Overall Success?

Have you have ever considered starting your own small business or working for a major corporation? Despite whatever your particular talents are, your long-term success in any field largely depends on your keen awareness and attention to detail. When I was asked to be a contributing author for the book, *Ready, Aim, Influence!: Join Forces, Expand Resources, Transform Your World*, publisher Viki Winterton asked me, "What do you think are the key skills required today to make a business thrive?" In my chapter, I shared the following information:

> For a successful business to thrive in today's economy, you need to start with a solid vision of what you want your business to look like. You also need to hire good employees (as future managers) that share your passion and goals for the business. Implement an evaluation system or method that enables you to evaluate not only what works, but also what does not work throughout your entire infrastructure. Most importantly, you must possess the ability to identify and satisfy your clients' needs and expectations better than any of your competitors. High customer satisfaction is paramount to ensuring the success of any business and you must never rest on your laurels.

Think of awareness as being synonymous with opportunity, and your mastery of the details will not only be crucial in obtaining and retaining a client's trust, but your ability to be aware and cognizant of their needs will also differentiate you from your competition.

Using the following stories to illustrate my point may seem silly or petty, but I think they will enlighten you as to why awareness can be crucial to your overall success:

I was recently in a restaurant and I asked my server to bring me an iced tea with no lemon. A few minutes later, she returned with my iced tea, and sure enough, there was a wedge of lemon floating on top of it. For a moment, I replayed the conversation in my head that I just had with my server—less than five minutes ago—to determine if I had omitted the fact that I did not want a slice of lemon in my iced tea. The simple realization I made was that either the server failed to communicate my request to omit the lemon from my iced tea when she placed my order, or she failed to recognize that the preparer added the lemon despite both of our requests to omit it. Either way, the server was in the wrong because *she* was unaware of the error—she either did not relay my request, or she neglected to prepare it correctly herself.

A couple of days later, I was in the Los Angeles airport and I stopped in one of those airport restaurant/pubs. I ordered a "cheeseburger but with bacon and no cheese" (which was a custom order because only "cheeseburgers" appeared on their menu). When the server finally brought over my food, the bacon was missing. Again, this was either a failure on the server's part to request the bacon burger I wanted, or it was his failure to notice that the order he picked up from the kitchen was not prepared as I had requested.

These two incidents really brought the importance of *awareness* to my attention. In both instances, the servers clearly were not aware that they did not provide me with the orders as I had asked. This led me to ask the big-picture question: Can an iced tea really impact your overall success?

So the next time you are in a position to assist someone, regardless of the task at hand, don't miss the opportunity to take that extra moment to really *listen* to what they are asking of you. Equally important, evaluate and be aware as to whether or not you have successfully provided them with their desired outcome. Not only will your efforts be rewarded by your boss (in this case, the customer who will leave the server with a well-deserved tip), but it could be the very thing that ultimately differentiates you from so many unaware individuals who will never "get it" or really understand why they are unable to achieve the success they desire. By fine-tuning your awareness and attention to detail, you will continue to increase your *probability* for success in the future.

Probability versus Possibility

As you will see throughout your life, you will constantly be presented with opportunities, both personally and professionally, and your ability to sharpen your awareness, trust your instincts, and manage your fears will definitely enable you to better achieve your desired outcomes. This is why, when I have new coaching clients, I always begin by stressing the importance of awareness because it truly helps strengthen their foundation for success.

Throughout my life, one constant factor that has enabled me to achieve my desired outcomes has been my ability to confidently *take action* once a potential opportunity arises. Good timing (which I also refer to as "identifying opportunities") is a crucial element in accomplishing your goals for your future success. You must take advantage of opportunities before they expire. Sure, there will be others, but the difference between a missed opportunity and deciding to jump in can make a huge impact on your outcome for success. For example, in 1984 I was able to save up $3,000 by the end of my sophomore year at the University of Maryland. On December 31, 1984, a single share of Berkshire Hathaway stock—

the company of legendary investor and billionaire Warren Buffett—
was trading for $1,275. If I had known, or had had the opportunity,
to invest in Berkshire Hathaway back in 1984, my two shares of
stock would have cost me $2,550 and as of August 26, 2013, they
would have been worth $344,400. What is the moral of this story?
Keep your eyes open, listen carefully to what is happening around
you, and make sure to take advantage of all potential opportunities
as they arise.

I would also like to share a big revelation of mine that greatly
enhanced my confidence and timing for taking action. I asked
myself the following question: Is there really a substantial difference
between a *probable,* versus a possible, outcome?

Once I began utilizing the power of *probability* versus possibility,
I greatly enhanced my awareness to achieve my desired outcome
for success. I discovered that this revelation served as an excellent
timing technique that would consistently help me make better decisions whenever opportunities arose. However, before I share my
timing secret with you, I want to elaborate more on this concept of
probability versus possibility.

I want to begin by asking you, which of these two statements sounds
more decisive and powerful?

Statement 1: There is a strong *probability* that you will
achieve success in your life if you read this book.

Statement 2: There is a strong possibility that you will achieve
success in your life if you read this book.

Doesn't a *probable* outcome (versus a possible outcome) have a
stronger bearing on whether or not you would even want to read
this book?

The truth is, successful people base the majority of their decisions upon *probable* outcomes.

If you have ever watched *Star Trek*, then you'd know the highly logical Mr. Spock never made decisions or recommendations to Captain Kirk unless he believed there would be a *probable* outcome for success. Like Spock, you have to be logical when making important decisions and life choices. It is more difficult than it sounds because instead of *pausing* to think, then act, on a strategic decision (which I will discuss in a later chapter), many of us simply react emotionally, in the moment. This is where most of us get into trouble because instead of basing our actions upon thought-out decisions, we set ourselves up for failure by acting on preprogrammed responses. And as human animals, we basically react in one of two ways: fight or flight—and both of those reactions are FEAR-based.

> **Probability** implies decisiveness
> (That WILL probably happen)
>
> **Possibility** insinuates uncertainty
> (That COULD possibly happen)

There really is no good reason to waste any time, money, or energy on a mere possible outcome unless you are convinced that there is a great *probability* down the road that this outcome would eventually happen.

Are you now beginning to see the power between awareness, *probability*, and success?

It will become more obvious as you become more aware that good *probabilities* lead to better and more successful outcomes, which lead to greater prosperity, which all stem from one's own desire to succeed.

Still not clear? Then I want you to take a moment to think back to the last bad, possibility-based decision that you most recently made.

Now, I want you to reframe that same bad situation or decision as if it were a *probability*-based outcome. For example, "If I make the decision to do X, what is the *probability* that this decision would lead me to a successful outcome, or get me something I really want?" Considering this new perspective, wouldn't it have made more sense to have just passed on that prior bad, possibility-based decision if it did not lead to a *probable* outcome for success? I hope you see it that way now because that is exactly how successful people think!

So here is that timing secret I promised you: To help enhance your *probable* outcomes for success in the future, from this moment on, I want you to *always* phrase any decision that you are planning to take action on by pausing to ask yourself, "What is the *probability* versus the possibility of this decision enhancing my future outcome(s) for success?" I like to call this important secret timing tool an "intellectual timeout." Because by reframing your decision question, you are allowing yourself the time to step back and really ask yourself, "Will this decision benefit my short-term and/or long-term goals, or will this decision derail my plans and/or set me back?"

When I first moved to Los Angeles from Bloomington, Indiana (after I graduated from Indiana University), my goal was to be involved with the creative aspects of the recording industry (produce records, work with the artists, etc.). However, the only position that was available and offered to me was the project coordinator position in MCA Records' recording administration department. Although it was not the path that I initially intended to pursue, this new job was still a great opportunity for me to learn the business end of the recording industry. I was involved with the administration of the various artists' recording projects (budgets, the booking of studios, engineers, etc.) and I got to work with the creative Artist &

Repertoire (A&R) staff, record producers and engineers, recording studio managers, and artists. Within the first two years of my job, I received a great hands-on education as to how albums and CDs were recorded, produced, and manufactured. After I began my third year, I found myself faced with a slight dilemma: apply for an open position as an assistant for one of the MCA Records A&R staff or continue working for the recording administration department. As I mentioned before, when I first moved to Los Angeles, I really wanted to be involved with the creative aspects of the recording industry (produce records, work with the artists, etc.) and had I gone for the A&R assistant position, it would have aligned me with those goals. But reminiscent of my indecision while an undergrad at Maryland, I was torn. Once again, fear (this time, financial insecurity) got the better of me; I chose not to relinquish my stability by losing my established foothold within the company. I decided to stay put.

Looking back at that crossroad in my career, I now wish that I would have known more about my timing secret. I could have asked myself important questions such as, "What is the *probability*, versus the possibility, of achieving what I truly want by getting more involved with the creative aspects of the recording industry by applying for the assistant position in the A&R department, versus remaining within the recording administration department? What would the *probability*, versus the possibility, be of ascending to become an A&R representative or record producer if I remained within the recording administration department?" By asking myself those questions, I would have allowed myself the time to step back and decide, "Which position would really benefit my short-term and/or long-term goals? And would my final decision get me any closer to obtaining my desired outcomes, or would it derail my plans and/or set me back?" However, since I had yet to discover my "intellectual timeout" technique, I never allowed myself that opportunity to ask myself those questions, so I ultimately decided to remain within the recording administration department because I saw the rapid potential for more advancement. I realize was very fortunate to have had the opportunity to spend 22 years with the Universal Music Group overseeing recording and marketing administration, corporate travel, and shared services for all of the North American record labels and operating companies. But I must admit, I do wonder what my career might have been like had I taken that opportunity to work within the A&R department or produce records like I had originally wanted.

The reason I shared this story with you is to illustrate that if you truly have a desire or passion for something that you love doing, then you need to learn, from an early age, how important it will be to *pause* to really weigh the *probability*, versus the possibility, of how your decisions affect your desired outcomes. By learning how to successfully "time" your opportunities so that your decisions positively align with your desired plans and goals, you will confidently learn how to quickly accomplish any goal you set your mind to achieving.

Life Lessons for Success

The final concepts I would like to share with you in this chapter are my three life lessons that revolve around my own personal revelations regarding awareness and *probable* outcomes for success:

1. Get out of your own way. When you know what you need to do but still choose to make the wrong decision as a result of your own fear of rejection, failure, abandonment, or something else, you really need to start learning how to trust your own instincts and acknowledge that you are a good person with a lot of unique talents and skills to offer. Having confidence in yourself and your abilities is not bravado. Knowing you can do something well is an acknowledgement of a fact. Never confuse believing in yourself with narcissism. Confidence coupled with humility is a sign of maturity and will be an attractive—not detractive—quality. Always be confident, *aware*, and proud of your own talents, strengths, and skills because if you don't believe in yourself, how can you expect others to believe in you? Secondly, always communicate your needs and wants openly with others in a respectful and honest way. Although we want others to acknowledge our needs, people naturally tend to be more focused on their own needs, wants, and issues. Therefore, you cannot expect them to be mind-readers. Gauge your audience and don't set your bar too high if it's not appropriate for that particular relationship. Be *aware* that the bar you are requesting others to jump over needs to be attainable for them, or they will get tired and give up trying to please you. Finally, relax and take life in. Enjoy what you have and stop worrying about what is yet to be. Life will happen whether you worry about it or not.

2. Be good to yourself first. Be generous with yourself—both emotionally and financially—as you would with others. Make sure you dedicate at least one hour of every day toward taking care of YOU. Also, commit to putting aside at least 10% of your income (from your job and/or from your allowance) into a savings account or money market account (e.g., personal account) so you can practice good basic money management habits in order to become a self-reliant adult who is *aware* and can manage their own finances. In addition, any income from other sources or investment profits you acquire should also be added to your personal savings or money market account(s).

3. You are not the smartest person in the room. Understanding that you are not the smartest person in the room will help eliminate tension and pressure with others, especially if you are in a committed relationship or business environment. Admitting your mistakes, showing vulnerability, and being *aware* of your own actions will add to your personal credibility with others. You do not need to feel like you have to compete with everyone in the room in order to be the best all the time. It is good to embrace learning from others.

Despite the abundant information available to you on the internet, in the classroom, workplace, amongst family, friends, and others, I strongly believe that to continue to become successful in today's society, you must still look within yourself for your own answers— to search even deeper to find your essential core values and beliefs necessary to protect your own integrity and awareness. Just like learning to manage fears, enhancing personal awareness is another major tool that successful people utilize to help them identify and take advantage of potential opportunities that will grow their future success. You will need to be more aware than ever, and even quicker to adjust your actions, in this fast-paced and ever-changing technological and global environment. That is why it is so important to think strategically and not emotionally. Do not let others, or outside distractions, cloud your judgment or awareness with their preconceived fantasies of what *they think* will be possible for you. Focus on what *you know* will be *probable.* By trusting and relying on your own inner strengths and instincts, *you will* greatly enhance your odds for success.

Call to Action

If you have not already done so, I would like you to take a moment to sit down in a quiet place and give yourself an honest reality check by asking yourself the three questions that I discussed earlier in this chapter. By taking the time to honestly address your current fears and emotional blocks, you will begin to learn how to get out of your own way so that you can become more aware as to how others really perceive you, how you wish to be perceived by others, and how you intend to manifest wealth in the future. By improving your ability to spot potential opportunities, you can begin to effectively "time" when to either act upon them, or pass them over.

In addition to completing your reality check, I would also like you to answer the following questions below as thoughtfully and honestly as you can. Remember, there are no right or wrong answers. The following exercise is designed to get you to focus more on becoming aware of your current reality.

How's that life working for you? What are some of the biggest fears or negative emotional programming obstacles that you are hoping to overcome and that may be preventing you from achieving your desired success?

1. _____

   _____

   _____

2. _____

   _____

   _____

3. _____

   _____

   _____

List three actions you now plan to take to help you get out of your own way so that you can begin to take ownership of your successful outcomes.

1. _____
_____
_____

2. _____
_____
_____

3. _____
_____
_____

Think about my iced tea story and write down three separate incidents where you believe you had an opportunity to improve a situation had your awareness been more heightened under those circumstances. Based upon what you have learned, how would you alter your actions, and why?

1. _____
_____
_____

2. _____
_____
_____

3. _____
_____
_____

"You can clutch the past so tightly to your chest that it leaves your arms too full to embrace the present."

~ Jan Glidewell (retired Times North Suncoast Columnist)

3
Who Are You Really?

Do you suffer from a bad case of mood-poisoning?

Self-esteem is often wrongly associated with validation. This is why you must first learn to become aware of your own feelings and sense of self so that you can stop worrying and overthinking how others may perceive you. It might sound trite, but it's incredibly important that as an individual you always strive to find peace and happiness within yourself. As a young adult, you need to learn to get out of your own way and stop feeling like your thoughts or feelings need validation from others. This insecurity never serves anyone well. Who are they to judge you anyway? Once you begin to become more aware of your own strengths, goals, and desires, and you start trusting your instincts, you will be able to begin overriding some, or all, of your early negative programming.

As I mentioned in the last chapter, success starts with awareness. So to help you become more aware of and understand how you currently perceive your own happiness and self-esteem, I would like you to honestly ask yourself the following questions:

1. **Do I feel happy?** If not, why?

2. **What in my life will give me immediate happiness, versus long-term happiness?**

3. **Am I aligning myself with positive influences and/or environments (e.g., friends, jobs, hobbies, etc.) that make me happy?** If not, why?

4. **Am I aligning myself with positive situations or experiences?** If not, why?

Happiness is a state of mind based largely upon how you feel about yourself. Therefore, enhancing your own self-esteem entails breaking bad habits or patterns while not giving others the power to validate your choices or decisions for you. Just because your parents' and friends' beliefs and choices work for them, does not mean they will work, or be good, for you. Don't hold yourself back. Instead, address and manage your fears and be willing to take risks in life. Just make sure those risks are right for you.

Sometimes you may find yourself stuck and not even know why. This could simply be due to a negative and debilitating condition called, mood poisoning. Without being able to pinpoint a particular reason why, you may just start to feel out of sorts or uncomfortable around certain types of people, or even a place or location in which you currently reside. Many people are incredibly sensitive to their surroundings (people, places, etc.) and it can seriously affect their energy and mood.

I first became more aware of my own surroundings when I started to travel to various cities to run marathons. It was during my travels when I started to realize that I was contracting bad cases of mood poisoning. I could literally feel my entire emotional and physical being change. Not only were the places I encountered starting to affect my mood and demeanor, but the more I actually stopped to look at how people were dressed, the way they ate, and especially the way they communicated back and forth with each other, the more it started to wreak havoc on my central nervous system. It got me thinking, what would happen to me if I had to stay in this uncomfortable environment for any prolonged period of time? What would be the long-term effects of my so-called mood poisoning? Would it start to lessen my self-esteem, my ability to motivate myself, or even worse, affect my self-identity? It may sound silly, but I wondered what would happen if I started to believe that this was who I was or that this was where I was supposed to be? Do you see how self-awareness is so crucial to your own well-being? Can you think of a recent situation when you felt this way too?

The next time you start to feel out of sorts, take a moment to honestly ask yourself, "Is it really me, or am I stuck in some holding pattern or transition place that has become an unwelcomed prison sentence?" For example, one of my prior Los Angeles apartments affected me this way a while back. It was an apartment I had vowed I would only occupy for a year, yet apathy kept me there for seven. Yes, I stayed in that negative environment for *seven long years*. Do you see why I want to help you, from an early age, become aware of situations or events that may temporarily be blocking or preventing you from achieving your long-term future goals and success?

Another obstacle that might be affecting your happiness and emotional well-being could be your early childhood programming. During your formative development—before you could walk and talk—you were already learning and forming new habits. All those experiences (good and bad) that you learned, watched, or personally experienced were embedded into your subconsciousness. Not only have they contributed to who you are today, but they have also had a profound impact on how you perceive the world. For example, have you ever noticed that sometimes you experience a weird feeling or knee-jerk reaction to something out of the blue that suddenly triggers a positive or negative thought or emotion? Then, based upon that thought or emotion, you either find yourself overreacting or freezing up? When this happens, your mind is basically going back to its own historical file cabinet of beliefs or experiences, and those memories dictate to you how to think or feel about a particular situation. If the situation in your past was pleasant, you will feel happy; if it was bad, you will feel sad, scared, or mad. Because your early programmed emotional responses ultimately impact how you act—or react—during any situation, you may have to deal with possible repercussions resulting from your emotional, versus strategic, actions. Therefore, unless you make a conscious effort to identify (tap into your awareness as addressed in the previous chapter) and change the negative triggers you learned back when you formed your early beliefs or habits, you will continue to get caught in the same emotional traps which result in the same negative outcomes. If you want to achieve different outcomes, once you start to really examine who you are, as early as possible, you can begin to change your perspective and reprogram your emotional responses to achieve those desired different results. At the end of the day, you are the only one who is ultimately in control of your own mind.

Now, I want you to ask yourself, "Why am I here on this planet?" General consensus answer: To procreate. Sure, anyone can cite countless existential reasons, but the answer really comes down to this one, pure and simple fact: The *only* reason *any* life form exists on this earth is to ensure that the species survives. So what are YOU doing, right now, to ensure that the human species, your future family, and you, yourself—10, 20, 30, etc., years from now— are better off, more secure, and well-equipped to handle adversity than you are today? Are you living a life of value and worth? Or do you merely exist? Some young adults say they are "drifting," or "leaving themselves open to possibilities," when in actuality they are stagnant...like a rock in a brook as life swirls around and passes them by. What they view as being "open" is, in effect, being unprepared. When opportunity knocks, anyone can open the door. But only the prepared will be ready to actually walk through it and handle the opportunity that has come their way. The famous first century statesman, Seneca, once said, "Luck is what happens when preparation meets opportunity." However, do not confuse "luck" with opportunity. Although in interviews and/or documentaries successful people often attribute their success to luck, they are, in actuality, not "lucky", but simply *prepared*. Due to all of their diligent hard work and persistence, they are prepared to pounce when the right opportunities arise. They make things happen. *That* is the real reason why they became successful—because they were prepared to "spot the opportunities," and then act upon them before they expired. Their continued success is neither a fluke, nor due to luck, because by acting upon their established good habits, they are consistently prepared to duplicate their positive outcomes for success.

As for equating obtaining lots of money with success, it is my belief that your perception of success should not be based solely upon how much money you can accumulate within a lifetime. Rather, it should be based upon how much happiness you can feel because you are able to earn a comfortable living while doing something that you enjoy on a daily basis. Additionally, many people find giving back to society (by whatever means) provides them with a deeper sense of purpose and meaning. While it is up to everyone to determine, on their own terms, what success means to them, I highly recommend that your perception or definition of success include more than just simply accumulating money, possessions, or wealth. My definition of true success would be incomplete if I did not have the people in my life with whom I share mutual love and support. Moreover, it might sound strange, but I wouldn't be able to accept their love if I didn't already love myself, and vice versa. That being said, I urge you to always try to cultivate your own personal happiness and success on a daily basis; because the truth is, one can only be loved to the extent that he or she loves themselves. And that's a good thing, because you have total control over how well you treat and love yourself, and all of your relationships will reflect the solid one you've built with yourself.

Christy Whitman, my spiritual life coach, once told me, "The past does not determine the future, yet we tend to bring it forward. The future can truly be what *you* want it to be." Remember, you will be no good to anyone else if you can't be good to yourself first. In an airplane, before you take off, what does the flight attendant always remind you to do in case of an emergency? Put your own oxygen mask on first before you assist your loved ones or others. Why? Because if you tried to help someone else with their mask first, as heroic as everyone may believe that to be, by the time you got to your own mask, you would run out of air and pass out. And then what good would you be to anyone? It's not selfishness, it's self-responsibility to learn to be good to yourself first.

Healthy Personal Relationships

Protecting yourself in terms of furthering your success is largely determined not only by your thoughts and emotions, but also by the people you choose to surround yourself with. In fact, there is a strong correlation between all three—thoughts, emotions, and the people in your life. Not only does surrounding yourself with the right people matter toward influencing your overall confidence and self-esteem, but the people in your inner circle can actually impact your overall ability to make good decisions that lead to *probable* outcomes for success.

Have you ever noticed that for better or worse, we tend to attract certain types of people into our lives depending on whether we feel happy or sad? Or simply based upon how we are perceiving ourselves at the time? Unfortunately, being unaware of your own emotional state interferes with your ability to quickly identify and protect yourself from self-loathing, disruptive individuals—people who pretend to have your best interests at heart. This leaves you vulnerable and more susceptible to succumbing to their detrimental, energy-sucking influence. Healthy successful people, on the other hand, are acutely aware of these unhealthy individuals and their negative intentions. As a result, they learn how to co-exist with them, maneuver around them, or avoid them altogether in order to protect themselves from any of their sabotaging behavior. So how do you quickly identify and protect yourself from these so-called emotional predators?

Like colds and viruses, people tend to attract these types of "emotional parasites" like a magnet when their self-esteem or emotional guards are down. These emotional parasites seem more than willing to aid us in our self-loathing mindset rather than challenge us to get out of our own way. The "boggled and debauched" (as I refer to them) are unhealthy, dysfunctional people that often intentionally (or even unknowingly) manipulate or use others for their own personal entertainment or distraction. These people tend to project their own fears and negative self-worth onto others rather than deal with their own self-sabotaging issues. They often pretend to be concerned or supportive of an unsuspecting victim's uncertain or negative circumstances, but in reality, they silently gain satisfaction and enjoyment by disclaiming and intentionally diminishing the success, spirit, or character of their targeted victims.

To make matters worse, emotional parasites will go as far as making their victims feel responsible for their needs as they prey on their misguided guilt or loyalties. I cannot begin to tell you how emotionally debilitating these cowardly people can be. They rarely own their own crap, they rarely apologize when wrong, and most importantly, they rarely respect YOUR needs, goals, or requests unless it somehow benefits their own short-term purposes.

Any important decision in your life always requires you to weigh the pros and cons. This especially holds true regarding the people you choose to include in your life. As I said earlier, emotional parasites often tend to strike when you are most susceptible—when your guard or social immunities are down. So I want to share three different scenarios that I have either personally experienced, or have witnessed, that should help make you more aware of how to spot them in the future:

1. The Bait and Switch. There are individuals you will come across that have become master manipulators. They study you and learn very quickly how to make you feel comfortable in their presence. They often tell you what you want to hear, pretend to like the things you like, or even worse, create a false sense of security so that you take their bait. The only problem is, their actions are not sustainable over time because they are not being authentic to who they truly are. They are simply trying to get you to befriend them, or even worse, fall in love with them. NEWS FLASH: These manipulators have an agenda! So you need to put their words on mute and study their actions. If you ask them questions and they become defensive, clearly you have unearthed a chink in their deceptive armor. If this uncomfortable moment occurs, do not apologize; just continue to trust your instincts, keep your eyes open, and be *aware* of any future inconsistencies.

2. Being dismissive of your needs. Recently, I witnessed a good friend of mine who reached out to a group of so-called friends requesting space and time to regroup her thoughts while going through her *tunnel of transformation*. In the past, my friend had hit some tough times and these same so-called friends gleefully cheered her on by supporting her bad decisions and choices simply because it fueled their own unfulfilled needs. Yet, when my friend finally figured out that her choices were no longer productive in helping her find her success, she decided once again to reach out to these same so-called friends for support and understanding as she worked on improving her life. Lo and behold, some showed their true colors and actually became irate and dismissive with her because she changed her mind about how she had been leading her life—the same spiraling out of control life they had been cheering her in leading only because it fulfilled their needs, not hers.

3. Getting defensive (yeah, but you did this...). The last red flag I would like to bring to your attention is a parasite's failure to apologize. Have you ever noticed when you call someone out on something that you did not like, rather than receiving a simple apology from that person, you get a defensive response? It is almost like they are angry that you called them out on their crap. In any healthy relationship, there are going to be times when you unintentionally do something that upsets or hurts the other person. Under these circumstances, the healthy and productive response is to own (take responsibility for) and acknowledge the fact that your actions negatively affected the other person. (Versus an emotional parasite's manipulative technique of deflecting their discomfort by pointing out additional flaws or weaknesses in you).

There is a reason we choose to categorize and compartmentalize the people in our lives as loved ones, friends, acquaintances, etc. Successful people often learn, from an early age, not only how to manage their fears, but their relationships as well. This is why it is so important that you protect yourself by learning how to differentiate the good types of relationships from the bad ones. Once you do, you can learn how to cultivate positive and supportive relationships with healthy people, while navigating around unhealthy people, in order to achieve your desired successful outcomes.

The biggest mistake that I see a lot of people make when it comes to relationships is when they falsely label "acquaintances" as "friends." I can remember (before there was Facebook) the pressure I felt at a young age to make a lot of friends. But the truth is, I quickly realized that this process was flawed because everyone's definition of a "friend" is different. We have all heard people say something along the lines of, "That person isn't a real friend, just look at the way she treats you," or "I am a better friend to Jim than he is to me!" The problem is, all too many have been programmed from an early age to just accept others at face value and label them a "friend" despite whether or not they even had a clear definition of what that term "friend" meant. I believe for most, there is no real logic as to why someone befriends another other than the fact that they had some positive emotional reaction to the other person when they met, and now because they "like" each other, it must mean they are friends. But isn't it true that we can also like acquaintances that we meet? So does that mean that we should immediately label that acquaintance a "friend" due to an emotional response? It doesn't really make much sense when it is put in those terms, does it?

As I consoled my friend, I shared with her what I believed defined the difference between a *friend,* versus an *acquaintance,* versus an *emotional parasite.* As humans, we tend to unconsciously gravitate toward certain types of people based upon an emotional level, yet the only thing that really sets us apart from all the other animals is our ability to reason...our power to *think* versus *react.* Therefore, it suddenly dawned on me that we humans should have some practical means of being able to differentiate relationships between one another that does not simply rely on an emotional response. It was during our discussion when I realized that if someone truly wanted to quickly differentiate and cultivate positive relationships in their lives, then they should be able to evaluate such relationships not based solely on emotions, but based on a set of criteria which evaluates their *actions.* As a result, I designed a *Friends Exercise* to help her, and others, quickly determine whether or not a friend properly aligns with their core values, short-term or long-term goals, etc. And like my friend, I think you are going to be very surprised by the results you get.

The Friends Exercise

The purpose behind this exercise is to enhance your awareness and help you cultivate positive relationships throughout your life based not only on your emotional connections, but also on the *actions* of others so that you may more accurately determine what their true level of friendship is, then interact with them accordingly. As I said earlier, everyone tends to have a different definition of what a friend is. So I would like to teach you a simple exercise that you can use based upon your own definition or criteria (needs, wants, expectations, etc.) for friendship. This exercise will help you differentiate between the good and healthy types of relationships/friendships for you, from the potentially bad ones.

To begin this exercise, get ready to write.

Step 1: Write down as many adjectives, or qualities that you can think of, which best describe what you believe define a friendship.

Step 2: Now, define each of those adjectives or qualities that you wrote down in Step 1. Describe what these adjectives or qualities mean to you, and why.

Step 3: Pick the top five adjectives from Steps 1 and 2 that you believe best align with who you are as a person. This step will provide you with an opportunity to reflect upon how you see yourself, and more importantly, how you really want others to perceive you. How do you see yourself? How do you wish to be seen? As this exercise is all about actions, write down these five "self" adjectives and hang them up in a prominent place (bathroom mirror, doorway, etc.) to remind yourself how you wish to be perceived so that your actions and decisions remain in consistent alignment.

Step 4: Pick the top five adjectives that you would like your friends to possess which you believe would best support your own five adjectives listed from Step 3. You can choose to pick the same five adjectives as in Step 3, or you now can choose any five adjectives from Steps 1 and 2. The reason that I give you both options is that sometimes people like to befriend others who share the same qualities as themselves, whereas others find themselves attracted to opposites. Since this is *your* exercise, *you* get to decide which five adjectives you would like to list in Step 4.

Step 5: I have created the following chart for you to plug in the top five adjectives (which you determined in Step 4) that best describe qualities you would like your friends to possess. You are personalizing this chart, so replace "Adj. #1 - Adj. #5" with your actual adjective descriptions from your own list.

	Adj. #1	Adj. #2	Adj. #3	Adj. #4	Adj. #5
Friend's Name	Loyal	Supportive	Driven	Creative	Honest
Example: Linda	3	4	4	2	5

Step 6: Now choose some of your current friends and write their names in the far left column on the chart above. On a scale of 1-5 (1-poor, 2-fair, 3-good, 4-very good, 5-outstanding) rate how well each friend ranks under each adjective (see the Linda example above). Each friend should rank "3" or more on at least three out of your five adjectives. I would be surprised if they didn't since Step 6 represents those qualities that you emotionally need or desire based upon your own programming. Let's face it, you got to pick the adjectives, right? On to Step 7…

Step 7: In creating the chart and filling it in with your personalized data, you can now move on to see how these same friends of yours measure up against a different list of qualities which I believe better represent one's *universal needs*—needs that when fulfilled by one's friends will positively enhance one's self-esteem, trust, and life. This next step will definitely help you to differentiate whether the people you come into contact with should be called (considered) friends, acquaintances, etc.

For this last part of the exercise, I would like you to replace your five adjectives from Step 5 with the following six new "universal" adjectives (I've added one extra for this new chart).

1. *Safe* – How safe do you feel speaking openly with this person? Can you share intimate and personal things about your life with this person without worrying about them using the information against you?

2. *Reliable* – How reliable is this person to you? Can you rely on them to be there for you or follow up on your behalf? Are they there for you? Do they do what they say they'll do? (Note that this question asks about their *actions*.)

3. *Trustworthy* – How trustworthy is this person to you? Are they truly being honest with you or do you feel they are manipulating you in some way to gain your trust for their own purposes? Are they authentic in their intentions? Is their personality consistent among different people and situations?

4. *Supportive* – Is this person supportive of your goals, dreams, and passions? Do they cheer for your efforts and give you their true support, or do you feel they have their own agenda for why they hang out with you? Do they let their own fears and insecurities sabotage your success? Are they truly in your court? Do they have your best interests at heart, or their own?

5. *Myself (lets me be me)* – Does this person let you be yourself around them? Do you feel like you can just be you, or do you feel like somebody else whenever you're around them? Do they try to change you, or want you to be someone else and claim it is for your own good?

6. *Guilty* – Does this person ever make you feel guilty for not wanting to go along with what they want to do? Do you feel like you are compromising yourself to be friends with them?

Friend's Name	Safe	Reliable	Trust-worthy	Supportive	Myself	Guilty

I hope that you are now aware, and understand how these six new universal qualities require some form of action or commitment on behalf of others, which I like to refer to as, "Don't tell me—show me."

To complete this exercise, re-rank your same friends (from Step 6) using these new universal qualities on the chart above with the same ranking scale of 1-5 (1-poor, 2-fair, 3-good, 4-very good, 5-outstanding—see example below). Remember, it is extremely important that you be honest with your rankings because these universal qualities represent what every person should be receiving from a "true" friend.

Friend's Name	Safe	Reliable	Trust-worthy	Supportive	Myself	Guilty
Linda	2	3	2	2	2	4

After she performed this same exercise, my friend soon came to realize not every one of her so-called friends continued to rank the same when using the two different sets of adjectives in Step 5 versus Step 7. In fact, some ranked very low on Step 7's universal qualities.

So what does all this new information tell us? If, upon meeting new people, you can identify that they possess high rankings on both your emotional and universal quality requirements, then, by all means, call them a friend.

However, if you meet someone who possesses high rankings on your emotional qualities, but has not yet proven themselves on the universal qualities, consider them an acquaintance until shown otherwise. Do not immediately fast-pass them to "friend" status. Based upon what you learned from the exercise you just performed, the term "friend" should really have a deeper meaning for you now. With this in mind, if you meet someone who may possess high rankings on your emotional qualities, but very low on your universal qualities, then you may want to revisit their motives for seeking your friendship. Worst case, you may consider keeping them in your life as an "acquaintance" unless they prove to be nothing more than an emotional parasite.

And finally, I would also like to suggest that you revisit evaluating your current friends even if they have been lifelong friends. As you become more aware, you may realize you have inadvertently fast-passed someone to still be included in your circle of friends when they are no longer pulling their weight as a true friend. You have the right to disappoint others. Like clothes, you may outgrow your current circle of friends. It is okay to move on and go against the wishes of others if doing so is in your own best interest. In order to enhance your *probabilities* for success, you are going to need to surround yourself with people who will not only support and encourage you to attain your goals, but those who will also help you to grow as a person. True friends will always support your decision to embark on new life experiences—even when your intentions do not align with their own. Other friends may not align with your new path and you will need to let those who can't, fade away. Always remember and appreciate those who have helped you to become the person that you are today, but don't be afraid to leave some of your old friends behind if they can no longer champion or support your desired outcomes for success.

For Better or For Worse

Throughout your life, you should always try to cultivate healthy personal relationships with your parents, boyfriend/girlfriend, spouse/significant other, child/children, and friends based upon trust, honesty, mutual appreciation, love, and respect. Like any good relationship, it takes two people to make things work. So a good rule I always try to follow is to love someone the way you would want to be loved. Because at the end of the day, you may not always agree with someone else's opinion, but you should always remember that you are both entitled to have one. Therefore, you should never intentionally go out your way to make someone you love feel small or stupid. And if you do so unintentionally and they bring it to your attention, do not hesitate to apologize immediately. Owning and acknowledging the way someone else feels goes a very long way in sustaining mutual love and respect. Surrounding yourself with a supportive infrastructure of healthy relationships will always serve to enhance your success in all aspects of your life. But the most important relationship you'll have (outside of the one with yourself) is the one you have with your chosen life partner.

A great lesson I've learned as I've gotten older (another one that I wish I had learned earlier in my life) is regarding how to choose the ideal partner (boyfriend/girlfriend or spouse/significant other). It was imparted to me by my father in my late 20s. He told me, "The person you want to ultimately spend your life with should help you enhance your strong points, while also helping you to deal with your insecurities." When I took a moment to really think about what he had told me, and I began observing my family and friends, it finally dawned on me why most healthy relationships endure and thrive, while many unhealthy relationships typically end in divorce or remain stagnant with both partners feeling stuck with each other (most often "for the sake of the kids" or for financial reasons). The key to success for most of these healthy relationships came down to the fact that they shared core values and beliefs on most of their life's major issues. Sure, opposites can attract if they have different hobbies or idiosyncrasies, but if they do not share the same core values and beliefs such as religion, having children, where they want to live, etc., then their relationship will most likely become harder to endure. To be clear, I'm not saying their differences in core values will doom their relationship to failure—of course some relation- ships can most definitely endure without aligned core values—but what I am saying is that you can probably count on the presence of some inherent struggles between the couple if their core values and beliefs are not in alignment.

Why are core values so important? Because unbeknownst to most of us, our core values are actually synonymous with our subcon- scious "must haves," and what some don't realize is that after the initial honeymoon period wears off, without having shared core values, we actually start to feel like we are compromising ourselves by sacrificing an important part of our life to be with someone else. Resentment will become a predominant emotion both sides will have to manage. So what are some of the biggest potential core value "deal breakers" that should be discussed and/or addressed before entering any potential long-term relationship? Marriage (one partner really wants to get married, but the other is either unsure, or does not believe in marriage); religion (one partner is very religious and the other is not); children (one partner really wants to have children, but the other is either unsure, or does not want kids); and money (one partner likes to spend and the other likes to save). I understand that these core value deal breakers may not sound as important to you now (especially if you are younger because other factors may be at play when you begin a relationship), but I can assure you that as you get older and more set in your ways, these same issues will become harder to ignore.

I am encouraging you to learn from my experiences and start identifying your core values and beliefs, from an early age, so that you can avoid potentially unhealthy relationships (e.g., emotional parasites) that not only drain your energy and focus, but also delay or derail your desires, intentions, goals, and outcomes. It is important to be patient and take the time to select your relationships wisely. Be very aware of how others make you feel and do not allow fear or insecurity to cloud your better judgment. Everyone has personal and emotional baggage of some sort. However, projection of emotional issues and/or someone else's unhappiness onto you is not only disrespectful, but it's unfair. If your partner or spouse brings baggage into your relationship, just make sure they don't put *your* name on *their* bags. In a healthy relationship it is always important to compromise, but when the compromise becomes the sacrifice, move on! It is important to remember that you do not have control over other people's needs or emotions. They get to believe and behave in any way that they think is best for them. They get to be jerks, and they get to make their own mistakes. And if they choose not to learn from those mistakes, you have no control over that either. Yes, that is a bitter, miserable pill we all have to swallow— that no matter what we do, how loud or how often we say it, or how dead-on right we know we are, not everyone is going to buy into our belief system. It is neither your job, nor your responsibility, to change your partner. Achieving maturity dictates that you focus and work on YOU! As a young adult, you have a responsibility to yourself to learn from your own experiences with others, and to apply that knowledge in the best way you can.

Why am I discussing intimate healthy relationships with you? For the same reason I am demystifying all the other important success concepts in this book. Because you must always make good strategic decisions in *all* areas of your life to be successful. And while being "in love" with your life partner is extremely important, unfortunately, love alone may not be enough to keep you both together for the long haul. Marriage and long-term relationships involve making lots of business-related decisions together, and these decisions ultimately determine how successful your union's personal and financial outcomes may be. This is why it is so imperative that you share your core values and beliefs with each other prior to committing yourself to your loved one because you want to make sure that your future partner is on the same page with you about what really matters to you in your life.

If you are part of a young couple currently involved in a difficult and/or challenging relationship, then I would like to suggest that you both step back and ask yourselves what you might be doing individually or collectively that is contributing to your current set of challenges. I want you to honestly take the time to understand what each of you needs and wants in your relationship, and make sure that your partner or spouse really understands how you feel. Keep in mind that you cannot expect your partner to always know exactly how you feel or what you want. Positive changes start with open and honest communication, as well as a realistic view and awareness of yourself and your relationship.

Remember, good or bad, every type of relationship that you have with another human being is a learning experience. Whenever a bad relationship ends, you should always ask yourself what you learned from that relationship (especially about yourself) so that you can make better decisions and do things differently the next time to avoid similar situations and outcomes. Sure, it is always easier to blame someone else when a relationship goes south, but keep in mind that it always takes two to make a relationship work or fail. If your relationship ends, you need to swallow your pride and do some self-reflection. It is important to not only focus on what the other person did or did not do, but rather to focus on how their actions impacted you and made you feel. Did you really share the same core values or were you simply compromising yourself? Keeping in mind that we cannot change another person's beliefs, values, or behaviors, analyze your past relationships and try to identify similar situations or patterns. Then ask yourself what _you_ can do differently in choosing your next relationship. By doing so, you will be providing yourself with invaluable insights and confidence to grow your future success concerning your personal and professional relationships.

King or Queen of Your Castle

It's a scientific fact that when introduced to a new environment, an organism has only two choices: adapt or die. When things don't go your way, you can complain or you can choose to overcome the obstacle. The only thing you can ever truly count on is that things will always change—it is the only constant in life. The best way to always feel safe in a constantly changing world is to have a deeply rooted understanding of yourself. Over time, as you emotionally grow and change, your grounded sense of self (i.e., self-knowledge, self-acceptance, and self-trust) will enhance your ability to be flexible in adapting to change in a more comfortable way.

With that being said, I want you to think of yourself as king or queen of your castle and visualize your self-esteem, self-awareness, and your ability to be your own person serving as your castle's emotional moat. This protective moat should not be viewed as a negative attribute; it merely represents your confidence, sense of self, talents, strengths, and empathy toward others. Therefore, as king or queen of your castle, I strongly suggest that you only lower your metaphorical protective drawbridge (i.e., your guard) for positive people, opportunities, or situations that truly have your best interests at heart. DO NOT allow negative people (e.g., emotional parasites) or situations to cross your emotional moat because they could possibly compromise the integrity of your castle. Keep in mind, your strong self-esteem and keen self-awareness should always effectively guard your castle; don't waste your time entertaining negative thoughts. At the conclusion of John Lennon's 1972 INS Immigration Services hearing when he finally received confirmation that his immigration status was approved to remain in the United States, a reporter asked the ex-Beatle if he harbored any resentment toward those who tried to hurt him and kick him out of the United States. John simply muttered, "Time wounds all heels." Like John Lennon, you want to protect your castle and keep potential negativity from ever crossing your emotional moat! It is important to remember that there is no need to harbor anger and animosity toward others; you only need to manage your own expectations accordingly so that you are not disappointed by others' actions (or lack thereof). A great rule that I love to live by is, "Expect nothing and be pleasantly surprised." By not fostering any expectations, you take the pressure off of yourself from expecting actions in return—no expectations, no disappointments.

This approach is helpful under any circumstance where you may be setting yourself up for disappointment by imagining how you want/expect someone to respond to your intentions. You may be pleasantly surprised by their appreciation, acknowledgement, or a returned act of kindness. But, more importantly, by not expecting any of those responses, you won't be letting any outside forces affect your emotions. You stay in control of your own reality, and any disappointment you may feel will be due to your own thoughts and actions. I apply this same philosophy of taking "personal responsibility" when it comes to people thinking they "deserve" what is supposedly owed to them. The word "deserve" insinuates entitlement, and I believe it is more self-empowering to use the words "choosing," or "earning" when going after what you want in life. Starting now, YOU have the power to change your current beliefs and attitudes by *choosing* to live and *earn* the good fortune in life you wish to achieve. And you can get going right here, right now, by ensuring that you are, and continue to always, truly protect your inner castle.

Mentors and Masterminds

Throughout my life, I have been extremely fortunate to have found several great mentors and role models who have taken the time to help me further my own creative talents, knowledge, and goals. Your chosen mentors should act as tour guides on your personal journey of self-discovery and insight. Mentors can be family members (mother, father, brother, uncle, etc.), a favorite teacher, a good friend, or even a respected professional (e.g., doctor, lawyer, accountant, police officer, etc.). But most importantly, they should be people you really look up to who are willing to help you accomplish your interests, goals, and passions. A mastermind is a group of admired individuals that provide advice, support, and even financial resources to help you enhance your chances for success. As such, this mastermind group should include positive role models and mentors on whom you can rely to help you make important decisions regarding your personal and professional life—especially during times of uncertainty and despair.

As I mentioned before, when I was a young graduate student at Indiana University, I really wanted to be a professional musician and record executive. During my time at IU, I was very fortunate to have had the opportunity to study drums with one of my favorite mentors, Kenny Aronoff (former drummer for John Mellencamp). As a teacher, of course Kenny was very influential in helping me enhance and expand my drumming abilities. But as a mentor, he was very inspirational because he generously shared and explained his personal experiences with me regarding the music business. Like a great mentor, to this day he continues to offer me words of encouragement and admiration for all of my accomplishments. I look forward to sharing Kenny's story with you later in this book. He has an amazing story that I believe will inspire you just as it has me. Besides Kenny, there have been other teachers and role models over the past 20 years who have also inspired my success. I strongly encourage you to reach out and find similar mentors and role models for advice and assistance as you progress along your path to success. When asked to be a mentor, most people will usually be flattered and open to accepting that role (barring time constraints). It is also a great opportunity for them to give back, especially if they, too, were the recipients of positive mentoring in the past. In fact, if you can't find a personal mentor to work with you, don't be afraid to either interview, or write emails/letters to potential role models asking them if they're willing to impart any guidance or advice. You could also research your favorite role models' biographies or autobiographies online, at the library, bookstore, or rent/stream a movie about them. Although creating a personal mentoring relationship with that person is fairly unlikely, you can still admire and learn from his or her accomplishments and experiences through those various resources. For me, one of those role models was—and still is—billionaire investor, Warren Buffett.

I first learned about the great investor and businessman in 1996. I was immediately intrigued by his success and accomplishments and I wanted to learn as much as I could about who he was, and more importantly, how he was able to become so successful. I launched into voraciously reading articles, books, stories...anything I could get my hands on to learn more about Mr. Buffett. I had become such a huge fan, that by 1998 I even decided to invest in his company, Berkshire Hathaway. As a matter of fact, I have now flown to Omaha, Nebraska five times over the past 10 years to attend his company's annual shareholders meeting. Imagine what a thrill it was for me when I got to meet one of my inspirational mentors, Warren Buffett, at my first shareholders meeting that same year.

In addition to studying Warren Buffett and applying his lessons, I always enjoy learning from any professionals I admire. So I make sure to read a lot of autobiographies and biographies on a regular basis. In fact, if there is someone out there you want to emulate, then learn all you can about them and how they achieved their success. Of course, it's even more helpful if you read their life story because it basically serves as a blueprint for you to achieve similar success. Personally, I am perpetually expanding my knowledge with continued education (beyond simply reading autobiographies and biographies). I still love attending as many free webinars (on my computer) and live seminars or workshops that I can squeeze into my schedule. Sometimes I will even drive down to a local hotel or convention center to attend a free seminar if I believe the topic will benefit me in the long run. By the way, initial seminars are usually free and I find that if you pay close enough attention, you can almost always walk away with some important piece of knowledge or advice (even if you decide not to invest in any of the speaker's or company's products—courses, books, software, etc.). So don't hesitate to sign up for webinars and stay active within your social media networks. Do anything you can that will put you in contact with people or information that interests you.

As I like to tell students, "Throughout your life, education appreciates, possessions depreciate." In other words, invest in yourself, not stuff. The more knowledge you acquire over time, the more opportunities you provide for yourself to move forward in attaining your future desires and goals.

Network, Network, Network

No one who was ever truly successful in life accomplished their goals alone. If you ask anyone who has ever risen to the top of their field or profession, they will most likely tell you it's "who you know," or "your connections," along with "tons of hard work," that helps you to get where you want to go. Their strategy is simple: seek out other people who could help further their goals. That is why it is extremely important that you begin, from an early age, to reach out and build a network of personal and professional contacts and relationships that can help you to grow your future success. Your network can include people you meet at various events—school, social, or business. They can be members of groups or organizations that you choose to join and affiliate with, or they can be people who you connect with through social media (such as LinkedIn, Facebook, etc.) who share similar interests or goals. Because networks provide potential contacts and resources, I suggest you get an early start by seeking out various clubs, or extracurricular activities if you are still in high school. There are usually several afterschool clubs, sports teams, etc. that you can join which will not only give you the time to spend with other members who share similar interests, but they also give you the opportunity to meet and get to know your peers who you may not normally get to interact with inside the classroom.

During college, as you continue to broaden your network, there are countless organizations you can choose to interact with: leadership groups, programming boards, student and resident life organizations, fraternities or sororities, as well as campus mixers and networking events. Beyond enhancing your college life experience, these organizations are designed to help you make important connections. After graduation, you should affiliate with your college's alumni association—it is a great opportunity to seek out other alumni members for advice or potential job opportunities.

If you recently relocated to a new city for school or work and you don't know many people, these same networking outlets are available in the real world. Consider joining a club, organization, or group that shares similar interests (collegiate, hobbies, religious, etc.), or a professional association that can help you meet other like-minded professionals. If you are shy, introverted, or you simply feel uncomfortable walking up to total strangers, then take advantage of any opportunity you can to join a club or event where you can practice speaking with people.

Through my associations with the L.A. Leggers running group, Toastmasters International, the Online Trading Academy, and various "meetup" groups that I joined in Los Angeles, I was able to meet and interact with so many great people who have not only become important contacts and resources for me, but have also become friends. We human beings are social creatures who crave belonging to a community; we have an ingrained need to spend time with other people that we can relate to and connect with through shared interests and common life experiences. However, despite having that need, it doesn't make it any easier to take that first step toward assimilating within a community. It is very natural for us to feel a little out of sorts when we begin networking with others. So I've listed some quick tips to help you feel more prepared and at ease when you being to reach out and approach others:

1. Be yourself! It is really important that people get to know the real you. When you are authentic and honest through your interactions and communication with others, it definitely goes a long way toward making it easier for others to connect with you (which could lead to recommendations and referrals on your behalf).

2. Explore beyond your comfort zone. Whenever you attend an event or function, instead of gravitating toward your regular crowd, try to engage with others outside of your usual group of friends, acquaintances, or "types." Make it a goal to try to reach out and speak to at least a few new people you wouldn't <u>normally</u> get an opportunity to meet. For example, "I will speak to five new people at this event." Then after the event, if you felt a connection and liked engaging with a particular person/people, it is extremely important to follow up by sending a short email where you include a "call to action" when you reach out by proposing a time to speak on the phone or meet for lunch, etc. Basically, a "call to action" is where you give them the opportunity to respond in a way that will move the relationship forward. Make sure you do not overlook including this in your email since that end-result is what networking is all about. As you establish your mutually beneficial (personal and/ or professional) relationship, don't forget to figure out if there are ways you can assist this new "connection" in the future to continue to build and grow your mutual trust.

3. Establish social connections. Try to expand your social network by reaching out to new contacts via LinkedIn, Facebook, Twitter, etc. Ask your current contacts if they can introduce or recommend you to someone online that you would really like to connect with or meet. Introduce yourself to new people and give them an opportunity to get to know you, especially if you believe you share common interests, etc.

4. Own your personal brand. In social or professional situations, always dress the way you want others to perceive, identify, and/ or remember you. First impressions do matter, so always project a positive self-image because you never know who you might meet or be introduced to. Dress for success, act appropriately, and carry business cards and a copy of your resume (if applicable). By the way, it's practically free to have a simple online presence. If you haven't already done so, consider purchasing a URL (web address) with your "name.com." Then you can go get a free blog (Word-Press is the most popular) using one of their free templates—pick something that looks clean and simple. Once you follow the site's intuitive prompts and post your contact information and resume (and any other professionally presented, pertinent information that furthers your personal branding message), copy your new blog page's link, then go back to the site where you purchased your URL address. Locate the forwarding feature and paste your blog's link there. Save it and wait a few minutes, then check it to confirm that when you type your personalized URL ("name.com") into the browser, it forwards to your blog. Once you've done this, you can now put your website branding on your business card, LinkedIn profile, Facebook page, etc., and it will demonstrate to prospective employers/schools that you are a person who not only pays attention to detail, but also that you are a person who goes over and above to succeed.

5. Don't be the smartest person in the room. Networking is all about meeting new people and building mutually beneficial relationships. You can't learn if you are always the one doing the talking. You need to also listen and provide space so that you both can connect and determine if you can build and create a personal and/or professional relationship with each other in the future. It is always a great idea to look for opportunities to get the other person to talk about themselves or their ideas. Ask them questions along the lines of: What do you do? How did you get started in your job? How are you affiliated with the organization hosting this event? What do you like about your company or organization? What advice can you share with me? What are some of the biggest challenges you foresee in the future of your industry, company, school, organization, etc.? Have you had a lot of success networking with other people at these same types of events? What tips can you share with me that helped make you successful? Of course, these are just some of the many questions you can ask to forge a relationship with a new connection. Remember, people tend to love talking about themselves and will appreciate people who are genuinely interested in listening to them.

6. *Never overstay your welcome.* If the conversation is going well, you will quickly get to know their interests (Why did you choose to attend this event or function?) and their goals (What do you hope to accomplish in the future?). Give your conversation enough time to grow organically so that you can take note of all the information they share with you to determine if you can provide them with any valuable help after the event. When the conversation starts to wind down and it is time to move on, ask the other person if it would be okay to follow up with them at a later time to continue your conversation. You do not want to monopolize the other person's time, suffocate them, or force uncomfortable conversation. Learn to read nonverbal cues!

7. *Pitch yourself, not your products.* Remember, your goal at a networking event is to acquire information to determine if you can possibly build a future relationship with another person based upon providing each other with valuable resources and potential referrals. You are not there to "pitch" them products or services. If you effectively network and build good relationships, there will be plenty of time to exchange ideas, etc. No one likes to feel cornered like their backs are up against a wall. If you are attending a social event, keep things light and festive. If you are attending a business or professional function, inquire why they are attending and what they hope to get out of participating.

Building a collaborative relationship through networking enables you to consult with others outside of your normal circles and to leverage each other's talents and connections. Therefore, I strongly encourage you to seek out professional networks or groups as a way of sharing new ideas and learning new ways of doing things so you can create more opportunities for your future personal and financial success.

Call to Action

For this exercise, I would like you to complete the following three actions:

1. Take a moment and think about the people who tend to inspire and influence you the most. These people can be parents, teachers, celebrities, spouses, coworkers, or even classmates. Now, write down five qualities that you admire most about these people.

Quality #1: _____

Quality #2: _____

Quality #3:_____

Quality #4: _____

Quality #5: _____

For this next list, instead of writing down qualities you admire, write down five qualities that you *least* admire as they pertain to people that you know. It is not important who these people are. Rather, it is more important that you learn how to identify these negative qualities in others to learn, from an early age, how you can avoid adopting these same negative traits as your own so that they do not become *your* habits.

Quality #1: _____

Quality #2: _____

Quality #3:_____

Quality #4: _____

Quality #5: _____

Now that you have compiled your list of the 10 qualities which came to mind (5 positive, 5 negative), I want you to take a moment and reflect upon what you have just learned about the person you now wish to become. In the space below, write down how you plan to start incorporating these newly identified positive qualities into your daily routine. Make sure to also address how you plan to eliminate any of the negative qualities that you've identified in others, as ones that you recognize you possess as well.

_____

_____

_____

_____

2. In an effort to help you cultivate happy, healthy relationships in your future, I would like you to take an honest look at what is truly important to you, and write down five core values that you hope to share with a future boyfriend/girlfriend, or spouse/significant other. By honestly communicating (and adhering to) your true core values with a potential boyfriend/girlfriend or spouse/significant other, you will be greatly enhancing your *probability* of meeting a partner with whom you will not be compromising qualities and beliefs that truly matter to you.

Core Value #1: _____

Core Value #2: _____

Core Value #3: _____

Core Value #4: _____

Core Value #5: _____

3. List two or three networking events that you can attend per month, and what you hope to accomplish at those events.

Network Event #1: _____

Network Event #2: _____

Network Event #3: _____

4. If you have not already done so, I would suggest that you watch the movie, The Pursuit of Happyness (or read the book by the same title). It is based on self-made million-aire and motivational entrepreneur, Chris Gardner's struggle in the 1980s to pursue an unknown path that he believed would create a better life for himself and his infant son. But in order for Chris to pursue a better life, it required him to quit his job—lose his safety net—and trust his instincts. The combination of his personal beliefs, positive attitude, and following the sound advice from his mother, helped bolster Chris's determination, inspiration, and strength to overcome his fears and obstacles to attain the better life he knew he really wanted. The reason I have added this last action is because I believe his story truly personifies the lessons we have been address-ing regarding one's ability to step up and protect their castle, despite all negative obstacles that may be placed in their path.

"If you choose to put such a small value on yourself, don't expect the rest of the world to raise the price."

~ Author Unknown

4

The Business of YOU

Be YOU, because everyone else is taken.

The popular quotation, "You never get a second chance to make a first impression," has been attributed to poet and playwright, Oscar Wilde. Although the quote's true origin still remains unclear, as I mentioned earlier, its message is not: first impressions *do* matter and they are often hard to change—especially if they do not go well. Have you ever seen or heard a loud, obnoxious parent scream-ing at a coach or player at a high school or college football or soc-cer game, or someone who wore clothes that were way too tight for their body type, or they looked poorly groomed (messy hair, bad teeth, etc.)? Do you remember what your first impression was of those people? I hope so, because it probably wasn't a positive one. This is why I stress how important it is to present your best self everywhere you go. Because your clothes (including your shoes, accessories, etc.), grooming habits (hair, teeth, shaving, makeup, etc.), strong mental and physical health (hobbies, spouse/significant other, friends, etc.), automobile (if applicable—and I'm referring to its upkeep, not its brand), and even your communication style (vocabulary usage, thought organization, speaking tones, listening and relating skills, etc.), all make up the foundation of a first impression that you consciously (or unconsciouly) choose to project to others. And if you continue to personify these characteristics or attributes long enough (intentionally or unintentionally), they *will* start to become identifiable by others as *your own personal brand*. Details do matter. Oprah Winfrey, Martha Stewart, and Donald Trump (to name a few) all worked very hard to create and establish their own personal brand/style to help others remember and identify with them. So again, it is extremely important to always keep in mind that whenever you meet someone new, or even when simply walking out your front door, you will always be taking *your personal brand* with you because this is how you (consciously or unconsciously) want others to perceive, identify, and/or remember you. Trust me, if you don't take the time to always be presentable, even when running a quick errand, you will eventually run into someone (a potential boss, an ex-boyfriend/girlfriend, etc.) who you do not want to see you looking like a wreck! Therefore, always choose to present a positive self-image and take the extra time to do so, because you should never expect others to see you any other way than how you present and promote yourself to the world.

In addition to your physical appearance, you also want to be very aware of your personal core values and beliefs, because they not only tend to influence your decisions, but also the way you choose to speak and interact with others. This is why it is so important that you become well-versed in what your core values and beliefs are from an early age. The sooner you do so, the easier it will be for others to genuinely connect with you. For example, Oprah Winfrey has done an amazing job over the years to not only project a strong sense of self, but to also craft a very polished personal brand that she intentionally designed to attract her specific target audience. This allows her followers to both relate to, and identify with her based upon that personal brand. According to Outsell, Inc. (a research and advisory firm focused on the publishing, information, and education industries), it is estimated that the budget allocated for advertising and marketing within the United States back in 2008 was $412 billion. Companies and businesses spend tremendous amounts of time and money each year promoting and advertising their personal brand messages to the general public. As the "marketing and advertising director" of your own life, it is equally important that you also choose how you want to advertise and promote *your* own personal brand. It should be consistent with your personal life mission statement (your intentions, core values, and goals). If you recall, in the last chapter we spent a lot of time discussing self-esteem, mentors, and role models. While establishing your own personal brand, I suggest starting off by incorporating some of the positive qualities that you have admired in your role models and/ or mentors. If you happen to favor certain types of professionals (athletes, businesspeople, actors, musicians, teachers, etc.), then start studying the personal brands of some of the more popular and successful leaders within those professions. Taking the time to educate yourself by understanding what has helped so many other people become successful, will provide you with ideas to enhance your own personal brand that you present to the world. I guarantee you that the people you choose to model yourself after did the very same thing with the people who came before them. We are all influenced by each other, so choose positive and successful influencers.

Establish your own signature look. Work on creating your personal brand by honing your image with your own unique look or style that you want others to quickly identify and remember you by (Jennifer Aniston's "The Rachel" hairstyle from *Friends*, or Donald Trump's signature red silk ties both come to mind). You'll want to try to distinguish yourself from others by being unique and memorable. But I do recommend you don't go too overboard where you come off as so zany and weird that you muddy your intended image (unless—as in Lady Gaga's case—that *is* your intent). In addition to your appearance affecting how others perceive you, your personality also helps define your personal brand. Some people may project a cool or laid back image, while others may come off as uptight or intense. Whatever your personality type is, the important thing is to be authentic, true to yourself, and embrace your personality quirks. Own them. If you are a geek, then be an *awesome* geek! Otherwise, you won't come off to others as unique and genuine. By the way, there are a lot of cool, successful geeks (e.g., Bill Gates, Albert Einstein, director Ron Howard, Larry M. Jacobson, etc.).

Have a clear understanding of who you are. Embracing and committing to your core values, character, integrity, and beliefs ensures that others will truly connect with you in a genuine way. The major element in exhibiting quality of character and high integrity involves *always* being true to your word ("Do what you say, and say what you do!"), and making sure that your actions back up your words ("Walk the talk, or put it on mute!"). By taking the time to further enhance your awareness and identify with your own personal strengths, skills, and abilities ("I am a great listener," or "I am a great problem solver," etc.), you will be empowering yourself with the opportunity to connect more deeply with others, and in turn, you will further enhance the personal brand you project to others.

Trust your instincts (using good common sense and trusting your intuition). Although "book smarts" are important, so is common sense (or "street smarts"). But unfortunately, it is not as common as you'd think. Using good common sense and trusting your intuition are more factors in what truly separates the successful from the unsuccessful. Your intuition is that little voice inside your head, or that uncomfortable feeling in your gut, which helps you differentiate whether something *feels* right, versus being off or wrong—even if your reaction doesn't quite seem logical at the time. In American culture, many young adults have been programmed to simply override their instincts because they've constantly been reminded to: "keep their heads down," "look the other way," "don't make waves," "let someone else handle it," "don't challenge authority," etc. Consequently, many have learned to tune themselves out and therefore they haven't learned to listen to, follow, or trust their own instincts. Instead, they often just ignore them and overthink themselves into paralysis. Or, they go in the opposite direction and give themselves permission to have knee-jerk reactions which they then follow up with second-guessing themselves and their decisions—after the fact. If they arrive at their decisions via either of those routes, they're led to possible, versus *probable,* outcomes for success. Why? Because there's a balance one needs to strike between listening to their "gut" (that intuitive "inner voice"), and reconciling that message with the one they get from their "head" (that indifferent "logical voice").

Of course, sound decisions are based on logic, but my whole point here is for you to wake up your inner voice and then listen to what you're telling yourself! Your instincts are actually the foundation for your own empowerment. Too often, people get swayed by negative or unsupportive comments made by others—despite what their own instincts might be telling them to do. They often allow others to "get inside their heads" and thus, overthink, or even worse, falsely predict how others might respond or react to their decisions or ideas. Unfortunately, these people rarely proceed as they initially intended, either out of fear of another's reaction, or even worse, to appease the other person at their own expense. At the end of the day, you have the right to disappoint others. This is your life—don't phone it in!

To be successful, you need to be able to identify opportunities by learning, from a young age, how to trust your own instincts. Your ability to confidently trust those instincts will allow you to grow your mental muscle to quickly run your cost-benefit (risk vs. reward) assessments in making speedy decisions. Being agile in that skill will enable you to be flexible, ready, and able to pounce on opportunities as they arise. Successful people "go for it." They check their fears at the door. They trust their instincts to spot the opportunities, which prompts them to reaffirm their intentions to motivate and empower themselves to take the necessary action steps to positively impact their desired expectations and *probable* outcomes for success.

One of the biggest regrets that I often hear from so many adults is that they wish they had begun listening to their instincts and followed their own path earlier in life. If they had just done that when they were younger adults, they would have gone after what they desired earlier in their lives, rather than going down the path they ended up choosing—trying to always please someone else by either working at a job they didn't really want, being in an unhealthy relationship because they sacrificed their own core values, or even worse, leading a fear-based life. When most of these people now look back in hindsight, they are convinced that if they had just listened to, and trusted, their instincts when they were younger, then their situations would have only been temporary and they would currently be leading a much more fulfilled life. If you do your inner work now, your older and wiser self will thank you later. And remember what my wife also likes to say, "Follow the path of least regrets!"

To help you get in touch with your emotions, and strengthen your own instincts, I would like to recommend the following exercise to help you get out of your own way, or more specifically, out of your own head. To be effective, this exercise should be repeated daily for the next 45 consecutive days (keep in mind what I have said about doing your inner work from a young age—improvement takes commitment and discipline).

For the next 45 days, during each daily exercise session, I would like you to choose a quiet place where you can sit down uninterrupted and become aware of your own feelings. This is *not* a "thinking" exercise, but rather, a "feeling" exercise. There is no time limit, so relax and take as much time as you need. It might help you to pick a specific time each day to do this exercise so that it's easy for you to remember to stick with it. This is all about acquainting (or reacquainting) yourself with your long-lost feelings and goals. By the end of the 45 days, getting in touch with your emotions, and trusting your instincts, will likely have become a habit which will have prepared you to quickly handle making big decisions in the future. You'll also be better prepared to determine who you can trust enough to support you and be in your inner circle.

Once you have found your quiet place, and have your notebook and a pen/pencil with you, relax. As you get comfortable and settle in, bring your awareness to any miscellaneous thoughts and focus on releasing them as you clear and calm your mind down. Now, reflect upon five different emotions that you recall feeling that day. Once you have identified your five emotions, handwrite each emotion in your notebook. DO NOT overthink this exercise. Simply jot down the first five emotions that immediately come to mind. Then briefly describe where you were when you felt each emotion, and more importantly, why you believe you felt that emotion at that particular time. Was there a person or an event that triggered that emotion? Again, there are no right or wrong answers. The purpose of this exercise is to help you learn (or re-learn) to listen to, and trust your own instincts and emotions (the "how" and "why" you may feel a certain way during a certain time). The goal is to get you out of your own head so you are able to begin tapping into, and utilizing, your inherent common sense. This will help ensure that your decisions and responses to others are properly aligned with your personal core values and goals.

I know that what we've covered in this chapter all sounds easier said than done, so I would like to quickly summarize and offer you the following four tips that I hope will further enhance your personal brand and help you strengthen your ability to listen and trust your instincts:

1. Whenever you find yourself feeling pressured and anxious about making important decisions or seemingly simple choices, stop thinking about everything—simply turn your mind off. Relax, breathe, and start listening to what your body is feeling. Let your body lead your mind. What is your body trying to tell you?

2. Notice whether your body is feeling calm (peaceful), or agitated (on edge) as a result of your pending decisions or choices.

3. In addition to getting in touch with how your body is feeling, especially in the beginning, start sharing your pending decisions or choices with your close friends, family (yes, including parents), spouse/significant other, mentors, etc.— basically whomever you think truly has your best interests at heart. Keep your trusted people in the loop on your thought processes until you start feeling comfortable enough to begin trusting your own instincts, then check in with them and see if they agree with you. This is called "holding yourself accountable." A lot of people often purposely avoid telling others how they feel about a decision or choice because, despite knowing their decision is wrong, they want to do it anyway and they are afraid the other person may try to talk them out of it. The truth is, if the person you are confiding in is truly on your side, then any objections they may have should be a screaming signal to you that something *is* wrong and you should rethink your intentions accordingly.

4. Sleep on it! Do not allow yourself to feel pressured into having to make any last-minute decisions or choices if you do not feel comfortable with what the expected consequences will be. At this stage, hold off on calculating a split-second cost-benefit analysis and leave the speedy decision-making for down the road when you will have mastered balancing your intuition, with your logic. Take the time you need to weigh all of the pros and cons and continue practicing the good common sense you were born with.

Your Actions Speak Louder Than Words

Understanding the reality of social media. If you are like most young adults, then you have probably posted "your brand" countless times on various social media sites (Instagram, Pinterest, Twitter, Facebook, etc.) and have possibly done so without thinking twice about what these postings might be saying about you. Like I said earlier, it is extremely important to always remember that whenever you walk out your front door, you will always be taking *your personal brand* with you because this is how you (consciously or unconsciously) want others to perceive, identify, or remember you. This advice especially holds true for social media sites, as your postings serve as portals to your personal life (and your brand) for others to observe (and judge) from the comfort of their own computer screens. And if you think there is no harm in posting crazy, irresponsible pictures, or verbal rants because you are "young and there will be no real repercussions," think again. Just like George Orwell's book, *1984*—"Big Brother is always watching." And like Las Vegas, what happens on the 'Net stays on the 'Net. This may seem obvious, but you really need to be careful and aware of what you choose to post on social media sites because once you post them, despite any future efforts to delete them, they will very likely still be accessible to others (including future prospective bosses and in-laws!).

Throughout the years, my teachers often reminded me that you don't want to say or do anything in your life that you wouldn't want to appear on the front page of the New York Times for all your friends and family to see. The same warning should hold true about your social media postings. If you are posting inappropriate things, you might think it is harmless and funny, but I can assure you, potential employers will likely find your inappropriate pictures and/or verbal rants to be unproductive and offensive. To help you avoid any embarrassing and potentially irreversible social media faux pas, I would like to offer you the following friendly advice:

As a general rule, I strongly suggest that you only choose to post things on your social media sites that truly support or represent your *personal brand.* Like your unique look or style, your postings should intrigue, not offend, potential supporters or employers. Your pictures and written posts should positively reinforce your personal brand, and describe how you would like others to perceive you.

What I would like you to keep in mind is that successful people utilize social media to help them share their personal vision and goals by explaining to their friends/followers/connections how they help other people to do "X." For example, I like to describe myself in the following way: I help young adults (ages 16 to 25) pursue their goals by making strategic decisions that positively impact their overall financial and personal success. To help reinforce my message (i.e., personal brand), I like to share my thoughts and insights at LarryMJacobson.com, as well as on my other social media sites, in order to help empower young adults, and adults of all ages, to discover new and different ways to succeed and define success on their own terms. To remain consistent with my personal brand, I often post pictures, videos, blogs, and articles that I believe help young adults make better decisions that will positively impact their overall personal and financial success. So by all means, use social media proactively to further enhance your personal brand and to maximize your success, but please, do yourself a favor, use it responsibly.

Know proper social etiquette. Just like in the virtual world, in the real world, nothing can tarnish a personal brand or make a worse first—or lasting—impression than bad manners or poor social etiquette. You always want to make sure that you act and behave appropriately in various social and/or professional situations and settings. Being aware of, and sensitive to, others' cultures and beliefs is an important part of diplomacy—which is an essential aspect of proper social etiquette. For example, if you were traveling abroad, you would (or should) do your research to find out if certain

American cultural behaviors might inadvertently offend your hosts. Why wouldn't you try to give yourself that same leg up in any new setting? If you find yourself invited to attend a new social or professional situation, I suggest you do your homework by finding out what the appropriate etiquette will be for that particular setting and occasion, so that you can always put your best foot forward.

Make sure when you're doing your research, that you don't overlook finding out what the event's specified proper attire is so that you dress appropriately and respectfully—there is a big difference between casual, business casual, cocktail, and dressy (or black-tie) attire. Again, your goal is to always make a positive first impression. It was Shakespeare who said, "All the world's a stage..." So call it what you will—costume, wardrobe, outfit, attire, etc.—the point is, dress the part! Also, all those polite niceties your parents taught you to say when you were little like, "please," "thank you," and "excuse me," were, and still are, very important. Always be polite to whomever you encounter and when anyone extends themselves to you, show them you are grateful for their kindness (e.g., sending "Thank You" notes). Doing so will go a long way toward establishing mutual respect and may potentially create a future ally. And if you're a young man, don't confuse respecting women as equals with not being chivalrous—equality is allowing all men and women equal opportunities for achievement. But that does not mean that men and women are the same: because the fact is, we're not. I believe our gender differences should be celebrated, not stifled. Therefore, I think men should always offer to hold a door open for others (both genders!) and be a gentleman at all times. You can never go wrong by honoring good, old-fashioned, traditional manners. Finally, pay attention to your table manners—do not talk with food in your mouth, no elbows on the table, place the napkin on your lap, etc.

Others may not recognize or acknowledge your good etiquette and manners, but they sure will remember your poor ones. If you feel like you need more information, I would suggest going online, going to the library, or purchasing a book to do further research on proper manners and social etiquette.

Communicate comfortably and effectively with others. Just as your physical appearance and mannerisms play a major role in your overall personal branding, so does how well you communicate with others. Therefore, it is essential that you acquire good written and verbal skills before graduating from high school so that your effective communication skills can (and will) further enhance your personal brand. If you do not feel comfortable speaking in front of larger groups of people, then I highly recommend that you consider joining a social networking group such as Toastmasters International or some other high school, college, or professionally sponsored program or organization that focuses primarily on public speaking.

Equally important, beyond taking the requisite "English 101" class, take an additional writing class (in high school and/or college). Doing so will help you delve deeper into HOW to apply the written English language (covering sentence structure and organization, using proper punctuation, grammar, spelling, etc.). In addition, refrain from using "big" words in conversations, emails, or reports if you do not understand what those words mean, or if you do not know how to use them correctly within the written or verbal context. Finally, please make sure that you always take the extra time to reread and spell-check your emails for errors and/or omissions before you send them out. You do not want to appear illiterate, uneducated, or lacking the ability to pay attention to detail. Remember, having solid written and verbal communication skills can make all the difference when it comes to enhancing the quality of your personal brand. Because, again, you are being assessed by others on all of the above factors I covered. Be conscientious about how all of your actions present who you are to the world. Make your message a great one.

There is a reason the popular old saying, "Know your audience!" exists. You can always learn a lot from others if you just simply study their nonverbal cues (i.e., communication through body language) and listen to their conversations (without interrupting, or being distracted by your own thoughts). Don't forget: never, ever, think you are the smartest person in the room. Because not only does humility go a long way, but by adopting this belief, you will be leaving yourself open to learning from others. And you never know where, or from whom, you'll learn your next lesson. By being observant of others, you can also determine a lot about what the other person is really thinking. In negotiations, they often call this a "tell" because it's used as a tool for factoring in how one wants to play their next "move." In fact, the general consensus among researchers is that humans actually communicate 90% of the time through nonverbal, versus verbal, communication. By now, I'm sure you understand why I have emphasized just how important nonverbal communication is, and why you should always take it into consideration when it comes to positively building your personal brand. Remember, it's not what you say, it's what you *don't* say—words are just words until they become actions, and actions speak.

One final thought on this topic...I'd like to share with you an anonymous quote I once heard: "Don't worry about what other people think about you, only worry about the information that you give them to think about you."

Your Health: Nutrition and Exercise

Although genetics do play a role in obesity, it has become clear that as a nation, our overconsumption of processed foods has led to a vast number of today's obesity cases. To stress my point, obese and "just" overweight children are much more likely to become obese adults. According to the Center for Disease Control and Prevention (CDC), an estimated 17% of American children and young adults (between the ages of 2 - 19), are now considered obese because they suffer from an imbalance between the calories they consume, and the calories they actually use (burning the calories off by metabolizing their caloric intake through physical activity). To put it simply, their food consumption (input) outweighs their exercise levels (output). A child is now considered overweight when the relationship between their weight and height on the Body Mass Index (BMI) is between the 85th and 95th percentile (when their BMI is above the 95th percentile, they are considered obese). Why is this important statistic alarming? Because overweight and obese children are usually more susceptible to acquiring life-threatening cardiovascular diseases (e.g., high blood pressure, high cholesterol, and type 2 diabetes) from an early age. The CDC also found that 25% of the children who were already overweight between the ages of 10 - 15, usually became obese by the age of 25 (at the time of the study, 80% of the children were already overweight).

Obesity in America has now become not only a health care epidemic, but also an economic problem for individuals and companies. In fact, while I am not implying it is a legal practice, there may even be an unspoken bias at some companies to avoid hiring obese employees because their high-risk medical condition could potentially impact the company's financial bottom line (due to an expensive health insurance liability). Not to mention the risk of short-term or long-term disability claims potentially being filed by employees as a result of their added health risks. And to make matters even worse, if being overweight or obese is not remedied as early as possible, their own future retirement savings could be severely impacted due to related health problems requiring potentially expensive medical care.

When it comes to being overweight or obese (in addition to the potential health complications caused by overeating), one cannot put a price on the real cost of being hindered while doing everyday activities in life. I hope you clearly see how having optimum physical health is yet another factor which contributes to your overall success.

I must stress this to you: there is more to physical health than just *appearing* fit—you've got to *be* fit. There are plenty of out of shape average, or even thin, people whose health is compromised because they do not exercise (usually their "good genes" let them rest on their laurels). I cannot emphasize enough how important it is that you learn to incorporate the following three habits, early on: exercise regularly, eat/drink healthily, and get plenty of sleep. While, of course, living a healthy lifestyle will make you feel good, it will also further support your personal brand—because how you look on the outside is definitely a reflection of how you feel on the inside. My wife, Kate, is one of those people who has "good genes" and has been thin her entire life. But she'll be the first to tell you that as she got older, she had to work at remaining thin. She realized how out of shape she had become when, despite being petite, she couldn't catch her breath when walking up a long stairway. After that wake-up call, she joined a gym, continues to watch what she eats, makes getting plenty of sleep a priority, and exercises not only to stay fit and strong, but to enhance her emotional state as well. It has been proven that people who tend to be stressed often try to fill their emotional voids by overeating. Or some respond by losing their appetite and starving themselves. Proper diet and exercise relieves stress and will help you avoid unwanted health problems, feel good about yourself, and keep you focused and motivated.

A good diet and exercise program is essential in helping you find balance within your life, so you should try to find time to exercise at least three to four times a week, for at least a half-hour a day. A strong body is a strong mind. Regular exercise will improve your confidence and help clear your mind to make better decisions, thus improving your overall outlook on life. I also suggest that, before you embark on a new diet and/or exercise regime, you do the following: discuss your intentions with a health care professional at your high school's or college's health center, or speak with a specialist at your university's gym or local health club, or schedule a visit with your personal internist. However you go about preparing to improve your health, consult with a professional prior, so you can create a good regimen of proper diet and exercise that will work specifically for you. Not only will you be able to start releasing a lot of tension and stress in your body, but you will also start to look and feel a whole lot healthier. One final reminder: I mentioned earlier that getting plenty of sleep should be a priority (I highly recommend that you get at least eight hours of sleep each night), because lack of sleep can also affect your weight and, of course, your energy level. By starting as young as possible, you'll improve your chances of avoiding health issues, staying fit, looking great, and most importantly, you will have turned good health into a strong habit.

Nutrition

An important aspect of ensuring you're eating a healthy diet, is managing your daily caloric intake to make sure it's the right amount for your current condition and body type. Just as I had suggested before about your exercise regime, you should consult your doctor or a specialist to determine what the right amount of calories would be for you to consume on a daily basis. I realize that for some of you calorie-counting might be time-consuming, so I recommend that you find a free website or smartphone app that can track and count your daily calories, as well as your workouts. Look for free sites or apps that also provide diet plans, exercise programs, weight-loss tips, recipes, support communities (blogs, message boards, articles, etc.), as well as helpful tracking tools. To use the website or app to your best advantage, all you will have to invest in is a small notepad to write down, and keep track of, your daily meals so that you can transfer that information to the website or app.

Try to balance your meals and limit your processed food intake. In addition, you must stay vigilant about hydrating throughout the entire day—especially after you exercise (since perspiration depletes your water reserves). So, you've heard it before and, because it bears repeating, I'll say it again: drink lots of water and *really* limit drinking sweet beverages (soda, energy drinks, juices, etc.) as much as possible. And don't delude yourself that just because diet sodas are called "diet," they are justifiably healthier for you to drink. Since they are loaded with artificial sweeteners, they are definitely not healthier. As a matter of fact, many would argue that diet sodas are actually detrimental to your good health. Moreover, carbonated drinks are *never* a good choice and, if possible, you should strike them out of your intake completely. Again, your future self will thank you. If you choose to eat out, it's a well-known fact that restaurant portions are greater than one needs to consume in one sitting—you do not need to eat all the food on your plate (contrary to my generation's programming, cleaning your plate will not alleviate world hunger). There is no shame in telling your server you'd like your food "to go." It will taste just as good, if not better, at home or back in your residence hall (especially when you're bogged down studying).

Speaking of residence life (for you college students)—save yourself from "The Freshman 15" (a reference to the pounds that new college students rapidly pack on) fast-food diet sabotage. Stock up on easily accessible, yet healthy snack foods such as nuts, fruits, and vegetables (unsalted almonds make an excellent snack), Greek yogurt, trail mix, and protein/energy bars. Above all, remember this: everything in moderation! If you follow this basic rule, by moderating the ratios of your food intake relative to your exercise output, you'll be striking the proper balance that is necessary to maintain a healthy weight. Whether you eat out or at home, you really should try to make as many healthy choices as you can. Because those unhealthy choices (calories) add up, and you don't want that addition to be to your midsection!

If you are in a relationship, encourage and support your partner to eat healthily. Make good food choices together that will allow both of you to benefit from the results—it helps to have each other as a teammate since it keeps you accountable to one another and more likely to stay on your healthy track. That being said, you do not need to completely deprive yourself from eating the foods you love, as long as you have been exerting enough physical energy (output) to justify the extra caloric intake of that indulgence (input). It is also important to reward yourself for all your efforts, so have that slice of pizza, a cheeseburger, ice cream, etc., but only in moderation. When you allow yourself an occasional indulgence, it makes you less likely to "fall of the wagon" and start binge eating. It also serves as an awesome reward for all of your hard work and effort.

Exercise

As far as your exercise routine goes, it's a good idea to shoot for an ideal weight goal. To help you figure it out, there are plenty of sites online that will calculate a good goal weight specifically for you. A site I've used is www.freebmicalculator.net. You just need to enter your information for results based upon your current height and weight. Again, I suggest you speak with your health care professional to help you determine what your ideal weight should be for your height and age.

To help you meet and maintain your fitness goals, participate in fun, exercise-related activities. Here are some suggestions: yoga, Pilates, CrossFit, bicycling, dancing, weight-training (again, consult your physician or specialist as to the appropriate amount of weights you should lift), running, walking, martial arts, or various other afterschool sports. To make it more enjoyable, make plans to exercise with your friends, boyfriend/girlfriend, or spouse/significant other. If you're a college student, you might want to look into various intramural on-campus sports, as well as various fitness classes (aerobics, spin class, yoga, kickboxing, cardio, etc.) that are either offered at your school's gym, or your local fitness center. You will be surprised at how many local fitness centers have discounted specials for college students. You could also look into joining your local YMCA or YWCA. Most importantly, take action and motivate yourself to either find a "workout buddy" or group of supporters (friends, family, etc.) that will push you to stay fit.

I want you to know that I follow these same healthy nutrition and exercise ideals. I practice what I preach, I walk the walk, and I run the run! In fact, in 2010, I even decided to challenge myself and run the 2011 Los Angeles Marathon. I had been a long-distance runner in high school, but never ran more than 10 miles—so I knew I couldn't do it on my own—I needed guidance and support to get myself up to speed. I joined a local running group in Santa Monica, California called, "L.A. Leggers" to help me train and stay motivated. I am proud to say that with the Leggers' mentoring and training program, along with their support and encouragement, I ran and finished my first marathon on March 20, 2011 in 5 hours and 38 minutes. I followed that success by continuing with my disciplined regimen of eating a healthy diet and exercising three to four times per week. As a result, I finished my second Los Angeles marathon in 2012 in 4 hours and 58 minutes—beating my first time by 40 minutes! I share a lot of the credit for my marathon successes with my Leggers running mentor and friend, Dan Manns, and with my nutrition and CrossFit personal trainer, Annie Mello.

When I first started training for the Los Angeles marathon with the Leggers back in August of 2010, I had only run 10K races (6.2 miles). Dan was quick to educate me on the differences between marathon, versus 10K, training and running. He helped me focus on the importance of proper breathing and stretching. He also directed me to purchase the proper tools: *dry fit* running clothes and accessories (salt tablets, electrolyte blocks, etc.) which I needed to utilize during training and the race. He taught me what to expect on the day of the marathon, and most importantly, how to pace myself during all long mile runs. Dan was an amazing coach and inspiration. I remember the first couple of weeks of training when I told him that I never ran more than 10 miles before in my life, and that I was nervous about being able to get through our upcoming 16, 18, and 20-mile training runs. Dan immediately told me not to worry about the future, and to just focus on what was important to learn and incorporate *now*. He told me he had no doubt that I was going to be a good marathon runner, and he complimented me on following all of the training suggestions and guidelines he shared with our group. I recently told him that during the marathon, there were several times when I heard his voice inside my head telling me what I should be doing, and focusing on, at different stages of the run.

What I waited to mention when I was telling you how very important good nutrition and exercise habits are in your life, is that I speak from a place of experience. Like I keep explaining, I really want to help you avoid making the same mistakes I've made in my own life. So I want to share my story of just how easy it was to go down the slippery slope of becoming overweight. I didn't realize until I started my marathon training in 2010 just how overweight I had become. As I mentioned earlier, I had been going through a period of feeling unfulfilled and unhappy. And through my own denial and self-sabotaging behavior, my weight had gradually crept up to 253 pounds. When I admitted to myself that my running would not improve unless I decided to commit to losing the weight, I reached out to my dear friend, who also happened to be a personal trainer, Annie. I humbly asked her to help me improve my diet and to design an exercise plan for me. I knew I had been compensating for my negative emotional state by overindulging with food. Thankfully, Annie explained to me why those unhealthy ingredients, that I was carelessly putting into my body, were so detrimental to not only my training, but my overall health. Through her support and guidance, she helped me lose 56 pounds in six months. But the best news of all, was that after 16 years, my doctor finally took me off my cholesterol medicine because I finally took control of my diet, sleep, and exercise. And as for my running...

My rude awakening about my neglected health came when, just to cross the finish line, I was forced to walk most of the October 2011 Long Beach half-marathon because I really had become just too overweight to run. It was the wake-up call I needed to finally stop procrastinating, get me off my butt, and begin incorporating my new diet and exercise routines. As a result of all my hard work and dedication (thanks to Annie and Dan), I was able to complete the following half-marathons while also improving my overall race times:

- Malibu (November 22, 2011): 2 hours, 38 minutes, 11 seconds

- Las Vegas (December 5, 2011): 2 hours, 34 minutes, 55 seconds

- Surf City (February 6, 2012): 2 hours, 11 minutes, 34 seconds

- Pasadena (May 20, 2012): 2 hours, 11 minutes, 26 seconds

- Disneyland (September 2, 2012): 1 hour, 58 minutes, 58 seconds

- Chicago (September 9, 2012): 1 hour, 57 minutes, 46 seconds

I honestly don't think I could have achieved those running successes had it not been for the support of Annie, Dan, and the other Leggers. I am extremely grateful that I had all of their supportive motivation at my disposal to inspire and enable me to accomplish my goals. See what I mean about having mentors? Never underestimate the important role mentors will always play in your continued growth and success throughout your life.

If you ever watch TV shows like "The Biggest Loser," or "Extreme Weight Loss" with Chris Powell, then you know there are many options for successfully achieving overall health. YOU are counting on yourself to rise to the challenge and commit to living a healthy lifestyle (which will also help support your strong personal brand and your overall success). The important thing is to: *Decide, Commit, Don't Quit!*

Decide to change, *commit* to it, and hold yourself *accountable* to achieve your desired results.

Call to Action

1. Grab your notebook and pen/pencil, and describe what your current personal brand looks like (clothing, style, hair, etc.). If you are in a relationship, you might want to ask your partner to give you their input.

_____

_____

_____

_____

_____

2. How would you like others to perceive you? What changes would you like to make to improve/enhance your personal brand based upon what was discussed in this chapter? Write down the action steps that you think would best enable you to achieve those improvements—and be realistic with yourself about your plan to accomplish your goals.

_____

_____

_____

_____

_____

3. Craft a brief, yet well-thought-out paragraph that you believe best describes and reinforces your personal brand, which you can then post in the profile sections on whichever sites you have established an online presence. While you are writing, keep in mind that you will be posting this on the internet. So don't forget to proofread it and remain aware of the vast and varied audience who will be reading it for countless years to come.

_____

_____

_____

_____

_____

4. List two different exercises or activities that you can either do individually, or you can do together with your partner three to four times per week. Now create your action plan to turn that goal into a reality. Then, as Nike so persuasively puts it, JUST DO IT!

_____

_____

_____

_____

_____

"Education is the ability to meet life's situations."

~ Dr. John G. Hibben (14th president of Princeton University)

5

Making the Grade?

How you choose to use your time determines your quality of life.

In this chapter, I'll be sharing my time-tested techniques with you on how to develop good study/work habits by learning how to enhance your time management skills. Your ability to master good study habits and manage your time effectively early in life, will ultimately be the same skills that will enhance your ability to excel once you've entered the work force. In general, I believe most (not all) people who tended to study poorly when they were in school, find themselves reaching adulthood still struggling to rise to their potential in both the workplace and in other areas of their adult life (finances, health, decisions, relationships, etc.). Therefore, it is incredibly important to address the quality of your study habits because effective study habits, established from an early age, provide the groundwork for effective time management skills as an adult.

So, how does one strike a good life balance in high school and college between studying effectively and having a social life? First of all, before we proceed, you need to be brutally honest with yourself, right here, right now, about the type of student you really are. Go ahead and ask yourself, "Do I study hard, or do I hardly study?" If you answered "hardly study," then it's time for a reality check: Are you really surprised by the low grades you may be receiving? If you are doing poorly in school, I'm sure you do not like the way it feels—it takes a serious toll on your self-esteem.

When I was a junior at the University of Maryland, I watched a friend struggle with feeling badly about how she could not seem to get out of her own way. We had both ended up in a couple of the same classes together—psychology and music theory. Elise was a really smart, funny, and talented girl. But she was having a hard time seeing that for herself. After getting to be good friends with her, I asked her why she was getting such poor grades in psychology. She said she was upset with herself, but couldn't bring herself to focus long enough to study properly. I told her I didn't buy it because I'd seen her laser-like focus when she practiced her flute. She said, "That's easy for me to focus on because I'm interested in it, so I've gotten pretty good at it. But I hate when I don't know, or understand something—it makes me feel like a loser." I told her, "I have a theory that you don't study very hard because you're afraid you won't get it, and won't become good at it, and since you're a perfectionist, you don't want to try really hard and end up doing poorly and feeling dumb, so you just don't try that hard at all. Then you have a good excuse for not doing that well." She was open to seeing her pattern. "Oh, yeah. Like when I only get a C but I justify it by saying, 'Well, I didn't really study that hard so...'" "So..." I continued, like the astute armchair psychologist I was, "...instead of studying hard to get the good grades you could potentially earn, you sabotage yourself by not studying hard enough so you can have an excuse because you're afraid of not being smart enough to do well. But that's just your perfectionism getting in your way." She looked at me, amazed that I had called her out on what she knew deep down, but no one had ever called her out on it before.

The truth of the matter is, it really wasn't so amazing that I could figure out where she was coming from. I had had that insight because years earlier, I had been in her shoes. I knew she had struggled with being perceived as a lazy underachiever who was not as smart as her fellow students and I could help her because I had dealt with that same issue too. I knew I could have done much better in high school and I had become fed up with myself over the average GPA I had when I graduated. So when I entered college, knowing I hadn't lived up to my potential, I finally got honest with myself and asked myself the same question I want you to ask yourself now: "Do I study hard, or do I hardly study?"

For those of you who do "study hard," and aren't relating to "not living up to your potential," please bear with me while I go over this with the soon-to-be-ex-underachievers. And to those of you who related to me and Elise, and are ready to own up to your reality check, good for you! When you answered that you're "hardly studying," then I'm sure you can relate to how crappy it feels to not be living up to your potential. Speaking from experience, you are sabotaging yourself (which, like Elise, you probably already know deep down) by using excuses like "It's too hard," or "I'm not as smart as the other kids in my class." Be honest with yourself. You know that your classmates aren't smarter than you. Harsh truth? Here it is: You are just lazier, more fearful, and less disciplined than they are. Ouch! The truth hurts sometimes, huh? Now here's a reminder to soften that blow: Change can be uncomfortable and even painful sometimes, but stay focused on the fact that you are reading this book to heighten your awareness and knowledge, so that you can live up to your full potential to be as great as you are meant to be. So, don't fool yourself anymore by coming up with lame excuses because I know firsthand that: 1. You're not fooling anyone but yourself (your parents and teachers aren't buying it), and 2. As cliché as it sounds, you really are only cheating yourself. In case I haven't made myself clear, I repeat: Everything you are doing right here, right now, amounts to you paving the way for your own future. And *every* action you take, will have a direct affect in determining how great and successful your life *can* be—so make the conscious decision to make good decisions!

Let that sink in.

Now, it's time you address just how bad your study habits have been due to your years of apathy and fear. Repeat after me: "I am getting bad grades because I have bad study habits." Remember in Chapter Three when we discussed building your castle as your source of protection? You are about to learn how to increase the height of your "castle walls" through the following techniques. If you are disciplined about adopting them, you should see a distinct improvement in your grades and work habits. Then, you will feel the boost in your confidence and self-esteem which will make it harder for others to penetrate the walls of your more fortified castle.

What if I told you that by simply applying better time management skills to your current study habits, you would not only improve your study time (which would lead to better grades), but you would also have more time to socialize or do whatever you wanted? Would that pique your interest? What if I also told you that I could show you an easier way to study so that you wouldn't have to stay up late or pull all-nighters (classic perfectionist/procrastinator move) to finish your homework and reading assignments? What if I could teach you how to use your time more wisely so that you could really understand the material you were learning *and* have better recall of the material for your tests and during class time? Does that interest you even more? It sure motivated me when I learned these study techniques and watched my grades go from C's and B-'s in high school, to B's and A's in college.

I'll fill you in on the secret I learned at the University of Maryland during my freshman year. I call it, "The art of taking something big, and learning how to break it down into more manageable pieces." We all know how quickly the workload piles up. But don't overwhelm yourself into paralysis by ALL that you have to do, and that you have to do it all WELL. That's perfectionism, which leads to procrastination, which leads to last-minute inefficiency and exhaustion (and poor grades). If you break down your seemingly insurmountable tasks into manageable, bite-size pieces, you will be able to complete your tasks in a timely manner. So don't "spin your wheels," and waste precious time without ever achieving your best possible results. By learning how to clearly define your study goals in advance, you will quickly learn how successful people utilized these same effective tools when they were students, and which they continue to utilize in the workplace. Are you ready to step up, take charge, and commit yourself to improving your study habits NOW, so that you can improve the rest of your life? Good. Let's begin.

Creating Study Plans

The first thing I would like you to do is to start getting in the habit of creating weekly lists of all your reading and homework assignments for school. Every weekend, review and revise your lists based upon what you have accomplished. For example, if you are in high school, over the weekend (and before the beginning of each new week), sit down with your new list of class assignments from the prior week and mark down all future quizzes and test dates, as well as all future due dates for your reading and homework assignments.

If you are a college student, sit down at the beginning of each new semester with all your new class syllabuses, and do the same thing. Mark down all future quizzes and test dates, as well as all future due dates for your reading and project assignments. Now, this is important—on a *weekly basis*, I want you to write down all of your reading and homework assignments that are due for that particular week, and map out what you plan to read and/or outline.

For example, if you have to read 100 pages of a particular book for that upcoming week, I want you to break down that 100-page reading assignment by dividing it up over the next seven days. Here is my logic (my "why"): rather than trying to cram and retain 100 pages of information over one or two days (which I know some of you are trying to do), by simply breaking the reading assignment down over seven days, you will now only have to read 15 pages each day (manageable, bite-size pieces)! This technique will help you to improve your studying in the following two ways:

1. You will be able to read all the pages assigned to you by the required deadline date, but more importantly,

2. You will be able to better understand and retain the information you have just read if you give yourself the extra time to really comprehend the material.

Repeat this same process for all of your class reading assignments. For your math homework, I suggest that you also break down your assignments over a certain number of days, so that you can take the time to really comprehend how to properly apply the mathematical equations to your various math homework problems. For example, if you have 10 math homework questions for the week, you should break them down over five days and then you will only have to focus on answering just two of the questions each day. Breaking it down that way would allow you more time to really understand and respond to the questions as thoroughly as you can. By giving yourself that extra time to understand each of the required mathematical steps needed to correctly answer each of your assigned math problems, you will quickly learn how to recognize and apply these same mathematical steps to any future quiz or related mathematical exam. My math grades went from C's to A's during my freshman year simply because I taught myself the secret of learning how to break down each of the mathematical steps so that I could recognize and recreate the same steps during the math exams. And there is absolutely nothing stopping you from succeeding like this too!

Here are some other techniques you can use when studying for upcoming quizzes or exams. I strongly recommend that you outline, and begin studying your class notes, teacher's lectures, and assignments a number of days before the quiz or exam. Like your homework and reading assignments, break down your study notes over a predetermined amount of days leading up to the quiz or exam. For example, if you have 20 pages of class/teacher's notes to study or memorize, if you start studying five days before your next quiz or exam, then you would only have to study or memorize four pages of your notes per day.

When I was in college and graduate school, I would start each new study day by first reviewing my notes (or the study pages) from the previous day so I would refresh my memory before moving on to review the new notes. This helped to reinforce the material that I had already learned, so that I would feel really comfortable with *all* the material for the quiz or exam. For example, if it were Friday, I would first review/recite the notes that I studied/memorized on Thursday, before I studied/memorized the notes for Friday. I also found that I often retained all of the material much better by doing it that way, instead of trying to cram and study it all the night before the exam. Granted, there are certain people who can do very well even when they cram all that accumulated material into their heads the night before a deadline. But having known plenty of people who operated that way, I can assure you, they did not enjoy dealing with that self-imposed pressure—which could have so easily been avoided. Trust me, if you develop good study habits in high school and college, it will be a whole lot easier to utilize these same well-defined time management skills once you enter the workforce.

Another technique I acquired that freshman year, was a little game that I liked to call, "Think like the Professor." I would try to pay close attention to whatever material the professor would be focusing on during their lectures, and if there were ever times when I was unclear about the material, I would try to schedule an appointment outside of class to meet with the professor to get further clarification. I would ask them what material might be useful to focus on as

I began studying for the quizzes or exams. I would ask if they could provide any examples of papers or practice tests that I could review to give me a better understanding of what they expected from me. I always tried to be respectful and I never overlooked the opportunity to stand out and make a good first impression. In fact, because of the positive impressions I made, and the relationships I forged with them, I gained their respect and trust. To this day, I still maintain relationships with many of my past college professors, which has resulted in their providing professional recommendations, references, and coordinating speaking engagements on my behalf.

Now, if you are one of those "Cool" people who think that these techniques are "uncool" and only work for "Nerds," I must warn you...Nerds are quickly becoming the New Cool in the 21st century. Yes, you read that right! Not only do Nerds regularly commit to their plans and often execute their visions and goals (which leads to attainment of their desired successes), but they also pay close attention to detail and tend to be more authentic to their true selves. They are less concerned about what other people think, and tend to place higher importance on how *they choose* to present themselves to others. Their intelligence and abilities—not their fashion sense—dictate their identities. In fact, Nerds attract like-minded people and choose to participate in groups and clubs in high school and college because of the common goals and purposes their members share. They seek deeper meaning and connection with others, and at the same time, they grow their network of potential employers, employees, and business partners. Whereas "Cools" waste a lot of unnecessary time and energy trying to impress others, or even worse, they attract personal and professional relationships that they cannot cultivate beyond the superficial because they are constantly distracting themselves by trying to maintain and improve their status or image. When instead, they could be learning about the newest and best technological advancements that Nerds are already plugged into, which they use to grow their success. If being one of the "Cools" is ringing true for you, I strongly encourage you to put aside your self-imposed cool constraints and embrace your inner "Cool Nerd." Start prioritizing what truly matters in life, use your time wisely, and dedicate yourself to growing your own success. Or if losing your cool edge sounds just too distasteful, you might want to start befriending that so-called Nerd sitting beside you in class...because one day, you may just find yourself calling him or her, "Boss."

From the Classroom to the Boardroom

Let me show you how, once you graduate, you can continue to apply these same time management study skills to your professional job or career. Just as these skills are effective to use in high school and college, they will also improve your habits and productivity in the workplace so that you will have more leisure time to enjoy your favorite activities.

Most Americans never learn how to "work smart" because they are always working too hard. Are your parents or your friends' parents workaholics? I can relate because I used to work way too hard. I was a self-described workaholic until one of my Pepperdine Business School professors taught me a great secret to managing not only my workload and productivity, but my boss as well. While the study habits/planning techniques which I had established back in college were deeply entrenched, I had yet to learn the art of managing the boss. It is most definitely another key to achieving your future success. Whether you work for a big or small company, or you are a young entrepreneur working for yourself, the first thing I would recommend that you do whenever your boss and/or your clients give you work projects or assignments, is to sit down on a weekly basis and review, then prioritize all of your current job projects. This may sound really simple, but you would be surprised how many people never do this in their professional lives—just like most neglected to do back when they were in high school and college.

Therefore, you should make it a priority to write down all of your current and future work projects and assignments, along with the necessary action steps that will be required, to help you accomplish these work goals as timely and as efficiently as possible. As such, it is really important that each week you familiarize yourself with all future deadlines, contacts, etc. to help you prioritize your work. In doing so, (just as I suggested regarding your homework assignments), you should be able to break down your weekly work assignments into manageable daily tasks.

Take the extra time (either at the end of your work day, or first thing when you arrive in the morning), to create your "To Do" list by handwriting all of the things that you wish to accomplish either the following day, or during the remainder of that day—and be as specific about the details of your tasks as possible. Your daily list should include phone calls, emails, meetings, project deliverables (if any are due that day), etc. As you complete each item, check or cross it off your daily list. This is a great way to not only keep yourself on task, but it also provides you with a great feeling of accomplishment when you review your overall progress at the end of each day. Remember, you only have eight hours in a typical work day. Try to make sure that your daily tasks are realistic enough to be able to complete them within the timeframe you've allocated so that you do not find yourself falling behind, feeling frustrated, or losing interest. The more aware you are of your deadlines and progress, the more successful and reliable you will become to your boss and/ or clients.

However, DO NOT overcommit yourself in order to try to impress your boss/clients. Like trying to cram for a high school or college exam, you may not achieve your best work, or even worse, find yourself making excuses for what went wrong. There's an old saying in business, "Underpromise and Overdeliver," which is an approach that leaves bosses/clients pleasantly surprised when they get more than they expected. Do yourself and your boss/clients a huge favor and learn how to incorporate good time management techniques into your professional life..."Do what you say, and say what you do!"

To help you prevent yourself from overcommitting your time and energy at work, as promised—here is the "secret" that I learned from my Pepperdine University MBA Professor, Richard Riordan, regarding managing the expectations of your boss/clients in order to make your project workload more manageable. Let's presume you can only manage five projects at a time, and you are unable to delegate any of your current workload. My professor's suggestion was to solicit your boss'/clients' advice to find out if they want you to take on any new or additional projects. And if so, ask them to help you decide which one of your current five projects you should remove from your list in order to feasibly incorporate their new request into your busy schedule. Essentially, you are being a good time manager by including your boss and clients in helping you evaluate how you should prioritize your work because it ensures they are on board with (and approve of) how you structured your workload. As a result, a healthy working relationship will be achieved by all parties because they will be on the same page with you regarding your current priorities and work deliverables (responsibilities, deadlines, etc.).

Being able to "turn on a dime" in school and at work is essential when it comes to unexpected circumstances. Therefore, it's important to always remain curious and to fuel that curiosity regularly. The inquisitive mind is the learning mind, and the learning mind is an agile mind. By creating and following written plans and goals for tasks you wish to achieve, you will be improving your time management skills. Once they become a regular habit, you will find that you have an extra cushion of time which you just may need to handle any unexpected problems, or better yet, opportunities, that may suddenly cross your path. So the more time that you can carve out for yourself to learn things from an early age, the more problems you can quickly and creatively solve, and the more opportunities for success you will be able to spot and attain throughout your entire life.

Word Associations

When I was younger, I had the worst time trying to memorize and retain information. It seemed like no matter how long or how hard I studied, I could never seem to retain all the information I had tried to memorize. Unfortunately, I was not like one of those lucky kids who could read a book once or twice and—*bam!*—remember everything. I was also not one of those students who could stay up all night cramming for exams and either barely pass, or better yet, ace them. Nope, not me. I was one of those slow learners (a "late bloomer," if you haven't already figured that out), and unbeknownst to me I had no idea that my luck was about to change when I turned 12 years old. Back in the sixth grade, I had a really unorthodox teacher named Mr. Novak, who used to torture my class with different reading and memorization techniques that he believed were meant to help us learn and retain information. For example, we had to learn, memorize, and recite all the multiplication tables from 1 to 12 within two minutes as follows: 1, 2, 3, 4, 5, 6, 7, 8, 9, 10, 11, 12; 2, 4, 6, 8, 10, 12, 14, 16, 18, 20, 22, 24; 3, 6, 9, 12, 15, 18, 21, 24, 27, 30, 33, 36; 4, 8, 12, 16, 20, 24...I think you get my point. And not only did we have to recite all 12 multiplication tables within two minutes, but we had to recite them in front of all our fellow sixth grade classmates. Talk about pressure! Ric Mandell, Toni Calo, and I *still* laugh, reminisce, and roll our eyes about those dreaded multiplication tables. But you know what? Mr. Novak was right! All three of us can probably still recite all those multiplication tables. And if that wasn't bad enough, he also made us all memorize and recite a poem from a famous poet—again in front of the entire class. I chose to memorize and recite Edgar Alan Poe's,

The Bells. Even today, I can still recite most of that poem without having to look it up. But the most interesting and helpful thing he taught us was his use of word association.

Word association is when you associate familiar things to unrelated things so that you can easily recall or remember them. For example, he taught us to remember the nine planets in our solar system by using word associations—mnemonics: "Mr. M. VEM J. SUN P." ("Mr. M"—Mercury, "VEM"—Venus, Earth, Mars, "J"—Jupiter, "SUN"—Saturn, Uranus, Neptune, "P"—Pluto.) As you can see, I have never forgotten that little gem and thanks to Mr. Novak, as I progressed through school, I utilized his techniques to help me associate other unfamiliar words and concepts to retain important information for quizzes and tests. As a result of incorporating word associations into my study habits, my grades improved and I found that I started to actually retain more and more information.

Let me give you an example of how I used word association when studying. Let's pretend that you are taking a criminal justice class and you have to memorize the definition for the Miranda warning. If you have ever watched any police or detective TV shows, then you probably know that when a criminal is first arrested, the arresting officer always reads that suspect their rights (i.e., the Miranda warning): "You have the right to remain silent, anything you say can and will be used against you in a court of law…" A type of association that I might choose use to help me remember the Miranda warning is: "Miranda is a girl who never shuts up! She's always talking and talking and sometimes I wish she would just shut up and remain SILENT!" Get it? Miranda = silent. Therefore, the Miranda warning is the right to remain silent. I have found these types of word associations to be incredibly helpful and I still use my favorite TV shows, songs, friends, toys, or anything else that I can associate to any type of subject matter to help me memorize information that I need to retain. So how do you think *you* could use these types of techniques to better help you study for your future school quizzes or exams?

Utilizing All Available Tools for Success

In addition to word associations and time management techniques, I have found that there are also two additional tools that every student *must* utilize in order to help them become more successful. And these two tools should always be used abundantly when you do *any* reading or writing: a dictionary and a thesaurus. Do not ever assume that you will always understand everything that you read in a book, magazine, etc. If you ever find yourself unsure of a particular word, look it up! You should always acquaint yourself with words that you either do not understand, or of which you are unsure (definition or usage). You *never* want to use a word incorrectly or in the wrong context when speaking or writing to others, as it may tarnish your credibility and personal brand. Also, as I said earlier, always proofread your school papers and emails before you submit them by running spell-check, catching typos, and to confirm that you have accurately and effectively used your vocabulary words to convey your intended message to the reader/ recipient. While I'm mentioning vocabulary words, I am compelled to remind you to use a thesaurus to help you find new ways to say the same old thing. A thesaurus helps you keep your words fresh and new to your reader. To this day, though having hardbound copies may be antiquated, I still keep these two important tools on my office desk and you can bet I used them both when I wrote this book. Always remember: You are never too old to learn!

Ultimately, how you use your time often determines the success you will experience in both your professional, and personal life. Time management really is all about managing yourself and creating the groundwork for your efficient and productive study and work habits. How you learn to manage time, early on, will definitely help to create your foundation for success throughout your entire life. Therefore, the sooner you learn how to control time, the sooner time will no longer control you.

Call to Action

If you are a high school or college student, take out your current class syllabuses, and in your notebook, outline your reading and homework assignments for the week. Then write down what you plan to read or work on this week. After reading your required amount of pages each day, write down the key themes or points from each day's reading assignment, and then see if you can attach various word associations to those key themes, ideas, or points that will help you remember them better in the future.

In addition, write down (on a separate calendar) the important assignment deadlines and test dates so that you can map out how many days you will need to break down the assignments and/or start reviewing your test and lecture notes into more manageable, bite-size increments prior to your deadline.

If you are a young professional in the workforce, then I want you to write down all of your current work projects and corresponding deadline dates. Immediately prioritize these projects, and if possible, try to manage only five projects at a time. Over the weekends, take time to review and familiarize yourself on the status of each of your projects. I also want you to begin focusing on whatever you need to do during the upcoming week to ensure that your projects will be completed and delivered on time.

To further ensure that you are meeting your weekly goals, begin writing down all your proposed daily tasks (either first thing in the morning, or just before you leave work every night), so that you can check or cross them off your list by the end of each day to help keep yourself accountable. Remember, you need to keep your daily tasks as realistic as possible so you can actually accomplish most all of them within a normal eight-hour workday.

"Act the way you'd like to be and soon you'll be the way you act."

~ Bob Dylan (musician)

6

See Your Future, Be Your Future

Dreams are for bedtime, goals are for success.

I realize I've covered a lot of information up to this point. So in this chapter, I will revisit those important concepts, while also introducing the next steps to further your success. We'll discuss how you can take your positive attributes and apply them toward manifesting new opportunities, so you can create successful outcomes.

Change Your Thoughts, Change Your Life!

In Chapter Three, I shared insights with you about how your early childhood programming (what you may have learned from your parents, teachers, and/or environment) affects how you think, believe, and internalize everything in your life—in both a positive or negative way. That, in turn, affects your emotional state of mind (happiness, fear, anger, anxiety, sadness, etc.), which influences how you respond to your opportunities. Therefore, your state of mind directly impacts your overall success, and consequently, whether or not you ultimately end up with your desired outcomes. So always be mindful that you are the one in charge of the way you think, and your actions will follow suit accordingly.

Most humans are wired to be loss averse—an emotional tendency to react more sensitively to possible losses than to possible gains. As a result, people tend to be more motivated by avoiding losses, than they are by acquiring gains. And sadly, rather than enjoying and living their lives in the moment, they consciously (or unconsciously) spend the majority of their time waiting for the other shoe to drop. They spend way too much time spinning their wheels and catering to their fears as they reside in their unhealthy comfort zones. However, unlike the general population, when making decisions successful people tend to be more cautiously optimistic about attaining their expected outcomes because they have learned, through their own life experiences and mistakes, how to manifest opportunities and turn them into successful outcomes. Over time, this repeated pattern of manifesting their own opportunities serves as positive reinforcement that they can consistently create and duplicate their desired outcomes for success.

Since you've already committed to reading this much of this book, I'm presuming you want to create a successful life for yourself, right? Well, in that case, in addition to adopting the success tools and secrets I've shared so far, you really need to put aside your past programming's influence, along with what anybody else might insist is in your best interest, and get in touch with what you are truly passionate about. Once you've figured that out, then you need to visualize successfully achieving that desired outcome. You can no longer allow fear, anger, prejudice, old programming, etc. to deter you from becoming the successful person you were meant to be. To move forward, there is no room for any of those distractions, there is only room for you to focus on what *you* truly want to achieve. Believe me, it is not always easy, but in order to attain your ultimate goals and desires, it is necessary for you to learn to listen to *yourself*, and then to visualize your goals coming to fruition.

What would you do if you weren't afraid? It's another simple question—one that requires you to just be honest with yourself. Get in touch with what your true driving force is: What are you deeply (and possibly, secretly) passionate about? What could you joyfully spend endless hours doing? What gets you excited to get out of bed in the morning? Once you've answered these questions, you will be that much closer to figuring out what your desires truly are...then there's that little matter of *fulfilling* those desires. And that is where PLANNING comes into the forefront. When you dedicate yourself to learning (or re-learning) how to visualize your desired outcomes (passions/goals), followed by creating the appropriate action steps (the plan), you will be primed to take advantage of your opportunities as they materialize.

One such opportunity that materialized for me was during my sophomore year at the University of Maryland. It took place when I decided to pledge the music department's honorary band fraternity, Kappa Kappa Psi. When I decided I wanted to join, the fraternity's membership was primarily made up of non-music majors who participated in the University's marching band. Unlike the majority of the membership, I wasn't in the marching band. I was a member of the Symphonic Wind Ensemble (SWE) and Jazz Ensemble, and I did not know any of the Kappa Kappa Psi fraternity brothers other than the two SWE members who encouraged me to join. During the pledge initiation ceremony, I can still remember standing in front of the chapter president for the first time and thinking to myself how much I wanted to eventually become president of the fraternity. But since I didn't know anyone other than my two fellow SWE members, and being a new pledge left me feeling somewhat intimidated, it just didn't seem like a real *probability* (let alone, possibility) at the time.

However, following my initiation into the fraternity, I continued to find myself *visualizing my desired outcome*—what it would be like to become the president and get the opportunity to accomplish all the great things that I could, and *would* do if it were to actually become a reality. Shortly thereafter, I started volunteering on various projects, and fundraising committees, assisting the Kappa Kappa Psi fraternity brothers, as well as the Maryland Department of Bands. The fact that the majority of them were not fellow music majors, didn't overshadow the fact that, for the most part, we shared a lot of common interests (music, movies, sports, etc.). My fraternity brothers and I quickly forged new friendships and as a welcomed member, I started to feel more comfortable and began *manifesting my desired outcome* of becoming president. By my junior year, I ran for, and was voted in as, recording secretary—which demonstrated to the brothers that I could take initiative and assume leadership roles within the fraternity. As recording secretary, I was only one of three brothers (third behind the vice-president and the president) who got to actively participate in the pledging rituals. While serving in this role, I quickly realized that I was only one step away from going for the presidency. So during my senior year, because I chose to no longer be afraid and felt I was finally ready to handle the position (having gained the experience, confidence, and support of my fellow brothers), I began *implementing my desired outcome.*

The majority of the brotherhood voted me in as their new president and I was both elated and honored that they entrusted me with the opportunity to serve the fraternity and the Maryland Bands. I was able to manifest the goal that I had envisioned just two years prior, because I overcame my fears of being a newcomer, chose to make new friends, and became part of their culture. I had *executed my desired outcome* to become president by staying focused and aligning myself with that opportunity when it arose. By changing my way of thinking, it positively affected my end result, which led to my life-changing outcome! So, the next time you feel afraid, remember to ask yourself that simple question: What would you do if you weren't afraid? Then challenge and conquer your fears to achieve your goals—*visualize, manifest,* and then *implement your desired outcomes* by *executing* your plan and taking ACTION!

Dreams are for Bedtime, Goals are for Success!

Motivation represents the *action* behind your success.

The most important step toward achieving your goals is to TAKE ACTION! That is the motivation behind the Call to Action exercises at the end of the chapters, so that you would take immediate action toward making your goals a reality.

So, do some people just have all the luck, or do they really just know how to always get what they want? If America is truly the land of opportunity, then why can't everybody land his or her dream job or manifest their desired outcomes? Most well-established young men and women who do land their dream jobs get to happily avoid working thankless, unrewarding, dead-end jobs because they focused their energy toward manifesting their desired outcomes (job success) from an early age. Most people tend to diffuse their focus by spreading themselves too thin, dabbling in too many things all at once, and end up being, "Jack of all trades, master of none." The solution to this problem is harder than it sounds (especially if you're a curious type who is interested in a lot of things and/or are good at a lot of the things you do). The truth is, you need to *focus*. Pick that *one* thing that sings to you the most—the *one* thing that tops your list of something that you really, truly, want to—no—*must* do. Meditate, marinate, and stew on it. Get in touch. Because when you combine what you love with your core values and beliefs, and you start to make intentional choices and decisions that are in alignment with your desired goals, you will ultimately lead a happier, more satisfying life. But first, you must figure out what you want.

So how do you go about creating steps, or guidelines, for achieving your lifelong success? I would like to offer the following: In order to help you achieve your true focus, I want to first explain why there is a clear distinction between dreams versus goals. I have come to understand (by firsthand experience, of course) that *there is a difference between a goal and a dream.*

Before I proceed, do you think you understand the difference? If not, you are not alone! I would venture to say that most people often confuse dreams for goals. Let me start by explaining that many people actually believe exclaiming, *"I want to be rich!"* is a valid goal. Well, it's actually not. Because by simply proclaiming, *"I want to be rich,"* one is making way too vague of a statement, which really only amounts to being nothing more than a dream. That's because there is nothing in that five-word statement that motivates one to take any immediate action. Whereas, by asserting, *"I want to make $100,000 a year by the time I am 25 years old,"* one is stating his or her inherently implied goal by specifying a concrete dollar amount, to be earned within a set period of time (by the age of 25). Because of this statement's specificity, one can now be held accountable to attain that goal by taking the required action steps to work toward achieving it. By now, you can probably figure out that one's next step would be to create an action PLAN! While the goal in this example is very specific, the path one can take to pursue it is wide-open. So, to get that action plan started, introspection and research would be your first order of business. For example, consider answering questions such as: What type, and level of education would be required to accomplish this goal? What type of job would one need to perform? What extracurricular activities/experiences would one need to have under their belt in order to reach this specific goal by the age of 25? Again, by simply stating, *"I want to be rich,"* one is not specifying any dollar amount or timeframe, and therefore, it makes it harder to create, or assign, any specific action steps to achieve this *dream*. I hope you now see the distinction between dreams versus goals. As you begin manifesting the life and things you want to accomplish, always remember: *dreams are for bedtime, goals are for success!*

My second suggestion for achieving your personal success is to *never focus too much on the negative.* As I said earlier, successful people tend to be cautiously optimistic. However, nothing kills a goal or desire faster than caving in to your own, or to others', fears and negativity. I am sure at some point in your life you have heard your friends, parents, or teachers say something along the lines of, "That's too hard," or "That's impossible; you can't do that!" Never be swayed from trying to achieve your goals or desires because someone else (or yourself) tells you that you can't do something. If you are one of those people who always seems to shy away from following through on your goals and desires because others tell you not to go for it, then I want you to pay very close attention to what I am about to tell you: *You have the right to disappoint others and pursue your own goals.* NOW is indisputably the time for you to identify your own true passions: trust your instincts, set your goals, create your action plan, and then GO FOR IT.

Refuse to live up to anyone's "misery loves company" expectations. "No" people tend to live in a world of, "would've, could've, should've" because *their* fears often prevent them from going for the same things that you desire. But the difference is, <u>you</u> will be brave enough to go for, and understand how to achieve, *your* goals. Just think, what if the Wright Brothers listened to those naysayers who told them they would never fly? What if Thomas Edison gave up working on his light bulb patent just because his 90th attempt failed? I am here to tell you, that unless you are planning on doing something illegal or hurtful to someone else, you should never give up on your goals or desires. You need to start replacing the words, *"I wish,"* with *"I will."* And do not be afraid of utilizing all of your potential resources (friends, contacts, mentors, teachers, partners, parents, time, and money) in helping you to further achieve your goals.

From this moment forward, every time you begin to feel negative, you need to immediately replace that thought or feeling with something positive. Because you need to always remember that your thoughts— good or bad—will affect your emotions, which will then impact your ability to motivate yourself to take action, which ultimately affects your positive or negative outcomes. Positivity inspires success. Therefore, rather than focusing on your shortcomings, or even worse, staying limited by your own comfort zone (which others [due to projecting their own insecurities] may hope is what ultimately holds you back and makes you settle for less), you will want to always keep your eyes wide open, remain aware of your surroundings, and envision the life and reality that you want.

So now that you fully understand just how important your specific actions are to achieving your overall goals and success, how do you begin creating the vision and focus needed to ensure that your specific action steps are *focused, consistent, and in alignment with your passions and desired outcomes?* Like I said earlier, you must first identify your passions and goals, and then ask yourself, "How do I want to live my life?"

For example, I felt compelled to write this book because I had been incredibly frustrated that growing up I had had so little real-world exposure to these success tools and secrets. I pictured myself helping young adults by giving them a book so chock full of needed tools, techniques, and personal/financial guidelines, that they couldn't help but to achieve their goals and get the life they truly desired. I've maintained my clear vision *to teach young adults by inspiring and empowering them to heighten their awareness so they may identify probable outcomes to successfully achieve their desired goals.*

I just shared my *vision* that compelled me to write this book. However, my *mission* in writing this book is to *demystify success for young adults (as well as adults of all ages) by teaching them the success tools and secrets they didn't learn in high school.* I intend to accomplish this mission *by inspiring and empowering young adults to facilitate their own change, earlier in their lives, so they can get a head start following, and achieving, their true desires. I will do so by teaching them how to make probability-based, non-emotional, strategic decisions—which is the ultimate success secret to positively impacting lifelong personal and financial success.*

To recap: by first getting in touch with my passions, followed by establishing a clear *vision* for my goals, I was able to pursue my primary aim in life—my *mission*. I made the intentional choice to manifest this new life path for myself. As a result, my vision and purpose to help educate young adults—as well as adults of all ages—to achieve personal and financial success, based upon who they truly are, has become my life's primary call to action. Because my goals and actions are now in alignment with my vision and purpose, I am able to practice what I preach by living a much more satisfying and fulfilling life.

The reason that I am so passionate about helping you make these course corrections, as early as possible, is because one of the biggest mistakes I made growing up was that I did not take the time, or create the opportunity while I was younger, to learn how to plan effectively. Sadly, as I have shared with you, I did not have the maturity, knowledge, insight, or guidance to ask myself, let alone, others, basic questions that would have empowered me to create effective plans with clear personal spending and savings goals for how I would utilize my hard-earned money. If I'd only had that foresight, having that action plan would have helped me to get off my butt and implement measurable action steps that would have led me to achieve attainable goals, from any early age. Moreover, it would not only have provided me with realistic guidelines on how to best invest in the right opportunities as they arose, but it would have also served as the tool I needed to help me live within my financial means. Unfortunately, all I knew how to do back then was to "wing it," and that approach only worked for so long before it caught up with me and derailed me from living up to my true potential.

Looking back, had I been more aware and diligent, I could have just taken additional classes, interviewed people, or found a mentor so I could have gotten a clear picture of what would have been required to accomplish my goals. But it never even occurred to me to pursue this information! I am not rehashing these "what ifs" with you from a place of regret, but rather from a place of experience so that *you* can learn how to become more proactive with your own future planning. I would love nothing more than for you to learn from *my* mistakes! And today you have the added advantage of having the internet at your disposal. Even though this everyday tool has been in your life as far back as you can remember, I hope you stop to appreciate what an amazing tool for learning it really is. Of course, when it comes to appreciating it myself, I have the added advantage of perspective. Because it didn't even exist when I was growing up. Ever heard of microfiche? No? Then just "Google" it! Today, you have a million answers just waiting to solve your burning Googled questions. With the vast wealth of information readily accessible, you can even enroll in online classes, webinars, etc. Don't be afraid to own your true goals, tap your resources, and pursue the life you want! One of the biggest mistakes most people tend to make is that they either deny, or do not acknowledge, their own strengths. They sell themselves short (and at the same time, they make matters worse by giving too much undeserved credit to others). As a result, their minds tend to spiral straight to their negative self-perception. Nothing kills a goal or desire faster than indulging in an insecurity-driven negative downward spiral. Fight the urge, and choose to stay positive. Cliché alert: there's only one you—and never forget it! As I said earlier in this book, do not be afraid to question your learned negative fears and emotions, and get out of your own way. Figure out how you want live your life, on your own terms. Then stay focused while you take action on your plan to achieve your *probable* outcomes for success.

As the famous playwright, George Bernard Shaw, once said, "Life isn't about finding yourself, it's about creating yourself." So how does one go about creating lifelong success? It all starts with an idea of what's important to *you*. This is *your* life. What is your goal? Your passion? Your ultimate mission in life? Once you have created your vision and purpose (your mission), begin creating specific action steps for achieving your goals by asking yourself simple, basic questions (like I've discussed) that will enable you to become clearer about the action steps you'll need to take in order to achieve your goals. It is *extremely important* that you create a plan *before* you start taking action because you will need to know who (mentors, professionals, teachers, friends, partners, family, etc.) will best align with helping you achieve your goals, as well as why, and how, they can best assist you. Remember, most people are busy with their own lives and their time is valuable. So you will want to have a good idea of not only how they can help you, but also how you can help them. Try to figure out how the relationships you establish will result in reciprocity—so you can always try to build mutually beneficial and positive professional relationships with others. Networking is essential to building your success early on, because at the end of the day, you never know how those relationships will benefit both of you in the long run.

Operation Three Sixty Five

By the fall of 2011, I had been working for the same company for 22 years, I was overweight, I wasn't in the type of personal relationship that I wanted, I wasn't really pursuing the things that I wanted to do, and I wasn't really happy living in Los Angeles. I slowly came to the realization that I needed a change, and as I discussed in Chapter Two, I decided to sit down and give myself an honest reality check by asking myself, "So, how's that life working for you?" Well…it wasn't. I knew that I needed to create a plan. So on October 20, 2011, I decided that I was going to try to completely change my then-current reality, 180 degrees in 365 days. I dubbed this new plan, *Operation Three Sixty Five*. When I made the decision to embark on my new goal, I immediately identified several smaller goals that I believed would help me to achieve my outcome by the following year, on October 19, 2012. To help me evaluate my progress throughout the year, I created my own "action board" that included multiple action steps with various deadline dates. I taped this action board to my bathroom mirror to ensure that I would see it at least twice a day—once when I woke up, and once when I went to bed.

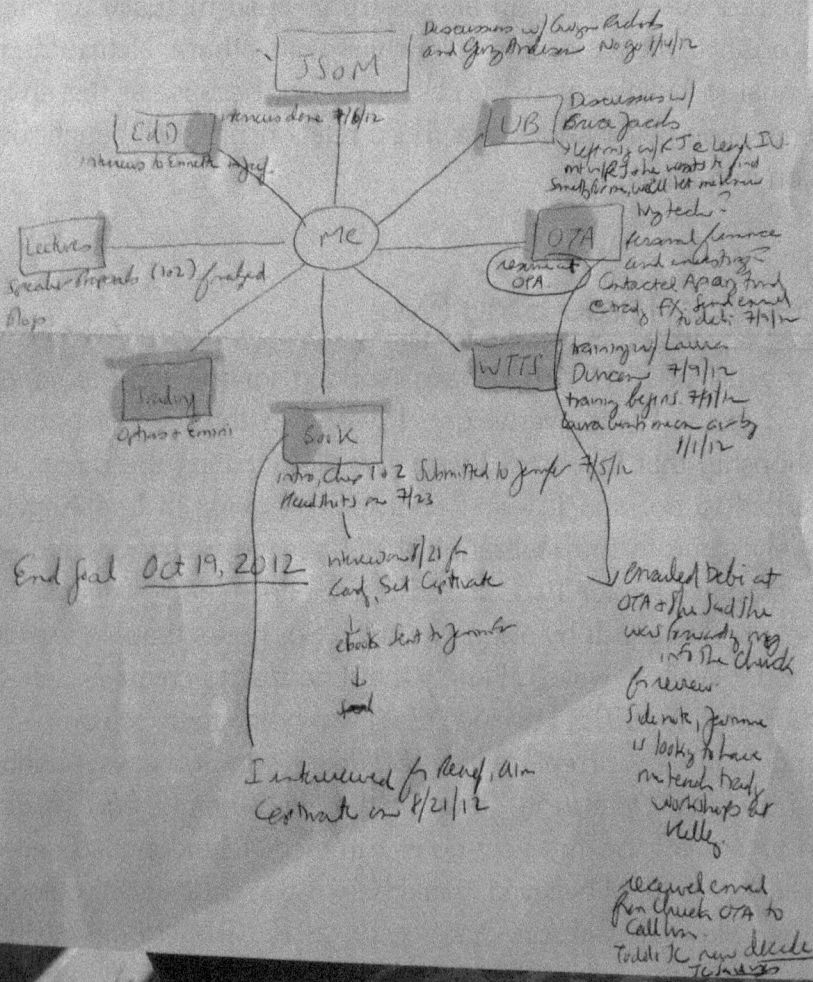

My "Operation Three Sixty Five" Action Board

In addition to my action board, I also chose to document (in my handwritten journal) all of my phone calls, emails, meetings, interviews, events, etc. that I either set up, participated in, or completed on a daily basis. The journal was a means of keeping myself accountable to the goals that I set, as well as a way of measuring my daily progress toward completing my overall 365-day goal of completely changing my life by 180 degrees.

I am happy to report that I did accomplish the majority of my 180-degree goals by my October 2012 deadline. After leaving my position at the Universal Music Group in March 2012, I moved to Bloomington, Indiana to be closer to the Indiana University campus (to further pursue my desire to educate and motivate young adults) and I lectured several times at the University. In September 2012, I became an international best-selling contributing author for the book, *Ready, Aim, Captivate! Put Magic in Your Message and a Fortune in Your Future* alongside Deepak Chopra and Jim Stovall, I lost 63 pounds thanks to Annie Mello's amazing personal training, and as of September 9, 2012, I had run two marathons (one personal record) and seven half-marathons (four personal records) due, in large part, to the guidance and support of the Los Angeles Leggers and thanks to the great advice I received from Dan Manns, and Rose and Ken Sewell. Also in September 2012, I co-taught my first stock options class for Online Trading Academy in Los Angeles, and on May 18, 2013, during the commencement ceremony at Pepperdine University, I finally got to wear my long-awaited doctoral regalia. Then, in August 2013, I once again became a contributing author for the international best-selling book, *Ready, Aim, Influence! Join Forces, Expand Resources, Transform Your World,* this time alongside billionaire, Carlos Slim, and ABC's Secret Millionaire, James Malinchak. But most importantly, in May 2013, I married the love of my life—my beautiful wife, Kate. Because I made the intentional decision to transform my life 180 degrees in 365 days, I finally got to create the life that I really wanted. Now, I get to do what I love *every* day—empowering young adults through my speaking and writing, while surrounding myself with the people who love and support me.

To get you started on your own journey to success, I have created the following checklist to help you organize your action steps. So let's recap:

1. What is your true passion? (What is that one thing that keeps you up at night and drives you to pursue your passion? What are you compelled to tell the world that you believe will benefit all who will listen?)

2. Create goals that lead you to live the life you want (live your passion). Remember: *dreams are for bedtime, goals are for success!* Do not confuse a dream with a goal. Unlike dreams, goals require specific action steps to be taken within a predetermined period of time in order to be achieved.

3. Clearly define your vision and purpose (i.e., mission). Be very clear and specific about what you want to achieve when you define your vision and purpose. Make sure that your mission's definition aligns with your passion and goals. It is extremely important that you communicate your goals in a way that allows other people to quickly understand, and identify with, what you are trying to accomplish. By doing so, they can more readily connect with you quickly to potentially establish a reciprocal relationship.

4. Implement and evaluate specific and realistic action steps. To help ensure that your action plan best aligns with your passion and goals, create action boards and/or keep written journals to help keep you accountable before you decide to take any action toward accomplishing your desired goals. Be very clear about the decisions, time, money, and people you decide to invest in because making the best decisions in those areas will positively affect your overall outcomes. Equally important, make sure you evaluate and adjust your plans when necessary, to ensure that you continue to achieve the results you desire—stay agile. Again, your action boards and journals will help you visually track and measure your progress.

Using the mnemonic device, *P.P.I.E.*, should help you remember these four simple steps (*Prioritize, Plan, Implement, and Evaluate*):

1. ***Prioritize* your goals.**

2. ***Plan* your actions.**

3. ***Implement* your plans.**

4. ***Evaluate* your actions and desired outcomes.**

As you can see, your goals and action plan become a whole lot easier to create, implement, and achieve once you identify your passion, vision, and purpose. So there is no more room for making excuses like, "I don't have the time," or "I'm too busy." Just take that first step (like we discussed in the last chapter) by simply breaking things down into smaller, more manageable pieces. And please do not make the same mistakes that I made growing up—don't be apathetic, lazy, or naïve. Take the time *now* to really discover your true passion and purpose, *early on*, so that you can immediately begin to align your life with your true core values. Then your short-term and long-term goals will become intentional and consistent with your actions. Once you begin reaffirming your passions, and focusing your intentions on establishing concrete goals, you will quickly learn to self-motivate and take the necessary action steps required to achieve those goals/plans. You will find that by doing this, you will be empowering yourself to make positive decisions that will influence your *probable* outcomes for success.

Positivity is a Key Secret for Success

Over the past several years, there have been many books, and a lot of hype, about the secret laws of the Universe. Some of these books (based on the Law of Attraction) actually profess that all you have to do to get what you really want in life (seemingly achiev-able even by staying put in the comfort of your favorite room or couch) is to merely focus and fixate on manifesting your desires and dreams to appear and—*poof!*—the Universe will magically deliver your desires to you. Don't you wish it could be that easy? Clearly, a lot of 21st century Gurus think it is. Just go online or down to your local bookstore or library and marvel at the large selection of books, articles, CDs, and DVDs that have flooded the market over the past several years on this subject.

Call me a cynic, but despite the existence of all of this literature, I find it hard to believe that only a handful of people over the past several centuries would be the only ones "chosen" by the Universe to possess all these so-called success secrets—secrets that remained hidden throughout the ages...until now! So back in 2008, to help me get to the bottom of all this, I decided to attend a Law of Abun-dance Seminar that was being hosted by the Learning Annex of Los Angeles. This Abundance Seminar was being held inside of a New Age bookstore in Venice, California. And I must admit that, at the time, the only real exposure that I had had to this genre of material prior to the seminar was through a highly hyped book and movie. As you can imagine, I was a bit out of my comfort zone as I tried to remain open-minded, sitting there patiently waiting with 20 other attendees in this New Age bookstore. I focused on containing my underlying skepticism while awaiting the expected stereotypical "New Age hippie woman" to stroll in any minute to start the semi-nar. I was shocked when, from around the corner of the room, a young and attractive woman dressed in a professional business suit appeared in front of us. She began telling us that she had person-ally experienced, and would explain, the true concepts surround-ing the Universe's Law of Abundance. In fact, she went on record right from the start of the seminar, sharing that she only believed in some of the elements taught in that crazy-popular book/movie and that no one would simply profit or benefit from sitting on their butts all day at home. What she said next was a paradox for me. She proceeded to hold a tennis ball up in the air and released it, then simply asked us, "What do you call that?" We answered, "Gravity." She replied, "Yes," then continued, "and isn't gravity a Universal Law that we can't see, but yet we all know exists? Why then, would it be so impossible to believe there aren't other Universal Laws that we can't see, but can also exist?"

New York Times best-selling author Christy Whitman, who wrote *Perfect Pictures* (GMA Publishing), and created www.7EssentialLaws. com, not only helped me get over my initial apprehensions, but her seminar also piqued my interest so much that I decided to work with Christy for an entire year as my abundance coach. I credit her with teaching me that *one of the major keys to the Laws of the Universe is to live your life positively with the Universe, as well as to honor your own belief system, and do not allow others to sway or block your beliefs because it will only create self-doubt.* She also suggested that I create my own daily affirmations. She instructed me to be as specific as possible when describing my intentions. So, for example, if I had you do this exercise and you were single but ready for a healthy relationship, I would instruct you to describe a potential girlfriend or boyfriend. Then, being extremely detailed, you would specify the core values and characteristics (physical and mental) that you would like them to possess. For example, humorous, athletic, blonde, religious, want children, etc. I think you get the point. When doing this, again, be as detailed as you can about the things you specifically want. Envision them so clearly that it's as if you already have them incorporated as a regular part of your life. I always like to read my daily affirmations once when I first wake up, and once before I go to bed. I suggest you do the same. And when you do, always make sure to read them with conviction so that you let yourself feel and believe in those people and things you wish to attract into your life.

In addition to your daily affirmations, you should also keep a journal or notebook of your daily accomplishments. Be proud not only of the things you have achieved each day, but also of the people that mean the most to you. As part of my personal abundance studies with Christy, she recommended that I utilize various symbols (objects, animals, people, etc.) to help me define my present reality, versus the reality I ultimately wanted to see for myself. This concept of utilizing symbols can often help you create a paradoxical shift within your life so that you can understand and value your new reality, along with those beliefs associated with it. For example, if you find that your life is challenging and full of struggle, you might choose a salmon to represent your current reality symbol because this fish constantly fights to swim upstream against the water's downward current. You could visualize this symbol as a parallel of your need to stop wasting your time and energy and to get out of your own way. Before struggles like these become habits and unwanted patterns in your life, sit down and choose a new, empowering symbol that you want to really signify your future success and freedom (a fast car, a soaring eagle, a historic figure, etc.). Choose something or someone that will continuously act as your guiding force symbol to specifically help you visualize steering your way toward the success and prosperity you desire. Your symbol should help bolster the support you receive from your trusted inner circle (mentors, friends, etc.) and your resources (education, money, etc.) as you pursue your life's goals and desires.

You've probably heard of a "vision board" which is used to help enhance and strengthen visualizations to manifest the people/things that you wish to attract into your life. You may want to try creating one of your own. They're simple to create by finding personal photos and pictures from magazines or catalogs, etc. (really just any image that speaks to you) that you then arrange and affix on your board. You end up with a customized vision board depicting exactly what you need to visualize on a daily basis to manifest the future you ultimately desire. As I mentioned earlier (when I shared my "action board" for Operation Three Sixty Five), I prefer to take this concept a step further and also use the "action board" to help me attain the things that I really want to attract in my life. So in addition to visualizing my desired future, I also convert my passions, desires, and goals into realities through taking action. When you create your action board, you will be creating a call to action for yourself to implement steps that will ultimately lead you to achieve your goals and desires. Remember: *dreams are for bedtime, goals are for success!*

The basic idea that I am trying to convey here is that, despite the struggles and obstacles everyone experiences, successful people choose to strategically work around their hurdles and remain positive by embracing the Laws of Abundance. Whereas, the majority of unsuccessful people tend to view their circumstances from a perspective of deprivation, which feeds into their fears, and they end up continuing to remain stuck in their comfort zones. Without getting too "New-Agey," hopefully you can now see the power your current mindset has over your life—by choosing to manifest your goals from a positive perspective, and having faith in the Law of Attraction, you will reap the Universe's abundant rewards. Think of the Universe as if it was Aladdin's lamp—it amplifies your reality by simply granting you more of what you already have..."Your wish is my command." If you are someone who always thinks positively and you believe in the Law of Attraction, then the Universe will bestow upon you more positivity in your life. Conversely, if you are someone who always thinks negatively, then the Universe will respond in kind with more negativity in your life. Because your thoughts carry such power, you are the one in control of the message you want the Universe to receive. It's a simple formula: negativity begets negativity, and positivity begets positivity.

As Christy often reminded me, positivity is a key "secret" for success. And after working with her that year, I began adopting a new way of thinking that integrated her lessons, combined with my own action steps (*P.P.I.E.—Prioritize, Plan, Implement, and Evaluate*), and came up with the following:

I BELIEVE, THEREFORE I AM

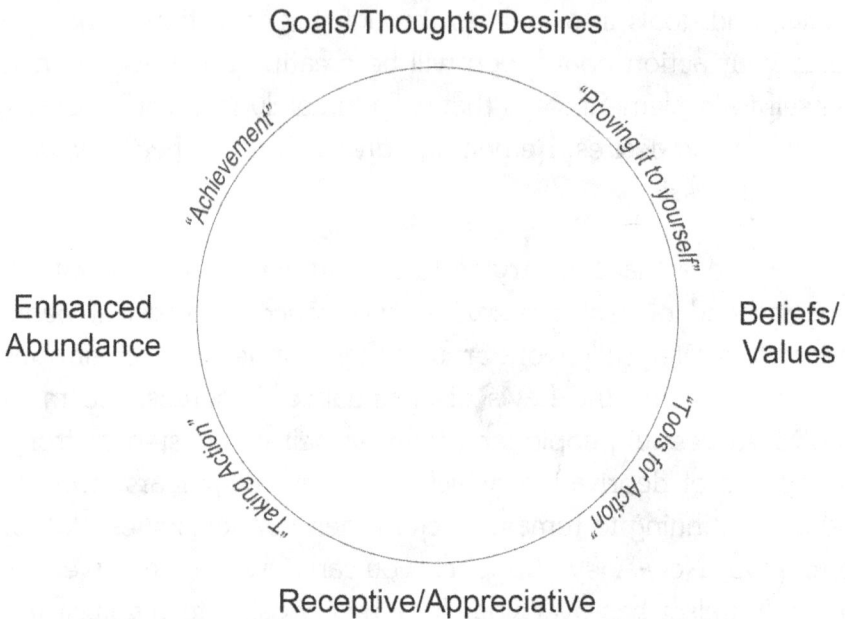

Goals/Thoughts/Desires

"Achievement"   *"Proving it to yourself"*

Enhanced
Abundance

Beliefs/
Values

"Taking Action"   *"Tools for Action"*

Receptive/Appreciative

By integrating my action steps (*P.P.I.E.*) with the Law of Attraction, my new way of thinking, "I believe, therefore I am," not only enabled me to attract the abundance I wanted in my life, but it also helped me to concurrently achieve the goals that I wanted to accomplish.

1. Creating your own abundant reality. The process begins with your own **goals, thoughts, and desires**, which need to become so real and vivid through your own focused vision and purpose, that your goals, thoughts, and desires manifest themselves into daily **beliefs and values.** I call this first step, "Proving it to Yourself." (*Prioritize*)

2. Creating your own tools for action. Once you have incorporated your goals, thoughts, and desires into daily beliefs and values, you need to look within yourself to enhance and refine your own inner tools for abundance (your creativity, intelligence, style, charisma, message, etc.). You should also expand your access to abundant resources (people, time, and money) in order to become more **receptive and appreciative** of your true gifts. At that point, you can begin to take **positive action steps** toward achieving your goals, thoughts, and desires. I call this second step, "Tools for Action." (*Plan*)

3. Creating your own call to action. The sooner you become receptive and appreciative of the positive gifts you will be receiving from the Universe (through the utilization of your daily beliefs, values, tools, and resources), the sooner you will take action toward achieving **enhanced abundance** in your life. I call this third step, "Taking Action." (*Implement*)

4. Creating your own successful outcomes. After you have taken action, and completed the three initial steps toward attracting what you want and desire, your positive energy (that you acquired by completing your goals) will only serve to further enhance your abundance, which will enable you to **achieve** even greater accomplishments. As a result, your positive emotions will not only help you to create more goals and take even more actions, but your new mindset will also continue to inspire you to start and complete the entire abundance process over and over again, perpetuating the philosophy, "I believe, therefore I am." I call this final step, "Achievement." (*Evaluate*)

It is my conviction that there are three prominent beliefs for attaining success which I call, "The 3 C's":

1. Commitment: You have to commit yourself wholeheartedly to your own goals, thoughts, and desires.

2. Conviction: You have to live your life by your own personal core values and beliefs, through your own convictions, and you must not let others steer or sway you away from your chosen path.

3. Confidence: Establishing confidence comes from growing your self-esteem (refer back to Chapter Two), along with the passage of time, which leads to repeated successes, and then culminates in building up your positive experiences. Being confident means always believing in yourself and your abilities no matter what others may think, or try to get you to believe.

Although there are no guarantees in life, there *are* infinite opportunities. And within those opportunities, anything can happen. Which is why you should try to always position yourself, from an early age, to identify, and take advantage of, your internal and external resources so that you're prepared to pounce on opportunities that will provide you with *probable* outcomes for success. To illuminate just how powerful attracting a life of abundance is, I would like to share with you an amazing story that I believe truly personifies "The 3 C's," *Commitment, Conviction, and Confidence.*

My mentor, friend, and legendary drummer, Kenny Aronoff, is probably best known for his drumming with John Mellencamp. As of 1980, he had recorded 10 albums and toured for over 17 years with the Mellencamp band. In addition to his past success working with John, Kenny has cultivated—and is still currently enjoying—an enormously successful studio and touring career (which he also started during the 1980s). The artists he plays with include such greats as: The Smashing Pumpkins, Bob Seger, John Fogerty, Melissa Etheridge, Jon Bon Jovi, Elton John, Bob Dylan, Rod Stewart, Alanis Morissette, The Rolling Stones, Lynyrd Skynyrd, Willie Nelson, Waylon Jennings, Puddle of Mudd, Avril Lavigne, Joe Cocker, B.B. King, Mick Jagger, Ray Charles, Alice Cooper, Meat Loaf, Bonnie Raitt, Ricky Martin, Santana, Jefferson Airplane, and the legendary, Johnny Cash (to name a few). As of today, Kenny still remains one of the most successful and requested touring and recording session drummers of all time.

I first met Kenny back in 1986 when I was a percussion performance and jazz studies graduate student at Indiana University.

When we met, Kenny had just finished touring for John Mellencamp's highly successful multiple platinum album, *Scarecrow*, and
the album's videos were all over MTV. I was 22 years old at the
time, and considered myself fortunate to have been introduced to
Kenny through a mutual acquaintance. I began studying drum set
with him over the four years that I attended IU. You would never
know it based on all his successes, but early on in his career, Kenny
had to overcome some pretty major obstacles to become one of the
most successful drummers in the music business. I hope his story
inspires you as it did me, because as you will read, it was truly only
through Kenny's commitment, conviction, and confidence that he
was able to achieve the levels of success he currently enjoys: being
the professional drummer/musician/artist that he is today.

When I asked Kenny to recount his background (to share his story
here with you), he actually attributed his earliest lesson in success
to one of his high school teachers at Monument Mountain Regional
High School in Great Barrington, Massachusetts. Like most male
high school students, Kenny was into sports, music, and especially
girls. However, he was terrified of his chemistry and physics teacher,
Paul Gibbons. During many of his chemistry classes, Mr. Gibbons
would encourage Kenny and his fellow classmates to approach him
after class if there was anything that they did not understand. One
day, Kenny decided to take Mr. Gibbons up on his offer, and he
began asking him questions until he understood the material. As
a result of his own commitment, conviction, and determination,
Kenny began receiving A's and high B's in his chemistry class—
successes which began enhancing his confidence. Mr. Gibbons
became one of Kenny's earliest mentors. What Kenny ultimately
learned from his chemistry class experience was that if you work
really hard on something you thought you didn't like, but you override that reaction and instead seek out help from others, then you
might find out that in reality, you actually like something that you
initially thought you either wouldn't like, or didn't like because you
were afraid that you could not succeed in it. This revelation turned

out to be a big paradox shift for him that would continue to serve him well throughout his life and career.

Following high school graduation, Kenny attended the University of Massachusetts School of Music as a freshman percussion performance major. Unlike the other percussion students, Kenny did not have a lot of experience studying music in high school. Although he did perform with his high school orchestra for one semester, he did not have any formal music training (music theory or music history). In fact, during high school Kenny mostly played sports and performed with a local rock band. As you can imagine, when he got to college, he was very nervous as a result of his lack of exposure to various classical percussion instruments. He believed this gave him a severe disadvantage compared to the other percussion students. However, rather than succumb to his fears, Kenny chose to utilize the same conviction and discipline he had exhibited in his high school chemistry class. During the summer between his high school graduation and his first freshman semester at the University of Massachusetts, Kenny decided to study percussion with Arthur Press from the Boston Symphony Orchestra. To help build up his percussive skills, endurance, and confidence, Kenny committed himself to practicing eight to nine hours per day: three hours practicing mallet instruments (marimba, xylophone, etc.), two hours practicing the timpani, one hour practicing snare drum, and one to two hours practicing the drum set. Yet despite all his hard work, dedication, and moral support that he received from his parents, Kenny still felt he would have trouble competing with the other percussion students (who, unlike Kenny, had studied music from an early age). Although he was initially afraid and felt out of place when he first arrived during his freshman year, Kenny realized that he would just have to stay the course, and just like in high school, work harder and commit to putting in the extra hours necessary to compete and succeed. Not only did Kenny practice more hours than any of his fellow percussion students, but what really set him apart during his freshman year was his ability to network and forge positive relationships with the senior percussion students. He didn't know it at the time, but he was honing the networking skills that would end up serving him so well in his future career. Forging those bonds helped him quickly work his way up the ranks within the University's percussion department. Prior to leaving for summer break after his freshman year, a female music student told Kenny about a music festival that was held annually in Aspen, Colorado. Despite his upcoming summer plans to study again with Arthur Press, play drums with his local rock band, and spend time with his family, Kenny chose instead to pursue an opportunity to audition for the Aspen Music Festival. In typical Kenny fashion, he practiced eight to nine hours a day in preparation for the audition. Because Kenny always likes to think ahead, he follows the tenet that "one should always have a game plan, but still keep one's eyes open for opportunities and changes to their situations and environment." Kenny's hard work and discipline once again paid off—he was accepted to the Aspen Music Festival and was about to embark on yet another life-changing experience.

Upon his arrival in Aspen, Kenny was introduced to the late, legendary Indiana University percussion chair and instructor, George C. Gaber. Kenny soon realized that Gaber was not only a great percussion instructor, but also a smart and compassionate mentor. Just like before, Kenny felt he was the worst percussionist at the festival and felt inadequate compared to the other young percussionists (who had attended various music prep schools growing up). Upon his arrival, Kenny spent the majority of the summer practicing more than any other percussionist at the festival—with the intent of wowing George Gaber so that he could transfer to Indiana University (one of the top music schools in the country) to study with him. When George told Kenny that he would have to wait until January to audition him for IU, Kenny told him that he could not wait that long to start studying with him, and through his own determination, convinced Gaber to audition him for admission to IU right there in Aspen. George explained to Kenny that he would need to work up a mallet piece, timpani piece, and snare drum piece, then be prepared to audition for not only himself, but four other IU School of Music department heads as well. Not surprisingly, Kenny's commitment, focus, and discipline once again paid off, and he began his sophomore year that fall in Bloomington, Indiana at IU studying with the great, George C. Gaber.

Kenny's constant commitment and positive attitude to push himself harder than any other percussion student at both the University of Massachusetts, and at the Aspen Music Festival helped him to *attract his own abundant reality.* Through his own vision, conviction, goals, and desire to attend the Indiana University School of Music, he *created his own call to action*—to ultimately impress George Gaber (which, from firsthand knowledge, was no easy task). Kenny spent his next four years studying with Gabor at IU, and through his continued hard work and discipline, Kenny was awarded the highly prestigious Indiana University School of Music Performer's Certificate (as an acknowledgement of his impressive senior percussion performance recital). Kenny also went on to compete and win the music school's prestigious concerto competition, and performed his winning *Marimba Solo Concerto* piece with IU's premier orchestra at the School's Musical Arts Center. These were all amazing accomplishments which resulted from the discipline and confidence he first learned from studying chemistry with his high school teacher.

Following his graduation from Indiana University, Kenny moved back to Massachusetts. Despite all his training and achievements in classical music, he decided his instrument of choice was the drum set. So after spending several years studying classical percussion, Kenny chose to trust his instincts and shift gears; he began studying drum set with Alan Dawson—a Berklee College of Music drum professor, and Gary Chester—a New York studio drummer. Again, staying consistent to his character, he launched into practicing drum set for eight hours a day. But then shortly after returning home to Boston, Kenny decided to shift gears again and moved back to Bloomington, Indiana to play drums with a jazz fusion group (who were performing throughout the Midwest) called, Streamwinner. After three years back in Bloomington, Kenny began contemplating a move to New York City to find musical work, but he hesitated because he kept hearing about this local guy named Johnny Cougar who might need a drummer. At that time, John Mellencamp had just finished recording his latest album under the pseudonym, "Johnny Cougar," and when Kenny got wind that John was auditioning drummers for his band, Kenny didn't miss a beat and called his old acquaintance, and Mellencamp band member, Mike Wanchic, to pursue that opportunity. (His networking skills were paying off once again!) Mike was able to arrange an audition for Kenny with John, and in preparation for the audition, Kenny practiced six to eight hours per day spending a lot of his time listening to the songs on that first Johnny Cougar record. Given his track record of hard work and success, it really is no surprise that following his audition in 1980, Kenny became the new drummer for the Johnny Cougar band.

Five weeks following that audition, Kenny was flown to Los Angeles with the rest of the Mellencamp band to begin recording John's new album, *Nothin' Matters and What If It Did*. Kenny, primarily trained as a jazz fusion drummer, was having a hard time interpreting the simplicity of the drum parts that John needed him to play for the album, and his ideas for the drum parts just didn't seem to jive with John's. As a result, on their first day of recording, John's record producer, Steve Cropper, told John that he wanted to replace Kenny using two Los Angeles studio drummers instead—Rick Shlosser and Ed Green (who would be more familiar with John's style of music, as well as the studio recording process). Kenny had lost his chance to play drums on John's fifth album after only one day of recording. However, when John tried to tell Kenny that his services would no longer be required, Kenny's healthy ego kicked in. As a highly recognized and awarded percussionist from

IU, Kenny rallied and confidently informed John that he did not want to leave L.A. because he wanted to stay with them during the recording process to study how the other drummers played *his* drum parts. He persuasively offered to stay without pay and to sleep on the floor of the recording studio. When Kenny confronted John with, "I am your drummer, right?" John was so shocked by Kenny's confidence, he simply uttered, "Well...yeah." As he had done with Gaber back in Aspen, Kenny used his charisma and powers of persuasion to convince John that if he agreed to let him stay and learn all the drum parts, when they got back to Indiana, he would practice until they were completely ingrained and that this would ultimately benefit everyone involved—Kenny, John, and the band. Despite John's reluctance, he agreed to let Kenny stay. And although Kenny felt like the odd man out (a role he had endured many times in his past) during the album's recording sessions, he actually wound up playing and was even credited on the *Nothin' Matters and What If It Did* album for playing some percussion (vibes). Upon returning to Indiana, Kenny kept his promise and practiced eight hours a day so he could imitate and perfect the way he heard the other drummers play on that album.

Following his unfortunate experience in L.A., Kenny promised himself that no matter what he needed to do, he was going be the only drummer on the next Mellencamp record. Sure enough, not only did Kenny play drums on John's sixth breakout album, *American Fool,* but it was his drum solo on the iconic song, "Jack & Diane," that became the most immediately recognizable part of the song. As "Jack and Diane" climbed to number one on the Billboard 200 music chart in 1982, Kenny's drumming career was officially launched. Despite any pressure or fear that he may have felt when he was dismissed from playing on the *Nothin' Matters and What If It Did* recording sessions in L.A., Kenny didn't let it deter him. Instead, he intuitively capitalized on his resourceful and tenacious personality, and chose to convert a temporary obstacle into a new opportunity.

He transformed himself from "odd man out," to "acclaimed Mellencamp band member, Kenny Aronoff."

It was really no surprise at all then, that when I asked Kenny if he always wanted to be one of the world's best rock and roll drummers, he simply answered, "Of course." Kenny's secret (while obvious, yet eludes many) is his positive attitude and determination—attributes which help him wake up each and every morning with the will and desire to "go for it," even through difficult and challenging times. Kenny shared this simple sentiment with me during our conversation: "I am basically a happy person, especially when I play the drums, because it brings so much joy to me that it helps me overcome a lot. If you can have some kind of happiness and joy each and every day, either by yourself, or with somebody else, that will make all the difference."

Doesn't this sound a lot like he lives his life applying the Law of Abundance?

Kenny Aronoff and me at a music industry event.

To wrap up his story, I would like to add some profound advice from Kenny that I believe will be helpful to you:

1. **There are no shortcuts.** Hard work will get you where you want to go, all of the time.

2. **Be passionate for the things you really want to do.** Go for it!

3. **Constantly keep learning.** Educate, educate, educate!

4. **To overcome your fears and obstacles, figure things out for yourself and do the best you can to help yourself out of all negative and/or uncomfortable situations.**

I think you will agree that Kenny Aronoff most definitely encompasses the many positive attributes that you, too, can cultivate to grow your own success.

Finding Your Right Balance for Success

In the summer of 2013, I became a number one international best-selling contributing author for the second time in, *Ready, Aim, Influence! Join Forces, Expand Resources, Transform Your World.* The book is comprised of interviews that editor, Viki Winterton, conducted and then compiled from the various contributing authors. One of the questions that she asked me in the book was, "Is our youth more aware of having a balanced and a more fulfilling life?"

That was a really interesting question that I actually began asking myself over 20 years ago. Back in 1992, when I was in my late 20s— fast-approaching 30—I used to jog around my old neighborhood in North Hollywood, California. During my runs, I would often reflect on where I was in my life and where I wanted to be in the future. I had just started working for MCA Records at that time and my overhead was greater than my income. So in order to make ends meet, I had to work a second job at a video and CD store in Burbank, California called, The Music Wherehouse. During that time, I started keeping my eyes open for inspiration about how I could become a more successful executive at the record company. What did my bosses know that I didn't? Then it dawned on me that while my bosses could be, and were, *considered* successful, I had no idea if they were according to my own definition of success. I concluded that in order to achieve success on my own terms, I needed to live a more balanced life. I began to honestly analyze different areas of my life, and through that process of honing my self-awareness, I ended up designing the diagram I called, "The Four Quadrants for Life Balance."

The basic premise of this diagram was inspired during that self-awareness journey when I realized well-rounded people find life balance when they focus on addressing the underlying principles shown in my diagram (divided into two sections within each of the four quadrants, creating eight overall sections). By adopting elements from all four quadrants (each of the eight sections), you could apply your newfound knowledge, strength, talents, and skills to help create both your short-term (one to three years), and your long-term (five to ten years) plans and goals for success.

"The Four Quadrants for Life Balance" is comprised of these elements:

1. *Physical* (physical health/exercise and overall well-being/diet)

2. *Emotional/Spiritual* (personal development and personal/ professional relationships)

3. *Mental/Educational* (hobbies, education, reading, general studies, seminars, webinars, etc.)

4. *Financial* (personal finance and investing)

Because the first three quadrants involve actions or decisions within your immediate control—physical, emotional/spiritual, and mental/educational—you can choose to morph negative or unhealthy situations into positive or healthy ones at any time...as long as you commit to your own self-improvement by no longer sabotaging your future success and happiness. In my case, I chose to become healthier by going to the gym and doing new things that involved fitness (Quadrant #1: Physical). I also decided to attract and pursue healthy and positive personal and professional relationships, while distancing myself from, and avoiding, unhealthy emotional parasites (Quadrant #2: Emotional/Spiritual). And finally, I decided to start reading more, and pursuing new educational endeavors because I firmly believe that education appreciates (...possessions depreciate)—which is why I went back to school to earn my MBA and Ed.D degrees (Quadrant #3: Mental/Educational). However, the final one (Quadrant #4: Financial) really stopped me in my tracks. Because, at that point in my late twenties (since I had never really learned about finances from my parents, teachers, and friends), I identified a gaping hole in my own life balance. I was quickly coming to the realization that I knew very little about personal finance and investing. So to help rectify this gap, I set off on a pretty involved quest to educate myself about the importance of not just understanding the value of money (how to save and spend it), but I sought to gather knowledge about how to create and attract wealth...that was the bigger challenge.

To help get you started on enhancing your own knowledge, strengths, talents, and skills to strengthen your life balance, I suggest you either photocopy (if you're reading the bound book), or print out (e-book) "The Four Quadrants for Life Balance" diagram provided for you in the appendix, then filling it in with as much current, or projected near-future detail as you can. Continue to update this diagram as your circumstances change so that you cultivate another useful tool to stay on top of tracking, measuring, and evaluating your success. I can attest that this diagram has worked (and continues to work) as an effective tool to help me maintain my life balance, and I hope it will serve you just as well while you grow your success.

1. PHYSICAL   2. EMOTIONAL/
                                                        SPIRITUAL

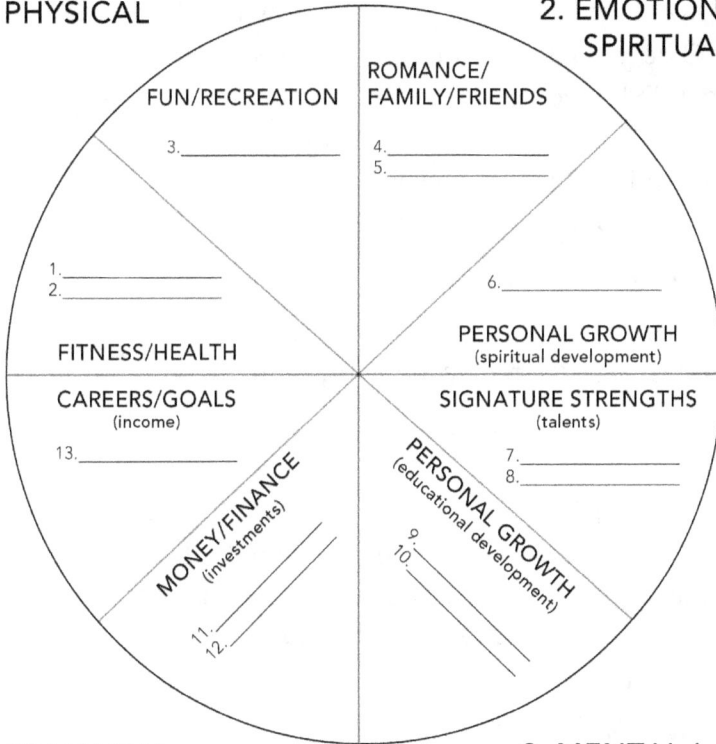

FUN/RECREATION

ROMANCE/
FAMILY/FRIENDS

3._____

4._____
5._____

1._____
2._____

6._____

FITNESS/HEALTH

PERSONAL GROWTH
(spiritual development)

CAREERS/GOALS
(income)

SIGNATURE STRENGTHS
(talents)

13._____

7._____
8._____

MONEY/FINANCE
(investments)

PERSONAL GROWTH
(educational development)

9._____
10._____

11._____
12._____

4. FINANCIAL   3. MENTAL/
                                                        EDUCATIONAL

The numbered activity questions that follow, can be used as a guide to help you get in touch with areas you intend to improve. They correspond to the numbers delineated within each of the eight sections of the specified quadrants, and are followed with spaces for you to fill in your answers. For example, take a look at the first question, "Quadrant #1: Physical *Fitness/Health* 1. Do you exercise regularly? If so, how often?"

On your copy of the diagram, you'll simply write your answer in the first section on the left within Quadrant #1 (the "Fitness/Health" section of the "Physical" quadrant), and on that first blank line (to the right of "1."), you could answer, "Yes, I exercise four times a week."

While there *is* a Call to Action at the end of this chapter, I'd first like for you to pause to do this right now and fill in as many areas within "The Four Quadrants for Life Balance" diagram (found in the appendix) as you can. Again, this exercise was designed to help you focus on areas where you might need improvement in order to help you find balance in your life.

Quadrant #1: Physical

Fitness/Health
  1. Do you exercise regularly? If so, how often?

  2. Do you play any sports? If so, which ones?

Fun/Recreation
  3. Do you take time out of your busy day to do fun or recreational things that you enjoy (hobbies, musical instruments, etc.)? If so, what do you like to do? If not, why not?

Quadrant #2: Emotional/Spiritual

Romance/Family/Friends
  4. Do you spend any quality time with your family, boyfriend/ girlfriend, spouse/significant other, friends? If so, how do you spend your time? What do you do? If not, why not?

  5. Are you kind and respectful to your boyfriend/girlfriend, spouse/ significant other, friends, etc.? If so, how? If not, why not?

Personal Growth (spiritual development)
  6. Do you have any positive role models or mentors you can look up to, or learn from? If so, who? How do they assist you and model the way? If not, seek them out!

Quadrant #3: Mental/Educational

Signature Strengths (talents)

7. Do you spend enough time enhancing your own unique talents, and/or do you look to try new things (hobbies, sports, music, dance, etc.)? If so, what are they? If not, why not?

8. Do you read any books, magazines, blogs, etc. on subjects that interest you? If so, name two or three from your list that inspire you, and why. If not, get on it!

Personal Growth (educational development)

9. Do you attend any seminars, online webinars, or classes that enhance your knowledge of subjects that either interest you, and/or support your goals? If so, what seminars, webinars, or classes have you participated in, and what about them inspired you? If not, you might want to consider incorporating these types of learning tools into your life (knowledge can never be taken away from you).

10. Do you practice good time management skills (study and/or work habits)? If so, how? If not, why not?

Quadrant #4: Financial

Money/Finance (investments)

11. Do you have any knowledge, understanding, or experience regarding personal finance and investing? If so, what? If not, you'll want to pay close attention when you read Chapter Eight!

12. Do you currently save money for your future in a personal savings and/or investment account? If so, good for you! If not, pay close attention when you read Chapter Eight!

Career/Goals (income)

13. Do you have any knowledge of, or experience with how to generate or create wealth? If so, what have you learned or attempted? If not, you guessed it...Chapter Eight!

Remember, you are reading this book to help you learn and acquire new skills to improve your habits to create successful outcomes. So at this point, if you are unable to answer some (or any) of these questions, please do not be hard on yourself. Just do your best to fill in as many of the quadrant sections as you can with either activities that you are currently performing, or ones that you are hoping to perform in the future. And if you're having trouble coming up with answers right now, by the time you've finished reading this book, I am confident that you will have a better understanding of how to respond to each of these 13 questions. Keep in mind, this exercise is designed to simply make you more aware, and to serve as a call to action for you to follow through on things that you either started, or told yourself that you would begin "eventually." The important thing here is that you begin engaging in activities that will enhance your talents, skills, and knowledge. As you enrich your life balance by growing and building your new strengths, I can assure you that you will also be increasing your personal happiness and successful outcomes.

I would like to leave you with one final thought before I conclude this chapter with your Call to Action, which is as follows: Clearly defined goals dramatically enhance your odds for success. If you truly want to achieve your desired outcomes, it is imperative that you start taking responsibility *now* for your own actions and decisions. Successful people "go for it." They consistently reaffirm their intentions to motivate and empower themselves to take the appropriate action steps, which are necessary to achieve their *probable* outcomes for success. Successful people set goals, create action plans, check their fears at the door, spot their opportunities, trust their instincts, manage their time well, and manifest their visions to achieve their goals and desires.

The sooner you begin to incorporate these important concepts into your own strategic life planning, the sooner you will begin to grow your success!

Call to Action

1. Take a moment to write down some of your passions and goals that you intend to achieve. Utilizing the first three steps of P.P.I.E. (Prioritize, Plan, Implement, and Evaluate), respond to the following: What is your true passion or desire (**Prioritize**)? Create and define your vision and purpose (e.g., mission) for your passion/desire, along with your goals for achieving them (**Plan**). Finally, outline and implement specific and realistic action steps that you believe will help you accomplish and achieve your passion, desire, and goals (**Implement**).

Prioritize your goals, thoughts and desires:

_____

_____

_____

_____

Plan and create your tools for action:

_____

_____

_____

_____

Implement and take action:

_____

_____

_____

_____

2. To help you measure and evaluate your progress toward achieving your goals (Evaluate), list the specific actions you plan to take to accomplish your goals on your own newly created action board. Once you have finished creating your action board with deadline dates, prominently display it so that you can view it (at least a couple of times) on a daily basis. I would also like you to begin journaling the various action steps that you have either undertaken, or plan to undertake, on a daily basis to help keep you accountable as you track your progress. By either handwriting (my recommendation), or typing your entries and documenting what you did to accomplish your goals on a daily basis, along with your method, you will be creating a historical blueprint to refer back to for guidance in the future. Like Kenny's practice schedule, you want to be as specific as possible about what you hope to achieve, and by what date, so that you can design the necessary action steps to achieve your goals.

7

No Nonsense Decision-Making!

Do your decisions dictate your situations, or do your situations dictate your decisions?

We all know that making bad decisions (or even remaining paralyzed by indecision or fear), will negatively impact or jeopardize one's personal and financial success. But knowing this still doesn't seem to stop people from continuously making bad decisions over and over again. Earlier in this book, I explained how important it is to enhance your awareness with more clarity by bravely and honestly facing who you are, and what you think about yourself and the world around you. I covered this concept early on because it is the foundation on which you build good decision-making skills. When you develop your heightened awareness, you will be empowering, preparing, and motivating yourself to make good strategic decisions, which will enable you to take the appropriate action steps to accomplish your desired goals. You will not only be more prepared to spot potential opportunities, but you'll also know more quickly when those opportunities are in alignment with your intentions (your vision and mission statements). Also, by knowing and understanding your perceptions with honest clarity, you will be in a much better position to jump on those positive opportunities when they come your way, because you will have prepared yourself to quickly make well-informed strategic decisions.

If you're reading this and wondering how to stop yourself from making bad decisions, then you will need to understand that there is a big difference between emotional and strategic decisions. Emotionally-driven decisions generally do not have nearly the same positive outcomes as do strategically-driven decisions because they are not based upon research, reality, and facts. You need to also recognize that when you are making emotionally-driven decisions, you will need to catch yourself, pause, and then strategize how you really should be approaching a particular situation.

Like most successful people, if you ever find yourself in a negative situation where you feel out of control, don't have many options, or simply feel the urge to let your emotional childhood programming kick in, before you render any decisions, just make sure those decisions are based upon *probable* (strategic), versus possible (emotional) outcomes.

Another emotional decision-making pitfall is when self-doubt creeps in and you talk yourself out of making a sound decision because you predict and fear someone else might negatively respond to your decision. However, when you take the time to base your decisions upon research, reality, and facts (while shifting away from making emotionally-driven decisions toward making strategically-driven decisions), you will definitely improve your *probable* outcomes for success. And by having done your "homework," you will know that the decision you made was a sound one, which will go a long way toward quieting any naysayers.

The Strategy of Decision-Making

Because young adults tend to spend too much of their time responding to their fears, low self-esteem, and the chaos that surrounds them, they often lean toward making choices based solely on reactions derived from their own negative emotions, as opposed to learning, from an early age, how to remain calm and make strategic, logical decisions that will benefit their ultimate outcomes.

So, how do you avoid making poor decisions during one of the most critical and emotionally-driven times in your life?

Like an anchor that holds a ship steady during a raging storm, whenever faced with an uncomfortable decision, you must first remember to stay calm and focused when weighing your alternatives and options (despite whatever appears to be going on around you) to avoid making any quick, emotionally-driven decisions that can derail you. To help you begin differentiating between strategic, versus emotional decisions, I would like you to revisit incorporating *probability*, versus possibility (which I discussed earlier in Chapter Two) as part of your decision-making process.

To help you improve your *probable* outcomes for success, I've created a list of the following questions that are designed to help you differentiate and start thinking more strategically (and less emotionally) whenever you are faced with making any decisions. Once you become clear on the difference, you will begin to execute *strategic decisions* that will not only better align with your overall goals, but will also consistently optimize your *probable* outcomes for success.

The next time you are faced with a decision (big or small), I'd like you to utilize these questions to work through your answers so you can strengthen your future insights, as you continue to improve your strategic decision-making habits.

1. What is the probability that my decision will lead to a successful outcome, and how will this decision get me closer to achieving my overall goals?

This would be a good time to step back and honestly ask yourself if this decision would really be a good strategic use of your time, money, and/or energy (rather than merely trying to convince yourself, or please someone else, by making an emotionally-driven decision). Determine if this decision is coming from your head or your heart, and how the outcome of this decision will ultimately benefit you personally, professionally, etc.

> ***Probability*** implies decisiveness
> (That WILL probably happen)
>
> **Possibility** insinuates uncertainty
> (That COULD possibly happen)

2. How do I hope to benefit from making this decision?

Whatever happened to the old expression, "Just sleep on it"? So many people have become so conditioned by the media, advertisers, and others that if they don't immediately jump and take advantage of a so-called opportunity, right then and there, then it may never be available to them again—it's a lost opportunity forever! "If you snooze, you lose!" Advertisers pay marketing professionals huge sums of money to subliminally (or sometimes overtly) manipulate their target audience by telling them what they are lacking in their lives and *cannot live without!* However, only you can truly know how your decisions will play out in the bigger picture. So step back and give yourself that extra time to really think about it, and ask yourself how your decision will ultimately benefit *you*, as opposed to the person on the other end who may be pressuring you. If you are not sure how that particular decision *will probably* (versus could possibly) immediately benefit you, do not hesitate to go ahead and sleep on it. Also, keeping the following tips in mind will help you to pause and give yourself more time to think about making your best strategic decisions:

Do not rush yourself into deciding immediately.

Do not talk yourself into making any decision(s) before you do your research and know all the facts.

Do not fall prey to anyone's pushiness—you have every right to demand that your boundaries are to be respected.

Do not allow yourself to feel manipulated into making any decision that you may later regret.

And finally, DO keep the old adage in mind: "If it sounds too good to be true, then it probably is."

3. How much hard work, time, and/or money will my decision(s) ultimately cost me?

You would not believe how many people (including myself) neglect taking the time to plan ahead and address how they will handle important scenarios before they happen. Here are some example scenarios:

How many times will you lend someone money because they tenaciously begged you for it, but you never took the time to figure out if they were trustworthy enough to pay you back, or even whether they *could* pay you back?

You agreed to help someone in a jam, and because you did not establish boundaries and express any expectations, they took advantage of your kindness and relentlessly continued to push their luck by asking you for more favors.

You told yourself you would, "only take this job for year," or you would, "only live in this lousy apartment for a few months," only to find yourself still working in the same unfulfilling job, or living in the same old apartment for more years than you'd like to admit, because you never sat down to figure out how much time you would need to give up, and/or money you'd need to spend/save before you could do "X."

Please take some friendly advice from someone who knows...I made *all* of these mistakes in the past. Therefore, I cannot encourage you enough to NEVER make *any* important personal, professional, or financial decisions in your life without first figuring out *why* you are choosing to commit to investing your hard work, time, and/or money toward supporting that decision. More importantly, do not neglect doing your research and taking the time to calculate just how long it would take you to recoup your invested resources to receive the return on your investment.

4. What additional opportunities would my decision provide for me?

You may discover, for all the hard work, time, and/or money you invested, that your reward (or return on your investment) will arrive in the form of future opportunities. For example, your fellow classmates today, are potential business contacts tomorrow. Which is another good reason why an investment in your education (college/university degrees, certifications, seminar or workshop classes, educational boot camps, etc.) can not only help improve your knowledge, talents, and skills, but could also lead to new, or escalated personal or professional opportunities. An excellent way to create those future opportunities is to network, collaborate, and meet new people wherever you can. Look to volunteer, join, or intern for companies, organizations, or events that interest you. Another suggestion is tutoring or consulting others for free, in return for referrals, references, or endorsements. Receiving "word of mouth" feedback, testimonials, and/or referrals from others is a valuable reward that will definitely make it worth your efforts.

By stopping to ask yourself the above four questions, and remembering these simple strategic tips, you will learn how to filter your decisions, from an early age, so that you can confidently identify your opportunities, research and acquire important facts (to strategically forecast your *probable* outcomes), and commit to making sound decisions that will improve your overall success.

Your Intentions Drive Your Decisions

When I began researching and studying why successful people tend to make better decisions than most, I quickly realized that although many people learn from an early age *how* to make decisions, very few will go the extra mile to really understand their intentions behind *why* they chose a particular decision—especially if those decisions tend to be emotionally-driven. Because intentions are such a major component in the decision-making process, they must be taken into account when making any new decisions.

5. What are my underlying intentions for making this decision? What reaction am I hoping to solicit from others, or benefit/gain from the outcome of this decision?

When I refer to your intentions, I am referring to the purpose or catalyst behind what is ultimately driving you to make your decision in the first place. When it comes to emotionally-driven decisions, if your intentions are fear-based, then you need to learn how to manage those fears so that they do not dictate how you handle a situation (which could prevent you from making the right decisions for your desired outcomes). If your intentions are anger-based or malicious, put a stop to those thoughts immediately. Never intentionally make any type of decision(s) that you know may harm others— nothing positive ever comes of that kind of thinking or behavior (regardless of whatever reason you tell yourself as justification for indulging in it). I can assure you, successful people are not driven by malicious intent when they are going through their decision-making processes. Whereas, emotional parasites seem to feel the need to inflict their malicious intent on others because they can't seem to help being hellbent on either undermining, or unraveling, other people's success or happiness. How can you tell if someone may be consciously (or unconsciously) trying to hurt you?

I would like to share a quick story I once heard which may explain why emotional parasites do what they do. It's called *The Frog and the Scorpion.* In this story, the scorpion comes up to a river, and realizes that he cannot cross because he cannot swim. To help himself get across the river, the scorpion tries to solicit the assistance of a frog. The frog, well aware of the dangerous nature and behavior of the scorpion, respectfully tells the scorpion that he cannot help him across the river because he is afraid that the scorpion will sting him and he will die. In an effort to convince the frog to assist him, the scorpion tells the frog that stinging him would clearly be the illogical thing to do because if he were to sting the frog, then he, too, would die in the river. The frog took a moment to think over the scorpion's logic and agreed to let the scorpion jump on his back. Soon after the frog and scorpion began crossing the water, the scorpion proceeded to sting the frog. The frog, clearly in pain from the scorpion's sting, screams out, "Why did you do that? Now we are both going to die!" To which the scorpion replied, "I know. But I am a scorpion, and that's what I do!" The moral of this story is simple: Be very aware of the scorpions in your life! Although they may not wish to intentionally hurt you, like the scorpion, this is their nature. It's who they are, and that is what they do. If you recognize yourself as the scorpion, stop that behavior (you're a human, *you* can change). We all need people in our lives. And we all have choices about who those people are going to be. The truly successful and happy people surround themselves with those whom they share in reciprocated love, admiration, and respect.

If my point is not yet clear, you really need to understand your intentions (what do you *honestly* want?) behind each decision you make. Because sometimes, despite any desire you may have to be well-liked and to gain others' approval, there will always be people who aren't in your corner because they are simply predisposed—for whatever reason—to dislike you, and trying to gain their respect and approval is a waste of time. To expound, I believe that as "human animals," we are all, as individuals, predisposed to think and behave in certain ways. Did you ever wonder why there are some people we seem to naturally gravitate toward (friends), while others seem to immediately get under our skin and repulse us? Human beings exhibit internal energy differently, which I believe causes us to energetically vibrate with others in one of three ways: positively (friendship), negatively (avoidance), and neutrally (acquaintances). As thinking organisms, we should always try to make decisions that are in alignment and harmony with our true instinctual self (core values, beliefs, etc.) so that we always vibrate in a peaceful and positive way. We often refer to these positive instinctual feelings as, "going with the grain," or "going with the flow." However, when we rush into, or emotionally try to justify our decisions that are not in alignment with our instincts, we tend to feel uncomfortable or out of sorts. This is why no matter how long or hard an emotional parasite tries to shield you from seeing their true intentions, they eventually feel compelled to expose their true selves (the habitual liar, the con artist, the addict, etc.). It's your job to be aware and notice their true agendas when they slip and let their guard down. Hopefully at that point, your emotionally-driven decisions will not have caused you too much damage to clean up.

Despite the fact that one's beliefs might actually be inappropriate and/or even harmful to themselves or others when making bad decisions, like the scorpion (regardless of all the lessons we human beings may learn about making good decisions), many will succumb to their true natures and preprogrammed beliefs. Meanwhile, when we're on the outside looking in, we can see another person's situation with clarity and be convinced that we'd choose the correct and best choice on how to proceed. It reminds me of the old saying, "Practice what you preach," which speaks to the hypocritical behavior we can all sometimes engage in. I believe that deep down, we all instinctively know what the right, and best decision(s) should be—for ourselves *and* for others. However, we get ourselves into trouble when we act against our own good instincts, and instead make the wrong, or bad decisions because of our own negative early programming (fears, insecurities, low self-esteem, etc.). This is why I believe that when one makes "bad" decisions, despite their better judgment, it's because they are instinctively acting out their need to be in harmony with their subconscious mind. To improve our behavior, we must first take the time to find our inner strength and confidence to empower ourselves to consciously change our pre-programmed thoughts and beliefs. For example, even though we all know that telling the truth is the right thing to do, habitual liars actually feel more at ease when they lie because they most likely learned, early on, that their lies helped them avoid unpleasant consequences (severe punishment or ridicule). We filter our realities through the lens of our true core values and beliefs, which is why they so greatly impact the various decisions we make throughout our lives.

Do not compromise your core values and beliefs in an effort to please, or impress someone else, if it means sacrificing your own happiness or success. When you are making decisions, by continuing to ask yourself, "*Why?*" you will be ensuring that your decisions not only align with your intentions, but with your desired outcomes as well (which will greatly enhance your *probable* outcomes for your continued future success).

Can Making Mistakes Enhance Your Success?

Over the past several years, I have been on a mission to spread the word that success is all about never being afraid to ask, "Why?" When we were all toddlers, we instinctively questioned everything and everyone by incessantly asking, "Why is this...? Why is that...? Why are you...? Why? Why? Why?" But sadly, by the time we become teenagers, we seem to have lost our ability to ask, "Why?" Over the years, the combination of standardized testing agendas, along with the widespread lack of core life skills being taught in our high schools' and colleges' curriculums (personal development, personal finance, time management, etc.), have contributed to the erosion of our youth's ability to ask, "Why?" They instead, simply settle for a more practical approach to their thinking and ask, "*How?*"

(e.g., "How do I get that job?" "How do I become rich?" "How do I make that happen?")

As a result, more and more young adults will simply continue to conform and stop challenging the norm, as they either develop a fear of mistakes, or they just become programmed to avoid them altogether, so that they end up refraining from even trying to take on new challenges. The irony is, the biggest mistake that parents, teachers, and society have made is not teaching young adults that it is okay to make mistakes. So I'm telling you right now: It's okay for you to make mistakes!

Mistakes teach people to learn, from an early age, how to develop tools for handling and managing life's inherent struggles. Mistakes educate people on how to overcome prior obstacles by helping them understand why things do not always work out as originally planned. Mistakes help people foster new and creative ways to overcome, or circumvent, prior negative experiences in order to find new, or improved, ways to produce their desired outcomes (without letting fear get the best of them).

By providing you with valuable life lessons, making mistakes and living through bad decisions empower you to overcome your fears to achieve your desired goals and success. Mistakes are a big part of everyone's overall learning process. Once you've come out surviving on the other side, having experienced making mistakes actually helps you by allowing you to re-create, then improve upon (innovate), what you have already learned was effective/ineffective through trial and error. Ultimately, you will have learned to trust yourself to know when it's time to, "throw in the towel," and move on when something no longer works.

Personally, I have become a much better leader in life as a result of living through, and learning from, my past mistakes. I highly recommend that you don't shy away from opportunities out of fear of making your own mistakes. Actually, let's strike that word, "mistakes," and call them, "learning opportunities."

A few years back, I had become truly fed up making so many repeated mistakes in my life. I made the conscious decision that I was ready to learn my lessons so I could finally move past making the same mistakes. When I actually took the time and focused on honestly doing my "inner work" to reflect on my past and current mistakes, I realized that I tended to focus more on how I thought others would react to my emotionally-driven decisions, rather than what would have been best for me at the time. This revelation about why I kept, as my mother used to say, "falling into the same hole," woke me up to the fact that I needed to start reexamining my overall decision-making process. So I focused on trying to better understand *why* I kept repeating the same mistakes over and over again. I decided it was time to get out of my own way, learn from my bad decisions, and finally walk *around* the hole. In fact, I learned so much from my past mistakes that I even came up with an easy-to-remember acronym to help me identify, adjust, grow, and move on from past mistakes so that I could begin focusing on my desired future success:

L.A.R. = **L**earning from the past, **A**pplying in the present, and **R**eaping (your rewards) in the future

---

1. Learning from the past is centered on your own self-awareness.

There are two major aspects to *learning from the past* in your decision-making process:

Intention: The understanding of your own internal motivation for making decisions. You need to ask yourself the following questions when analyzing your decisions: What is the underlying intention for my decision—strategic or emotional? Is my decision in alignment, or in conflict, with my core values, beliefs, etc.? Or am I simply trying to please or impress someone else?

Lessons learned from others: As I mentioned earlier, knowledge-sharing (mentors, books, lectures, webinars, online courses, live presentations, etc.) is essential toward helping you make better decisions. Ignorance is not bliss—it is catastrophic! To be successful, you need to check your ego at the door and understand that you are not always the smartest person in the room. More often than not, a successful person is the one that usually observes, listens, and learns, rather than being the one who is always trying to speak. You cannot learn anything new if you are the only one in the room talking. Which leads me to share some common mistakes most people tend to make (again, I wish I had the foresight to avoid these when I was growing up!):

Thinking you are the smartest person in the room. I know I've mentioned this a few times, but it bears repeating. Despite what your parents, friends, significant other, or "mirror reflection" tells you, you are not the smartest person in the room. Don't try to be a "know it all." Like the old saying goes, "A smart man always finds the right words to say, but an even smarter man knows when to just listen." Listen more, talk less. You may actually learn more from others if you give them an opportunity to speak.

Not getting out of your own way. One of the main reasons why so many people never seem to achieve their goals and success is because they simply succumb to their fears and never make any real efforts to get out of their own negative comfort zones.

Always looking for the other shoe to drop. Stop expecting things to go wrong. That type of negative thinking is unproductive and could lead to self-fulfilling prophecies. You need to try to trust yourself, the process, and others, and stop assuming the worst. A good rule to remember is, "When there is no smoke, there is no fire."

It's my way or the highway. If you are someone who must always see or do things your own way, your own rigid behavior may create unforeseen barriers and prevent you from attaining your overall success. Remember, people never become successful strictly on their own. Everyone needs help from others at some point in time. And sometimes that involves swallowing your pride, asking for help, and then compromising your original ideas to implement their input. Learn to compromise with others, but just remember not to sacrifice your own core values and beliefs to please the others. Find your shared voice.

Whining and playing the victim. Stop beating yourself up and feeling sorry for yourself. No one has control or power over your life unless you choose to give them that power. If you want things to change in your life, then start taking responsibility for your own actions and circumstances and stop blaming others for your poor decisions that you chose to make—or avoided making—out of fear.

Keeping up with the Joneses. Stop trying to compare yourself to others. Do not allow the negative comments or views of a select few dictate how you choose to perceive yourself. Always comparing your success or failure to others is the quickest way to lose your own way in life. Respect yourself by following your own path so that you avoid the drama of making rash or emotional decisions in an effort to keep pace with someone else. Stay true to your own unique and authentic self.

Getting stuck in your own head. Your negative thoughts can turn you into your own worst enemy. To quote the Chinese Tao philosopher, Lao Tzu, "Watch your thoughts; they become words. Watch your words; they become actions. Watch your actions; they become habits. Watch your habits; they become character. Watch your character; it becomes your destiny." Stop worrying about how other people will perceive your ideas or actions, and don't overanalyze every little detail to the point where you become too paralyzed to take any action.

2. *Applying in the present* is centered on taking action.
When you begin applying what you've learned from the past, you will find that making better decisions will naturally become more habit-forming as you break your pattern of repeated mistakes. Another great tip you can utilize when taking action on your decisions comes from my old boss, mentor, and friend, Vinnie Freda. He often told me before making any important business or life decisions to always "trust, but verify" that the information you are given is accurate, trustworthy, and reliable so that you can ensure *probable* decisive outcomes.

Here's a simple example of why it's important to verify your information before you take action. Let's presume that an acquaintance you don't really know very well recommends that you should go see a movie you've never really heard of. Would you choose to trust their recommendation and spend a steep amount of money to see a movie that you know very little about, based solely upon an acquaintance's recommendation? Or would it make more sense to verify, and find out what a family member or friend who saw the movie thought about it? Or take the time to look up what established critics had written about the movie? How relevant is the cost of the movie to your overall financial plans and outcomes? If that money could be used for something more important, some people may not be willing to spend their hard-earned money to see a movie they've never heard of simply because some acquaintance told them to see it. When you do your prior research by incorporating the concept of "trust, but verify" into your decision-making process, it helps you weigh your options to make a better decision which will yield your highest *probable* outcome for success.

While it may be an admirable quality to see the good in people and trust they'll do the right thing, you must still do your research to make sure that what you find out, matches up with what you're being told (promised). Depending on the reliability of your source, you can hopefully trust most of the information you receive, but it's always a good strategy to verify the information before acting on it. You'll have the time to do your research because you will have made it clear you need to "sleep on it." Right? This is called doing your *due diligence*. Do not be lazy, or in such a rush, that you avoid doing your research. Confirm that the words you are told, match the actions you see, look for consistency in character, and make sure that all promises are kept. Ask every question that comes to mind, and request to see tangible (physical) evidence from them that backs up what they are saying. You can also go online and investigate their information yourself to help confirm its accuracy. Personally, I may even run my findings by my friends or family to get their opinions about my pending decision. Trust me from experience, the extra work you do upfront to confirm that you are dealing with an ethical and honest person (or business), will go a long way in preventing headaches down the road. Taking those preventive measures may just amount to saving you from making another bad decision.

Earlier in this book, we discussed how we project our personal brand while out in public and online through social media. I recommend that you apply that same awareness of your public persona when it comes to considering how the outcomes of your decisions will be perceived by others when filtered through the lens of their own thoughts and beliefs. Here's a little trick to help give you the gift of foresight: mentally project yourself into the future, then consider "in hindsight" what the positive or negative ramifications of your "past" decisions might be. I could have definitely used my own advice back in college when I was getting ready for an awards event. Turns out a friend of mine decided to challenge me to a dare as I was preparing to leave for the event. Unfortunately, I succumbed to his needling and ended up wearing an inappropriate outfit to this formal event. Of course, it did not go over well because it was a *formal event* and I disrespectfully looked like an idiot. I am sure that, because of my shortsighted mistake, many of the people at that event formed a negative opinion of me, which not only likely impaired my credibility, but tarnished my personal brand as well. By thoroughly considering all of the ethical and social consequences that could result from your decisions, you will be conscientiously protecting your personal brand, and potentially, your future.

Since you never want others to challenge or question your character or integrity, here are some ethical questions that you can ask yourself before making any important final decisions:

Will my decisions negatively impact or hurt others?

Are these decisions my own? Do they align with, or go against, my core values?

How will my decisions be perceived through others' ethical or moral filters?

Successful people often lead with high moral character and integrity which is why Gulf War General, Norman Schwarzkopf, believed that "99% of all leadership failures in this country in the last 100 years were not due to failures in competence, but rather a failure in character. Greed, lying, prejudice, racism, intolerance, sexism, hate, immorality and amorality are not attributable to competence failures—they are all character failures."

To help ensure that your decisions always comply with society's ethical filters, I suggest you ask yourself, "Would I want the outcome of this decision to appear on the internet, the front page of the New York Times, or my local town newspaper for all my friends, family, and future employers to see?" It is important that you always remember that ill-conceived decisions might eventually lead to undesirable outcomes and unfortunate consequences. Thus, before you decide to make any rash or quick decisions, either out of impatience or frustration, take some time to really understand how those decisions might impact not only your own success, but also the well-being of others. Be authentic, aware, and respectful.

3. Reaping (your rewards) in the future is centered on abundance and success.

Reaping your rewards is your big payoff for taking the time to ensure your strategic decisions always align with your goals and desired outcomes. As I have mentioned before, once you decide to take the appropriate action steps to attract what you ultimately want and desire in your life, the positive energy your actions generate will only serve to further enhance your abundance and foster your commitment to achieve even greater goals and accomplishments. In choosing to trust your instincts, while no longer allowing yourself to be emotionally manipulated by either your fears or others' expectations, you will be perpetuating your positive ascent toward reaching your ultimate rewards.

In fact, I am really amazed how well "L.A.R." can be applied to almost any situation. For example, I recently went to the movies and I noticed that L.A.R. could be applied to almost any Hollywood protagonist/antagonist character's development throughout a movie.

Quite often, the lead characters are flawed and faced with some huge personal dilemma that ultimately prevents them from getting what they initially wanted. Throughout the course of the movie, the audience gets to watch how these lead characters transform themselves through the lessons they learned from their various mistakes, setbacks, or situations which they encountered while engaging with the other characters and settings. Then we watch them morph as they start applying their newly learned behaviors as they work to rectify their prior mistakes, setbacks, or situations. So by the end of the movie, we are cheering them on as we watch them ultimately reap the benefits and rewards from their efforts. (Which usually consist of them either getting the girl or guy, receiving some huge gift or sum of money, and/or finally getting to live out [whatever their version was of] "that perfect life that they had always wanted.")

As the leading man or woman in your own life's movie, it's time for you to start taking control of your own decisions by first learning from your past mistakes, so that you can apply those important lessons toward your future outcomes and always receive the abundance and rewards you ultimately desire in your life. As long as you always align your core values and beliefs with your goals and desires, your good decisions will continually improve your chances for success.

The Art of the Pause

There is an old saying, "The shortest distance between two points is a straight line." The only problem is, if traversing that straight line happens to take more time than one anticipates, some people will actually attempt to forego the obvious route by taking some unproven shortcut. Sadly for some, taking this approach will always be in their nature—to try to find hidden detours that they *think* will save them time and/or money, and will help expedite the results they want. Never mind the fact that they have prior knowledge of others' unsuccessful attempts, they still believe that they will be the first to successfully complete such a unique undertaking. As a result, their arrogance, ignorance, or naïveté tends to override their common sense and leads them to shun their own instincts. They ignore their good common sense, despite their rational inner voices trying to reason with them, and (to continue with the road metaphor) they start their life engines (without a GPS device!) and embark down their own mental highway only to find themselves lost on the interstate, and stuck in the middle of life's nowhere.

So what's the urge that possesses normally intelligent people (young and old alike) to ignore basic common sense and pursue unproven shortcuts, when clearly staying on the straight and proven path is what most often enhances one's success? Once again, it comes down to one simple answer: emotionally-driven decisions.

Irrational, emotionally-driven decisions are usually ill-conceived and their outcomes could be dismal. How many times have we all responded to someone and said something that we later wished we hadn't? Or made a rash decision in the heat of the moment—especially because we were feeling impatient, tired, or upset? If you ever find yourself upset or agitated, refrain from responding or making any final decisions until you are in a proper frame of mind. As a general rule, you should try to wait at least one or two hours before calling or emailing someone back if you are not in a calm state of mind because you might make a decision, or say something to someone, that you may ultimately regret. This is especially true when making decisions that involve business, relationships, and money.

In fact, I can still remember how out of sorts and frantic I felt when I was divorcing my ex-wife back in 2003. All I could think about was how I was going to make back all the money I was paying out to her each month as part of the alimony settlement. You know how I keep mentioning that I'm writing about all the mistakes I've made because they have taught me valuable lessons I'm now teaching you? Well, here's another one. In my panicked state, rather than just stepping back and taking the time to simply pause and slowly figure things out, I ignored my instincts and started telling myself I knew better, and that I could find a quicker and easier way to get out of my money woes. Here's a little fact that I neglected to take into account: Whenever we humans get overwhelmed, feel trapped, or fearful, our minds shut off and our bodies go into an instinctual fight-or-flight mode. Rather than taking the needed time to research and analyze my financial situation before I began making important life decisions, I foolishly set myself up for failure by turning to the path of least resistance (shortcuts).

Back in 1996, I discovered the stock market. Discount brokerage firms such as e-Trade, Ameritrade, and Charles Schwab were enticing wannabe investors with a new trading platform which facilitated online trading. For only about a third of what traditional discount brokerage firms previously charged for commissions to execute your trades, one could go online, research their own stocks, and execute their own trades. At this same time, I began studying the investment strategies of value investors, Ben Graham, and his very successful protégé, Warren Buffett. The investing tenets of both Graham and Buffett were simple: Be patient and wait for a company's stock price to become undervalued (cheap) compared to its fundamentals (its financials). And then, as Buffett likes to say, "Be greedy when others are fearful, and be fearful when others are greedy."

That was pretty simple and straightforward advice, but not for someone like me who, back in 2003, was suffering from a bad case of mood poisoning caused by my fight or flight instincts. Rather than utilizing the sage advice from the world's greatest investor (as I had done in the past), I now found myself enticed by late night foreign exchange (Forex) and stock option trading television infomercials (yes, I succumbed to late night infomercials!) that showed just how simple trading could be if you just followed the little green and red arrows, or used their simple trading platform. Like a dog to a bone, I was signing up and attending their free seminars at the local airport hotels in Los Angeles. Story after story was shared about how people like me quickly turned their financial lives around simply because they chose to take advantage of investing in their trading courses and systems. Before I knew it, without reading any online reviews to see if any of their current or previous customers were happy or profitable, I simply chose to forego my previously successful strategies because, ironically, my aversion to losing money (risk) became too great. All I knew was, it was a bull market and supposedly everyone was making money hand over fist. So, because I was so caught up in my negative spiral of impatience and ill-conceived decisions, and failed to just pause, take a moment to breathe, and listen to my own basic common sense, I decided to buy and trade their "get rich quick" courses and systems, and I actually wound up losing money—a lot of it—with two companies in particular. There are no quick detours to success. To quote the great opera singer, Beverly Sills, "There are no shortcuts to any place worth going."

So please, please, learn from my mistakes. Don't take shortcuts in life! You always want to be in the position where your decisions control or dictate your situations (thinking strategically), not where your situations (work, finances, relationships, etc.) control your decisions (thinking emotionally). We tend to be the most susceptible to failure when we don't have a plan and we succumb to our reactionary animalistic impulses, as opposed to proactively taking control of our situations. And as we get older, the more we continue to instinctively react to our fears, the more that behavior tends to become an ingrained and solidified habit. Therefore, you want to make sure to develop good decision-making habits, early on, so you can plan for the life you want to create, not react to.

Mastering the art of the pause involves—literally—pausing. This means taking the time to research your options, weigh your outcomes, and choose the best strategic (not emotional) decision that best aligns with your long-term objectives (goals), and true core values (beliefs). This can prove to be more challenging for those who are emotionally "under the weather" (e.g., mood-poisoned) because they often become more vulnerable to being enticed or manipulated by others who are trying to find the fastest or easiest way to alleviate their pain or fear. Therefore, it is extremely important to always be aware of how others may be trying to take advantage of you while you are in your susceptible state of mind (by telling you they have the solution to all of your problems—the "quick fix"). Do not take their bait because, at the end of the day, there are no "quick fixes," "sure things," or, for that matter, "overnight successes." On the contrary, truly sustainable success requires patience, dedication, determination, and most importantly, persistence. These attributes are most often attained through years of hard work, learning, experimenting, failing, and of course, achieving. So the next time you start to feel impatient or anxious, do not simply react and barrel forth. Pause, weigh your options, and think before you strike!

Follow Your Passion for Success

If America is truly the land of opportunity, then why can't everybody land their dream job or career? This begs a couple of questions: Are well-established young men and women just better at focusing their time and energy toward manifesting their job success from an early age? Or do most people just lack the attention to detail, knowledge, and ambition required nowadays to attain their dream jobs? I believe the answer is, "yes," to both questions. If I haven't been making myself abundantly clear, people are not only successful because they're lucky, they're successful because of all the reasons we have been discussing throughout this book (awareness, confidence, goal-setting, strategic planning, good decision-making, etc.).

I have long held the belief that the single greatest road to one's success is their ability to find a job, business, or career that truly sparks and inspires their passion and interests. So before you begin searching for your ideal job or career, or think about starting your own business, you should take the following into consideration:

1. Quality of life – You should do your best to find a job or career that will resonate with who you are, both personally and professionally. Not only do you want find, or start, a business that you would like to either work for, or create, but you will also want to consider working in a location (city, state, country, etc.) that you believe will best support your natural pace and peace of mind. If you are someone who resonates better at a slower pace, then a big city may not be a good fit. If you are someone who loves the nightlife, then a smaller, quiet town may not be your thing. Just as aligning core values is very important, so is getting a handle on what your ideal living environment is *before* you decide to uproot yourself to accept a job or open a new business. Also, if you choose a location that positively resonates with you, there will be more likelihood that you could have greater opportunities to establish your social circle by connecting with like-minded people. That said, if you decided to pursue your dream job by moving to a particular city which didn't end up resonating as well with you, of course eventually you would find others with whom you connected and shared similar goals and values.

2. Job growth or stepping stone opportunities – You should try to pursue a job or career that will either challenge you by providing educational opportunities to further advance your skills or talents (supporting your continued growth), or it should serve as a stepping stone toward getting you even closer to your ultimate job, career, or business goals. As I mentioned earlier, by leaving the music industry, I was finally able to pursue my true passion—helping young adults, as well as adults of all ages, achieve their own lifelong successes.

3. Financial reward – I intentionally listed this pursuit last. Don't get me wrong, I am all for finding a job, business, or career path that rewards you for all of your hard work and efforts, but I just don't believe that money should be the sole driving force for why anyone should choose to pursue a job, business, or career path. Money should be viewed as a tool for opportunity—a financial means for continuing to pursue your passion—because I honestly believe that if you follow your heart's desire, while living within your means, you should be able to save enough money to support yourself as you continue to pursue your passion and ultimate success.

"Act the way you'd like to be and soon you'll be the way you act." ~ Bob Dylan

Don't be like so many people who often wind up working thankless, unrewarding, dead-end jobs because they either decided to settle, or they made bad personal or financial decisions that prevented them from moving on to pursue doing something that they loved. If you are a junior or senior in high school, and you are still not quite sure what you would like to do after you graduate, then you might want to pause and consider your options. If you are undecided about what field of study you would like to pursue in college, then you might want to consider applying to your local community college as an "undecided" (or "undeclared") major. Because the tuition tends to be more affordable (manageable) than most four-year institutions, a community college could be the perfect place for you to get in touch with who you are, and what field of study you might want to pursue (your "major"). After attending a year or two at a community college, you could simply transfer to another college or university that you would like to attend, and which specializes in your desired field of study.

Whether you decide to take the community college route and transfer, or spend all four years at a college or university, acquiring an undergraduate degree can be an incredibly expensive endeavor, and unfortunately, many young adults are now graduating with extremely high student loan debt. And if that isn't bad enough, because of the imbalance of supply and demand in the job market, new openings can be scarce in their chosen fields. More and more college graduates are now finding themselves having to move back in with their parents and/or accept part-time or full-time job positions that have nothing to do with either their majors or interests.

So let me go on record here and say that there is nothing wrong with temporarily deferring your decision to attend college straight out of high school. In fact, if you are a young entrepreneur, or someone who is interested in pursuing a career that does not require you to have a college degree initially, then you may want to find a really good mentor or company and pursue an apprenticeship.

There are many options for young high school graduates to educate themselves—options which do not initially require college degrees. Instead of working for a large corporation or business, consider working for a start-up or small business so that you can learn the structure of that small business from the ground up. It's not an accredited education, but you will most definitely be acquiring useful knowledge as to how a business makes money and/or manages cash flow, marketing, sales, etc. Employees of small businesses wear many hats, so they acquire firsthand knowledge-building experiences carrying the weight of many departments. Another facet about business that is not often discussed is the issue of emotions in the workplace. Regardless of how professional one can be in their chosen field, they are still human and emotional highs and lows are unavoidable (unless of course, you're Star Trek's Mr. Spock).

So while it goes without saying that students can learn countless things while attending college, not many professors will teach their students how emotions factor into the business landscape (especially if they have only studied and worked in academia). If you choose to defer enrolling in college and go straight into the workforce, you may feel at first like this fast-paced global and technological world might swallow you whole. Okay, perhaps I'm exaggerating, but my point is, even if you choose to go to college right away, life after your structured high school world may initially feel overwhelming there as well. And just so you know, no college can really prepare you for how you'll react emotionally when you must handle making your first work-related decisions, engaging with your bosses or coworkers, and/or surviving on next to nothing (or worse, your bank account dropping past zero, "into the red"). These are all emotional situations that you must experience for yourself in order to build your character and figure out if you have the guts to do whatever you ultimately want to pursue in life.

Follow your path of least regrets. I don't want you looking back on this period in your life and wishing you had done things differently.

If you find yourself feeling indecisive or on the fence about whether or not to attend college right out of high school, do yourself a favor, go online and start researching the admission requirements for the colleges or universities you might want to attend. Many colleges and universities now offer online virtual campus tours to provide potential students with an idea of what college life might be like if they chose to attend that particular institution. I graduated many, many, years ago and I still love to go on college and university websites and take their virtual campus tours. It's a great way to get an idea of what your future might look like if you chose to roam that campus. And while you're at it, go ahead and research what those schools are renowned, or known for (medicine, law, music, business, etc.), as well as checking out the school's educational requirements—such as grade point average (GPA), SAT scores, etc.

This really is the perfect time in your life to figure out what you might want to do. So don't make any emotional decisions until you have taken the time to create a plan of what you want your future to look like. In addition to viewing the online virtual tours, you should plan on visiting the college or university's campus and city/ college town in person to confirm that the college or university's location positively resonates with your core values, as well as your educational long-term goals. Make sure that you do your research and consider your options.

Here's an anecdote to illustrate my point: Back in 1992, I had just started working for the record company and I was involved with reviewing contracts and interacting with the MCA Records legal department. I really wanted to go to law school at night while working full-time, but unfortunately, despite beginning my prep work for the LSAT (law school entry) exam, I allowed myself to become sidetracked. Years later, after I graduated with my MBA degree from Pepperdine University, I once again considered applying to law school because I still had an interest and passion for the law. At that same time, I was approached by Pepperdine University's

School of Education and Psychology to apply for their new doc-toral program in Organizational Leadership. Without really taking the time to sit down and review my options and long-term plan, and because I believed I could soar through the program within three to five years (and then pursue a law degree), I impetuously applied to the Pepperdine University Organizational Leadership doctoral program. The problem was...it actually took me *10 years* to complete my doctoral work. In hindsight, had I just learned the art of the pause from an earlier age, I might have decided to pursue my interests, skills, and talents for negotiation and the law first, before pursuing my doctorate degree. Again, the reason I am sharing this information with you now is the same reason I've been so forthright throughout this book—I want you to learn from my mistakes to achieve your success as early as possible. Take the time to strategically research and weigh all your options so you always ensure the most *probable* outcomes for achieving your goals and success.

Now, if you do ultimately decide to postpone college and go straight into the workforce after high school, or if you are currently a young professional already in the workforce, in order to best align your talents, passions, and goals with your job, you really should take the time to do your research and find the companies and/or mentors that interest and challenge you. If you find a company whose vision and purpose tends to align with your own, then check out that company's website, products, and news articles/events, and make sure that you research that company's industry as well. To see how the business community ranks various companies and industries, you can look up *Fortune* or *Forbes* magazine's annual company and industry rankings, the *Investor Business Daily* newspaper, as well as various online websites such as *MSN Money, Yahoo Finance*, and *Finviz.com*. I still hear many adults, of all ages, ask the question, "What will I be when I grow up?" Sure, they may pretend they're kind of kidding, but don't believe it. Don't fool yourself and end up being like most people who will spend their entire lives asking this question while they continue to be dissatisfied with how they earn a living.

Finally, attitude and work ethic are everything. Many years ago, I attended a National Business Travel Association conference where I heard Tom Peters, a great motivational business speaker, utter five really important words: "Be distinct, or be Extinct." And it got me thinking...it is extremely crucial that you learn, from an early age, how to really differentiate yourself from the crowd if you wish to grow and achieve long-term success. Most people simply go with the flow and never challenge themselves, or the status quo. Now, this is fine for someone content to live a mediocre life. But if you are someone who truly wants to experience a high level of success, you will need to be very clear about your intentions and decisions. Successful people do not coast through life. They make very strategic decisions to break out of their own boxes and make things happen!

To help you distinguish yourself from others, here are some suggested questions for you to ponder:

1. What job do you really want to pursue, and how do you want to create a life of service, purpose, and passion?

2. Visualize what those successes (service, purpose, and passion) will look like for you.

3. Create goals and action steps for acquiring those successes.

4. Make researched strategic (unemotional) decisions and take action!

Most people fail to achieve their goals because they remain fearful and indecisive. Don't let emotions, negative programming, or fear stop you from achieving what you ultimately want—success. You *can* do this! Believe in yourself!

Call to Action

To help you get in the habit of making more strategic (versus emotional) decisions aimed at assisting you to complete your goals, I would like to suggest that you begin incorporating the following actions immediately:

1. To start developing good decision-making strategies before you make any new decisions, ask yourself the following four questions (pulled from the chapter). For the next few months—until this process becomes second nature—write down your answers to these questions (in your separate notebook) so that you can analyze and evaluate how, and why, you strategically came up with your decisions.

Question 1: *What is the probability that my decision will lead to a successful outcome, and how will this decision get me closer to achieving my overall (big picture) goals?*

_____

_____

_____

_____

_____

Question 2: *How do I hope to benefit from my outcome due to making this particular decision?*

_____

_____

_____

_____

_____

Question 3: *How much hard work, time, and energy will my decision ultimately cost me?*

_____

_____

_____

Question 4: *What are my underlying intentions for making this decision? What reaction, if any, am I hoping to solicit from others? And what benefit/gain am I expecting to receive from acting on this decision?*

_____

_____

_____

2. List some of the common mistakes (e.g., acting like you are the smartest person in the room, thinking, "it's my way or the highway," etc.) that you are currently making in your own life. Then describe how, in the present, you plan to apply the lessons you've learned from making those mistakes, so that you can reap the rewards in the future. (I am only providing you room for three, but write down as many as you believe apply in your separate notebook.)

Common Mistake #1 _____

_____

Common Mistake #2 _____

_____

Common Mistake #3_____

_____

3. Recall three decisions that you recently made and write them down. Then I want you to be totally honest with yourself and ask if each one of those decisions was made strategically (logically) or emotionally. If they were emotional decisions, how could you have used the art of the pause (research, options, etc.) to have helped you make a more strategic decision? If they were strategic decisions, write down what research and/or options you used to help you arrive at your logical outcome.

Past Decision #1 (What was the decision?)

_____

_____

_____

(Check one): __ Strategic __ Emotional

Research/Options _____

_____

_____

Past Decision #2 (What was the decision?)

_____

_____

_____

(Check one): __ Strategic __ Emotional

Research/Options _____

_____

_____

Past Decision #3 (What was the decision?)

_____

_____

_____

(Check one): __ Strategic __ Emotional

Research/Options _____

_____

_____

(Check one) ___ Binary ___ Sequence

Research/Options

8

The Dollars and Sense for Creating Your Wealth

Are you a wealth creator, or do you suffer from "financial obesity"?

Growing up during the 1970s, to help prepare me for adulthood, I was required to take home economics and typing classes in middle school so I could learn practical skills for the real world. Fast forward almost 40 years, and it's saddening that in this 21st century, the majority of our U.S. middle schools and high schools have eliminated providing this type of practical education to young adults. As if that wasn't bad enough, by neglecting to incorporate crucial money management (e.g., personal finance) and personal development (e.g., planning, time management, etc.) classes into their students' current curriculum, society at large ends up sustaining the negative impact. Studies have shown that the majority of young adults in the United States continue to suffer from financial illiteracy. In fact, according to an April 2012 *USA Today* article, this is a trend that has remained consistent over the past decade and shows little promise of improving. In a study from 2010 to 2012, the U.S. Treasury Department and the Department of Education teamed up to assess financial literacy in U.S. high schools, and the results were not pretty. In 2010, almost 76,900 students' financial literacy scores were averaged at 70% (in grade terms, that's only a "C"). The following year in 2011, that number bumped up to 84,000 students' financial literacy scores being averaged and calculated at a point lower—69% (just shy of a "C" grade). And in 2012, 80,000 students were tested and they also scored an average of 69%.

While acknowledging those high school students' financial literacy test scores all flowed out of the housing crisis, low savings rates, and poor retirement planning, Secretary of Education, Arne Duncan, assessed the issue, stating, "We have a long way to go as a country. There has been a devastating cost to a lack of attention, urgency, and seriousness of taking this on." What's worse, despite the lessons the nerve-racking 2008 financial crisis should have taught us, following this crisis, only 13 states recognized the importance of requiring that students take a personal finance class. Moreover, in 2009, only 19 states (less than 50% of America) still enforced that high school students be required to take an economics class. Two years later, that number was reduced to a mere 16 states that were enforcing that requirement (according to the 2011 biennial survey for the Council for Economic Education). It would be simpler to just blame the majority of adults and teachers for withholding this important information, but when they most likely also lack this crucial knowledge themselves, the problem runs deeper. The fact that the majority of our U.S. schools still neglect teaching financial literacy in their curriculum, despite all indications it *should* be taught, demonstrates the degree to which politicians, administrators, and educators continue to disappointingly overlook the importance of remedying this generational deficiency in education.

If you are a young adult between the ages of 16 and 25, I have to imagine that life must seem pretty uncertain and somewhat scary to you right now. If it makes you feel any better, you're not alone. It has been well-documented that young adults are not only finding it increasingly difficult to obtain employment after graduating high school and college, but they are also finding that their lack of financial education has left many of them ill-equipped to make good personal and financial decisions, which hinders their opportunities to become successful and financially independent. The affliction from which so many American adults between the ages of 40 and 60 suffer ("financial obesity"), leaves them trapped in an unhealthy, self-sabotaging, and vicious cycle of living beyond their means. In much the same way one self-medicates through their addiction of choice, the financially obese are obsessive-compulsively driven to soothe themselves through their "drug" of choice—spending money they don't have in order to fill their emotional voids. Eventually, instead of the intended outcome of making themselves feel better, they ultimately end up feeling worse, as if they were financially starving themselves.

Lawmakers, administrators, and educators are long overdue in stepping up and taking action to help introduce new educational concepts, tools, and techniques that will finally help address the ongoing issues surrounding financial illiteracy in our country. As such, communities must now band together to ensure that the powers that be shift our nation's educational focus away from the overburdened "no child left behind" standardized testing efforts. The focus should instead be shifted back toward productive and effective practical financial life skill programs for the real world—like the home economics classes of the 1960s and 1970s. At the same time, as a nation, we must also raise our collective consciousness to help eradicate financial obesity so that it no longer continues to plague adults in our society. In doing so, we will be giving young adults a fighting chance to no longer blindly follow in the financially misguided footsteps of so many generations before them.

My goal for this chapter is to help educate you about the misconceptions regarding personal finance so that you can learn how to become an excellent money manager. I will be sharing important information and tools to help you avoid the drama and struggles usually associated with poor money management and overspending. Don't get me wrong, I'm not implying that spending money is an unhealthy practice. But what *is* healthy, is living within your means. When you apply what you'll learn in this chapter, and become wise about how and where you spend your money, you can begin building a solid foundation toward acquiring your financial success.

So What IS Personal Finance?

To help you better understand my definition of personal finance (which encompasses both the value of, and one's strategic relationship with, money), from this moment forward, I think you might find it helpful to think of your strategic relationship with money in terms of the following car/driving analogy: Think of money like it's the gas pedal (accelerator) in your car. Just as you would apply pressure to your car's accelerator to make the car go faster, the more money that you save and invest, the more it will help you accelerate reaching your financial goals. To achieve your financial success most effectively (the most direct route), you will need to manage your money efficiently by avoiding reckless spending. Just like reckless speeding can derail the driver, reckless spending can also result in serious financial and emotional setbacks. However, like an experienced safe driver, by being financially aware of your surroundings (your savings and spending habits) and always driving within your life's financial speed limits (living within your means), you will be creating the opportunity to acquire the financial freedom to really enjoy life's beautiful scenery (your family, friends, career, travel, etc.).

I used to ask myself, "Why would U.S. schools spend so much time, effort, and money to educate and test students on such important subjects such as math, English, history, science, foreign languages, etc. but then fail to teach their students anything regarding proper money management?" Then it dawned on me...the politically correct answer would be: "Well, money is a personal subject, and therefore finances should really be discussed in the home between children and their parents." However, I believe the real reason why most schools do not teach students about personal finance or money management is because there is no universal, or formally accepted, educational model to teach them about the value of, or one's strategic relationship with, money. This realization blew my mind because not only is money one of the most debated topics in our society, but it is also extremely controversial because most people tend to have different experiences, emotions, and opinions regarding money. That is, people have their own personal relationship with money, just like they do with other personal things in their lives (e.g., people, food, fear, risk, etc.). The way people tend to learn about and develop their own relationship with money is often most likely based upon their early childhood programming by having observed their parents, teachers, friends, and/or the media. For example, you may have heard someone projecting their own personal relationship with money (values) on others by making generalizations along the lines of, "That Robert is way too conservative for me," or "Look at that Ashley, she spends like there is no tomorrow!" These generalizations tend to be a reflection of one's parents' relationship with money. So, lets say your parents are, or were, conservative with money, and you embraced that value, then you will most likely follow suit and be more conservative with your own money. However, if you disliked the way your parents either frugally saved, or recklessly overspent their money, then you might ultimately decide to manage your own money the opposite way.

The overall point I am trying to make here is, there is no standardized way of educating young adults on how to respect and value money. Instead of learning practical money management (savings and budget strategies) early on, most people tend to develop their own bad personal savings and spending habits based upon what little knowledge they have obtained by simply observing others around them.

As I reflect back on my own childhood, I am both miffed and amazed about why nobody ever thought to discuss these important financial topics with me (including, of course, my parents and teachers). Like most kids today, I was educated by a constant barrage of commercials created by manipulative advertising and media executives to show me how much better off my life would be if I spent money on things that would help me materialistically compete with my peers and neighbors. And if I didn't go buy it right away, then the inherent subtext was that "I was not cool," or "I was behind the times."

Prior to the 1960s and 1970s, most Americans tended to practice good money management by working (earning), saving, and then buying (yes, in that order!). Yet today, most have been led to believe (as is the norm in our consumer-driven society) that we must have it now, charge it now, and pay for it...later. Except what they don't teach you, is that you *really* pay for it later.

So how did corporate America go about programming consumers to dismiss the preceding generations' long-standing financial values of earn, save, then buy?

Due to their foreseeable increase in profits, creditors and lenders in the late 1960s and early 1970s began to broaden their reach by extending credit to Americans for things that they were led to believe they absolutely *had to have* in order to satisfy their life's desires. No longer did people have to wait until they paid retailers in full—consumers could now simply borrow money on credit from lenders (e.g., MasterCard, Visa, etc.) and all they had to do to get their instant gratification was to pay a compounding interest rate on the money they borrowed. Because consumers didn't seem to mind making instant purchases in exchange for interest payments on money borrowed, buying on credit made it deceptively easy for people to live beyond their means. In fact, by the time the 1980s and 1990s rolled around, these corporate lenders became so profitable that they decided to further expand their business models to include targeting financially vulnerable young college students by generously offering them: "Free Water Bottles along with Fast and Easy Credit!"

As a result of several decades of easy credit, in combination with years of economic uncertainty, many people now find themselves financially obese and desperately falling deeper into the vicious cycle of being trapped in their financial holes. They are overextended and unable to pay back the total balance of the money that they borrowed (beyond just making the minimum monthly payments), and as a result, they just keep incurring higher and higher outstanding balances. As their balances grow, their interest continues compounding, their credit card bills increase, and their financial holes become deeper and deeper.

Unfortunately, too many people still continue to rely on living off of borrowed credit and find themselves one or two paychecks away from bankruptcy. Needless to say, living that way will not provide the quality of life that comes with financial success. By incorporating disciplined money management habits early on, you will be giving yourself the healthy financial infrastructure you'll need in order to avoid the kind of financial distress that most adults currently end up enduring today.

As I said earlier, most young adults tend to learn their good or bad saving/spending habits by observing their parents, friends, etc. This early exposure often dictates how that child will either emotionally, or strategically, manage their relationship with money as an adult. Will they be confident, fearful, frugal, thrifty, etc. When one has an unhealthy emotional relationship with money, it becomes the catalyst for so many "financial obesity" issues. This is why it is so important that young adults be properly educated financially so that they can develop normal and healthy strategic relationships with money. The truth is, most people believe that understanding personal finance is nothing more than learning about the fundamentals (value) of money: how to earn, save, spend, and grow it through investments. However, in addition to understanding the value of money, I strongly believe that personal finance is also about understanding the importance of learning how to manage one's strategic (versus emotional) relationship with money. This is why I stressed the importance of having you do all of the strategic foundational work, as well as all of the Calls to Action in Chapters Two through Seven.

Defining Your Own Financial Success

Before you can create wealth, it is important for you to be able to clearly define what wealth truly means to *you* (just like when I asked you to define what success truly means to *you*). If I were to ask 100 people to define what wealth meant to them, I would once again (just as with success) probably get 100 different answers. Would a family that lives in a large multi-bedroom house, in a wealthy neighborhood, owning expensive fancy new cars, be considered wealthy? Would a family that lives in a smaller house, in a less affluent neighborhood, owning affordable plain old cars, be considered less wealthy? What would a person's wealth status be if they attended a prestigious Ivy League college or university? Or how about a person who comes from a poor neighborhood and never got the chance to go college? Well, the truth of the matter is, the typical stereotypes of who is actually wealthy or not, just aren't true! Depending on what their strategic relationship with money is, anyone who fits any of the above descriptions could be the opposite of what you'd assume. I personally know a millionaire who basically wears the same uniform every day: stained navy T-shirt, faded jeans, and work boots. He drives a Toyota SUV from last century (the 1990s) and is so under the radar, it wouldn't be surprising if people assumed he struggled to pay rent (versus the mortgages he actually pays). My point is, he is so down to earth, and feels no need to "keep up with the Joneses," that he shows no visible evidence of his true wealth. Meanwhile, he quietly contributes to his nieces' and nephews' college educations and continues to mow his own lawn. He is among thousands of other millionaires who consciously choose to lead their lives modestly. Conversely, a lot of flamboyant people who choose to drape themselves in expensive jewels and drive extravagant cars may appear, or want others to presume, that they are wealthy. But in reality, they could just be amongst the multitudes living one paycheck away from bankruptcy. So any preconceived idea you may have had about what a wealthy person looks like, or lives like, can be thrown out the window. Nowadays, countless millionaires avoid being ostentatious about their wealth and steer clear of calling attention to themselves. These unassuming millionaires intentionally choose to live simply within their means (even the super-rich can overspend and end up bankrupt). They lead regular, comfortable lives by implementing and evaluating financial goals that align well with their own monetary core values and beliefs. This is why it is so important that you start getting in touch with your core values now, while also figuring out what *your own* definition for wealth and success is. Think of this period in your life as a time to get "conditioned," like an athlete does before a competition. That process will require you to do your due diligence ("prep work") so you can execute your plan when the time is right. Begin leading the financial life that you want now, so when your earnings do begin to materialize, and as your money accumulates, you will be getting a jumpstart on your financial plan (by having already aligned your core monetary values with your wealth as it was growing, in real time). By doing so, you will have averted derailing yourself from potentially succumbing to wasting money on cultivating any preconceived image you think you're supposed to project to others based upon presumptions and stereotypes.

If you are feeling motivated to start working through your own definitions for wealth and financial success right this minute, before you do, I would like to first share some basic money management techniques and strategies that I believe will help you better understand wealth creation, as well as good personal financial management. When I was a graduate music student at Indiana University in 1988, to make ends meet, I had to work three different jobs while keeping up with my full-time classes. These jobs included:

being a part-time on-air radio personality (previously referred to as a "disc jockey") for two local FM radio stations, teaching drum lessons at a local music store (on the weekends), and working part-time as a telemarketer raising money for the University's capital campaign. Let me emphasize, once again, that I was not exposed to any personal finance or money management courses when I was in middle school, high school, or college. So it should come as no surprise that back then, I barely had any understanding of the financial concepts that I am about to share with you—which is why I am so passionate about teaching you these valuable concepts right now. One night, while working through my overnight radio shift, it occurred to me that between all three of my part-time jobs (despite all the hours I worked and the income I earned), I never seemed to have enough money to go out with my friends. I soon came to the realization that it wasn't so much a shortage of income from the three jobs, but rather a lack of awareness in terms of where my income was going. In reality, I was clueless about how much money I was actually spending (throwing away) at the time.

That revelation allowed me to finally pinpoint the true origin of my negative financial situation—my own lack of financial oversight. So, in an effort to get a better grip on why my cash flow always seemed to stop flowing, I started writing down and tracking all of my daily expenses (what I was actually spending each day) in a small notebook. I would write down the date, place, and exact amount I spent on each and every expense, so that I could visually track and understand where all my money was going. Again, I did this on a *daily basis* (tedious, but necessary). Then, at the end of each week, I would enter each individual expense item into different categories (food, gas/fuel, rent, entertainment, etc.) and I would come up with weekly totals for each of the categories. After a few weeks, I began expanding these weekly totals into monthly totals. I was shocked when I realized just how much money I was actually spending on a daily, weekly, and monthly basis—my expenses were adding up like crazy. Once I compiled all this new information, I decided to take it a step further so I could continue to keep better track of where all my money was going so I created a monthly spending budget based on my prior daily/weekly/monthly expenses.

Sample Monthly Budget
The amounts below are fictional, for explanation purposes only, and do not reflect actual costs.

RENT	$ 200.00
FOOD	$ 100.00
GAS (fuel)	$ 25.00
UTILITIES (electric, etc.)	$ 30.00
ENTERTAINMENT	$ 50.00
CREDIT CARDS	$ 100.00
TELEPHONE	$ 20.00
MISCELLANEOUS	$ 25.00
TOTAL	**$ 550.00**

At the end of each month, I would compare my monthly total spending (comprised of each and every daily expense) against my overall monthly budget ($550). As long as I stayed within my monthly budget of $550, I knew I was practicing good money management. I would not get upset if one of the line items (e.g., food) turned out to be a little higher than anticipated, as long as I made up for that overage from one or more of the other budget categories.

For example, if I budgeted $100 to buy food for the month and wound up going over budget spending $125, but then in my entertainment category, I had budgeted $50 but only ended up spending $25 for the month, I knew I would be fine because I could just take the extra $25 I hadn't used from the allotted $50 entertainment budget, and use it to cover my $25 food overage. I stayed within my budget because my overall expenses did not exceed my allotted monthly budget total of $550.

After a couple of months of successfully tracking my expenses, I began to realize some important things:

1. There would be certain months where I spent more money than the other months.

2. Although I budgeted $550 per month for expenses, I didn't always actually need to spend that entire budgeted amount.

TIP: Even though you may decide to only budget $550 toward your monthly expenses, this does not mean that you have to spend the entire $550 each month. Your personal financial goal should be to always stay within your monthly budget, but if you ever spend less money than you budgeted, take that opportunity to save the additional money and deposit some, or all of it, into your personal savings account. If you don't already have a personal savings account, go open one (*and by the way, your savings account is not to be used as an ATM for your checking account*).

Creating Your Personal Income Statement
(The Tracking of Your Income and Expenses)

After carefully reviewing my monthly expense budgets, I decided to take things to the next level to further improve my overall money management skills. I wanted to strengthen my discipline—like I was running a real business—by tracking my spending (expenses) as a percentage of my overall cash flow (income).

So that I could better control how I managed my cash flow (net income) of $650 per month from all three of my part-time jobs, on a monthly basis, I decided to allocate a certain percentage of the $650 toward all my various monthly expenses (food, entertainment, etc.) which was not to exceed $550. This would leave me with an extra $100 per month after expenses ($650 - $550). This will become clearer to you as you read through the following pages.

Sample Personal Income Statement

The amounts below are fictional, for explanation purposes only, and do not reflect actual costs.

MONTHLY INCOME (cash flow)

RADIO STATION	$ 450.00
TELEMARKETING	$ 100.00
TEACH DRUM LESSONS	$ 100.00
TOTAL	**$ 650.00**

MONTHLY EXPENSES (spending)

	Budget Allocation* (percentages rounded)	Budget Amount	Expenses
RENT	30%	$195.00	$200.00
FOOD	15%	$100.00	$100.00
GAS	5%	$33.00	$25.00
UTILITIES	5%	$33.00	$30.00
ENTERTAINMENT	10%	$65.00	$50.00
CREDIT CARDS	15%	$100.00	$100.00
TELEPHONE	2%	$13.00	$20.00
MISC	5%	$33.00	$25.00
TOTAL	**87%**	**$572.00**	**$550.00**

Unallocated Income   *(Income $650 - Budget Amount $572) = $78*

Budget less Expenses   *(Budget Amount $572 - Expenses $550) = $22*

> *The formula for calculating a **Budget Allocation:**
> Budget Amount divided by the Total Monthly Income
> (e.g., Rent Amount $195 / Income $650 = 30%)*

Budget Allocation Formula example for the monthly rent: To calculate, you would divide the budgeted rent amount ($195) by the total monthly income ($650) as follows:

The rent budget allocation is: $195/$650 = .3 (expressed as a percentage would be .3 multiplied by 100, or 30%).

> **TIP:** Repeat this same budget allocation formula calculation for all the other monthly expense categories (food, entertainment, etc.), and then add up all of your expense budget percentages (rent 30%, food 15% [rounded down], etc.). For example, the total percentage for all of your budget allocations on the Sample Personal Income Statement was 87% (rounded down), thus 13% of your monthly income is still available and unallocated (100% - 87% = 13%).

The *Unallocated Income Amount* ($78) represents the remaining amount of money that is left over (unallocated) once you have subtracted your total budgeted amount ($572) which is comprised of all the monthly expense categories (rent, food, etc.) from your overall monthly income amount ($650).

Unallocated Income: $650 - $572 = $78

> **TIP:** As discussed earlier in this book, you should try to save at least 10% of your monthly income in your personal savings account.

10% of the $650 income would be $65 ($650 multiplied by .10) so you should consider depositing at least $65 of the unallocated $78 into your savings. If you think this doesn't add up, think again. If you were to deposit $65 per month for a year, at the end of one year you would have saved $780 ($65 multiplied by 12) and after five years it would be $3,900.

The *Budget less Expenses* on the Sample Personal Income Statement represents the total allotted budget amount for the monthly expenses ($572) minus the *actual* expense amount that was incurred ($550).

Budget less Expenses: $572 - $550 = $22

Personal Money Management Tool #1

If you were to look at the Sample Personal Income Statement as if you were analyzing an actual, real world business budget, what might this information tell you about how you are choosing to budget and track your monthly expenses? What assessments or conclusions could be made from the Personal Income Statement data?

Assessment #1: There is an additional $78 (13%) of income still available (monthly income of $650 minus the total allotted budget amount of $572 = $78) which is extra money that can now either be saved or spent on something else.

Assessment #2: Based on the Personal Income Statement data, the *actual* expenses are *under budget* by $22 ($572 - $550). As a result, you now have another $22 available to deposit into your personal savings account (in addition to your monthly 10% savings contributions), or to be used for something else. If the actual expense total ($550) had exceeded the monthly budget amount for expenses ($572), then you would have come in *over budget* for the month.

Conclusion/Outcome: Based upon our two initial assessments of the Personal Income Statement data, we can now confirm that our actual monthly spending remained within budget by $22, and that our monthly overall cash flow remained profitable by $100 — the $78 (unallocated income) plus the $22 (under budget expense amount). As a result, we are now free to save, invest, or use this additional money toward other future expenses as we so desire.

Welcome to Personal Finance 101! That wasn't so hard, right? Congratulations, you are now more knowledgeable than the majority of your fellow high school or college classmates! But before you go ahead and pat yourself on the back (and you should), I have two more suggestions to help you become even more profitable using your Personal Income Statement data:

Suggestion #1: Based on the information in the Personal Income Statement, you could decide to lower some of your monthly budget allocation percentages and budget amounts in order to help increase your unallocated monthly income total. For example, you might consider lowering your monthly rent budget allocation from 30% to 25%, which would lower your monthly budget amount from $195 to $163, thereby increasing your unallocated income by $32 ($195 - 163). Using the *Budget Allocation Formula*, instead of 30% allocated toward rent, you would now simply multiply your monthly income ($650) by 25%: $650 x .25 = $163 (rounded) per month.

Suggestion #2: Rather than adjusting the budget allocation percentages for each category, you could decide to just lower the budget amounts that you are willing to allocate each month for each expense category. For example, even though your monthly budget amount for food is $100, try only spending $75 which would save you an additional $25 each month.

These are just two examples of the many ways you can experiment with tweaking your budget amounts and percentages to help you gain better control over your monthly budgets and spending. And here's the best part: You can use these Personal Money Management Tools throughout your entire life! Whether you are receiving an allowance, have an after school job, or you are a young professional just entering the workplace, you can begin tracking and saving your income starting right now.

Understanding the Value of Money

To help guide you toward prioritizing the importance of saving versus spending, I would like to walk you through the process of creating your own monthly budget of income and expenses.

Step #1: Calculate how much after-tax money—"net income" (not *gross* income, which is what you make *before* taxes are taken out)—that you anticipate receiving (from whatever your income sources may be). Then take that net income dollar amount and multiply it by the number of weeks in a month (which ends up being four or five weeks, depending on the month). If you are paid *every* two weeks, then instead of multiplying by four or five weeks, just multiply your net income dollar amount by two.

For example, if you receive $100 after taxes (also known as "take home pay") per week, and there are four weeks in that current month, then you can estimate your monthly income to be $400 ($100 multiplied by 4).

Step #2: Once you have calculated your *monthly net income amount*, the next thing you want to do is calculate your *monthly budgetary allocations*, breaking them down by category and percentage (like I had done in the Sample Personal Income Statement).

For example, you'll want to include food, gas, entertainment (that would include app downloads), and any other expense category that you can think of. Once you have your category list compiled, decide how much of the $400 (your monthly net income from the previous example step) that you want to budget toward covering your expenses (spending) each month.

If you think you will spend $100 in the food category each month, then your budgetary allocation for food will be 25%. This percentage is calculated by dividing $100 (food) by $400 (your monthly net income): $100/$400 = .25 or 25%.

Now, you'll want to do this same *budget allocation percentage* calculation for all of your other budget expense categories. But keep in mind that your total monthly expense budget cannot exceed $400, and your total budget's allocation percentage across all of your expense categories cannot exceed 100%. Also remember that you do not have to allocate all $400 of your monthly net income. As you saw with the previous Sample Personal Income Statement, 87% or $572 of the available $650 (monthly net income) was allocated to cover the monthly expenses, which left an additional $78 to be saved or spent on any future expenses or purchases.

TIP: As a general rule, you should never allocate more than 30% of your monthly budget toward your rent (or mortgage, if applicable), and if you do have credit card debt, aim for carrying a balance of no more than 10 - 15% of your monthly budget until you can pay it off in full.

Step #3: Now that you have created your monthly budget and assigned various dollar amounts to spend on each category, you are going to want to begin tracking your expenses on a daily basis.

Make sure that you write down *all* of your daily expenses in a either good, old-fashioned notebook, or a computer/tablet/smartphone, etc. Whatever method you choose, just make sure it will best support you to consistently track your categorized expenses (spending) against your allotted monthly budget. By documenting your daily spending, your awareness will help ensure that you're staying within your budget. To track and easily reference each of your daily expenses, I suggest using the following format:

Date	Payee	Amount	Category
8/1/2013	McDonald's	$ 3.25	Food
8/13/2013	Unocal 76	$ 20.00	Gas

Step #4: At the end of each week, you are going to be transferring, and then totaling up, all of your daily expenses (see the following example chart) so that you can track how much money you have been spending on each expense category, and compare against your monthly budgeted amounts.

Monthly Expenses

AUGUST	RENT	FOOD	GAS	UTILITIES	ENTERMT	CREDIT	TELE	MISC
1	$200	$3.25						
2			$5		$5			$5
3		$4.50				$25		
4		$3.75		$25	$10			
5							$20	
6			$5					
7						$ 25		
8					$20			
9								$12
10								
TOTALS	$200	$11.50	$10	$25	$35	$50	$20	$17

Remember, the whole idea of tracking your monthly expenses is to make sure that you stay within your budget. You should continue to review and modify your monthly budget allocations on a monthly basis so that you can continue to make your financial future as profitable as possible.

Step #5: Finally, at the end of the week, you'll want to transfer your weekly expense totals from Step #4, to your Personal Income

Statement under the third column, *Expenses*. At the end of each month, you will then be able to see exactly how much money you spent on each category against your budgeted amounts (see the following chart). Again, the purpose of this Personal Money Management Tool is to help get you in the habit of always staying within your budget. As I mentioned earlier, you can choose to exceed an individual expense category (e.g., spending more than your allotted $100 for food), but then you must also strategically decide to spend less in one or more of the other expense categories, so that you do not exceed your overall monthly expense budget ($572).

Sample Personal Income Statement
The amounts below are fictional, for explanation purposes only, and do not reflect actual costs.

Monthly Income (cash flow)

RADIO STATION	$ 450.00
TELEMARKETING	$ 100.00
TEACH DRUM LESSONS	$ 100.00
TOTAL	**$ 650.00**

Monthly Expenses (spending)

	Budget Allocation (percentages rounded)	Budget Amount	Expenses
RENT	30%	$195.00	$200.00
FOOD	15%	$100.00	$100.00
GAS	5%	$33.00	$25.00
UTILITIES	5%	$33.00	$30.00
ENTERTAINMENT	10%	$65.00	$50.00
CREDIT CARDS	15%	$100.00	$100.00
TELEPHONE	2%	$13.00	$20.00
MISC.	5%	$33.00	$25.00
TOTAL	**87%**	**$572.00**	**$550.00**

The purpose of this exercise is not only to help you learn how to keep track of, and budget your expenses, but also to help you build your awareness to ensure that your future purchase decisions are always strategic ones.

Personal Money Management Tool #2

As I recommended earlier, set aside and deposit 10% (or $0.10 of every dollar) of your monthly income into your personal savings account (e.g., $62.50 per month of your $625 monthly income). The 10% savings is merely a guideline for you to follow so you begin to learn good savings habits. If you can afford to deposit even more than the 10% minimum each month into your savings account, I strongly encourage you to do so if you really want to get a good head start on creating your wealth. And if *that* sounds appealing, then I would like to suggest that you step it up by setting aside 20% (or $0.20) of every dollar of your income. You can incorporate this habit as part of your monthly budget by doing the following:

Consider setting aside the other 10% of your monthly income to go toward your future retirement by depositing the money in either a pre-taxed IRA, or company 401(k) plan. You may also want to consider investing some of your saved money in stocks or electronically traded funds (ETFs) so that you can begin to generate even more passive streams of income (in addition to your earned wages).

For example, publicly traded companies like the Walt Disney Company offer what is called *The Walt Disney Investment Plan* that allows you to directly buy shares of their company's stock each month, without having to utilize either a stockbroker or stock trading account (which saves you on commission fees). In addition, Disney's investment plan offers its investors dividend reinvestment (DRIPS), whereby all the cash dividends that you are entitled to receive as a current shareholder, can be automatically reinvested back into the company in exchange for additional shares of Disney stock. If you are interested in getting more information, you can research this (or other companies that offer similar programs) by either looking up their website(s), or contacting that company's investor relations department directly. (I will briefly discuss more about investments later in this chapter.)

Whichever way you choose to save that additional 10%, consider the 20% that you set aside each month as a bonus or reward you will be giving to your future self for properly and efficiently managing your monthly budgets. In case I haven't quite conveyed it yet, I cannot express to you how disappointed I am that I was never informed, from an early age, that by simply saving 20% ($0.20) from every dollar I received throughout my life, by my 60th birthday, I would have a seriously hefty savings account waiting for me. Once again, you know what's coming...please do not make the same mistakes I did! Start saving now, and it will be yet another positive strategic decision that your future self will thank you for.

Creating Your Personal Balance Sheet (The Tracking of Your Assets and Liabilities)

To the extent that your Personal Income Statement helps you track your monthly income and expenses, your *Personal Balance Sheet* will help you track your overall wealth.

<u>Assets and Liabilities</u> – Similar to the income and expenses on your Personal Income Statement, you have what are called *assets* and *liabilities* on your Personal Balance Sheet. An *asset* is something of value that you own, and if sold would generate income for you in the future. The most obvious asset you could own would be cash because "liquid" money is something that you could immediately use or give away.

Cash aside, there are several other possessions that can be classified as assets, and depending on how easy these items are to acquire or sell, determines the degree to which these assets are considered "liquid." If the asset is easy to acquire or sell, it is considered "very liquid," and if the asset is harder to acquire or sell, it is called, "less liquid." Once again, money/cash is the most liquid asset because money has an immediate value and use.

Below is a list of *assets* that could potentially appear on your Personal Balance Sheet:

Cash—money deposited into personal savings or checking accounts.

Investments—stocks, bonds, certificates of deposit (CDs), mutual funds, IRAs, etc. which are financial instruments that either pay you interest on the money invested, cash dividends for stocks purchased, or they grow in value based upon increases in demand in the stock or bond markets.

Real Estate—land, apartment buildings, commercial property, etc., are each considered an asset (versus a liability, as discussed below) when they are either owned outright (including one's home), or they generate monthly rental income from tenants.*

Intellectual Property—patents, trademarks, and copyrights are registered to protect the creator of intellectual property for their inventions, songs, apps, books, etc. The rightful owner then licenses the use of their work to others in exchange for money initially paid, and from future "royalties."

Collectibles—stamps, coins, fine art (such as paintings, sculptures, etc.), jewelry, baseball cards, dolls, or other items that either retain their value, or increase in value over time ("buy and hold").

Short-term liabilities represent current debt that usually takes more than a month or two to pay off in full (e.g., credit cards, loans, etc.) so they remain on your balance sheet (unlike expenses fluctuating on your Personal Income Statement).

Long-term liabilities are debts that tend to take a lot longer to repay, such a home mortgage (generally 30 years), student loans (10+ years), or a car payment (3 to 5 years). For example, if you buy a car and you incur monthly car payments, then the overall car payment is considered a *liability*. If you charge something on your credit card and do not pay off the entire balance each month, the overall balance is considered a *liability*.

*Although my opinion might not be popular among homeowners, I contend that until either the mortgage is fully paid off, or the house is sold for profit, an "owner occupied" primary house (not a rental property) should be considered a liability. Until that time, I consider the property mortgage payments as liabilities and all costs associated with the ongoing maintenance of the house as either an expense, and/or a liability, depending on how long one has to repay those expenses. That said (my personal opinion on this subject aside), if you wish to consider your home as an invest-ment (e.g., asset) because you truly believe that your property will appreciate in value over time, just keep the following in mind: you can't cash in on that investment until you choose to sell it. So if are looking to purchase a primary home as an investment, then before you buy, you really need to have a clear picture of how long you plan to own that house before you expect to sell it. Be strate-gic and do your homework (planning). Make sure you do your due diligence and research the community, schools, neighborhood, businesses, etc. that could possibly impact the future value of that home. Have a plan!

Sample Personal Balance Sheet

The amounts below are fictional, for explanation purposes only, and do not reflect actual long-term income or expenses.

ASSETS (long-term income)

Cash (savings, checking accts.)	$ 100,000
Investments (stocks, etc.)	$ 100,000
Baseball card collection	$ 10,000
Retirement accounts (401(k), IRA)	$ 200,000
TOTAL ASSETS	**$ 410,000**

LIABILITIES (long-term expenses)

30-year home mortgage	$ 250,000
Car payments	$ 25,000
Student loan payments	$ 25,000
Credit card balances	$ 5,000
TOTAL LIABILITIES	**$ 305,000**

NET WORTH	**$ 105,000**

As you begin to pay off your outstanding long-term expenses each month, you will naturally see a reduction in the amounts stated within the *liability* section of your balance sheet. Likewise, every month when you deposit 10% (or more) of your monthly income into your personal savings account, the asset category *Cash* in your Personal Balance Sheet will increase. Ideally, of course, you always want your assets to go up and your liabilities to go down—this is what generates your positive *net worth*.

Your *net worth* ($105,000) is determined by how much money you would have remaining after you subtracted your *total liabilities* ($305,000) from your *total assets* ($410,000): $410,000 - $305,000 = $105,000.

Based upon the data provided on the Sample Personal Balance Sheet, we can determine that there is a positive net worth because there are more assets ($410,000) than liabilities ($305,000). If the total liabilities were greater than the total assets, then there would be a negative net worth.

How to Strategically Define and Create Your Future Wealth

Based upon the data provided from your Personal Balance Sheet, you can use this information to help you forecast how much wealth you would need to accumulate in order to live the lifestyle that you desire. As we discussed, a person's net worth (positive or negative) is calculated based upon their total assets and liabilities. Therefore, your ultimate goal should be to generate enough monthly *passive income* (profits and interest payments) from your total assets (savings, investments, real estate, etc.) so that you could live off of just that income.

Let's pretend that you wanted to buy a new sports car that costs $50,000. If you were like most people, you would probably need to take out a car loan in order to finance this $50,000, and your monthly car loan payments (paid from your working net income) would also include interest fees that lenders charge you for borrowing their money. Now let me explain how a wealthy person would likely buy this car. Before they even hit the car lot, they would have planned ahead and generated passive income (profits) by investing their working net income, let's say $10,000, to purchase stock in Company XYZ. They would have then waited for the stock's price to rise (as anticipated). Now let's pretend that they waited long enough to be able to sell their $10,000 worth of stock for $100,000, earning them a great profit of $90,000 ($100,000 - $10,000). So instead of having to use their working net income paying off a $50,000 car loan, they would simply purchase it outright using only some of their passive income (the $90,000 profit) generated from selling their XYZ stock.

To summarize, other forms of passive income (profit) that can be generated from your assets include:

- Sale of stock, bonds, mutual funds, etc.
- Stock dividends or interest paid from a bond or CD
- Rent from apartment, house, or commercial business tenants
- Licensing fees for use of a copyright or patent
- Sale of a collectible

This is how a wealthy person thinks:

1. Preserve and use working net income (cash) to make investments that generate passive income.

2. Use passive income (profits) to pay for everything (make purchases, cover monthly overhead, etc).

TIP: Wealthy people generate more assets than liabilities and strategically generate enough passive income from their assets so that they do not need to spend any of their own hard-earned working net income when paying off their monthly expenses or making any big purchases (cars, houses, etc.).

As a result of this mindset, wealthy people continue to grow their net worth because they increase their total assets (cash, investments, etc.), while at the same time, they keep their total liabilities (debt) low.

To help you manage your future wealth, I would like share a simple formula that I often use based upon the data from my Personal Balance Sheet. This formula helps me forecast how much money I believe I would need in order to live the lifestyle that I desire. Similar to many retirement calculations, I based this forecast calculation upon how many days I could potentially live off of solely relying on my passive income (just my positive net worth [total profit from assets]), while also projecting that no paychecks (earned net income) were in my future.

Step 1: Add up all of your current monthly expenses (which would include your monthly mortgage payment, car payment, credit card debt, etc.) so that you can figure out just how much money you would need to cover those expenses in any given month. For the purposes of this example, let's say $10,000 represents your monthly expenses.

Step 2: Divide your monthly expense total ($10,000) by the current positive net worth total ($105,000 from the Sample Balance Sheet): $105,000/$10,000 = 10.5 months.

Conclusion/Outcome: What this calculation is telling you is that if your net worth ($105,000) remained the same, and you continued to pay out $10,000 per month in monthly expenses without receiving any more paychecks (earned income), then you would only be able to live off of your current net worth ($105,000) for another 10.5 months (that's less than a year).

However, if you were to continue to invest your working net income into growing your assets and passive income (through investments) over a longer stretch of time (e.g., growing $410,000 into $1,000,000), while concurrently reducing your monthly expenses ($10,000 or less per month) and total liabilities (down from $305,000), then you would not only continue to grow your overall wealth by increasing your positive net worth, but you would also allow yourself to continue to live off of your positive net worth for even longer.

Welcome back to Personal Finance 101! We just discussed another important aspect of personal finance that you should have been taught in high school—Wealth Creation: Assets versus Liabilities.

This is why it is so important that you learn, from an early age, how to manage your personal finances. The sooner you begin tracking and evaluating your income and expenses on a monthly basis, the sooner you will ensure achieving your desired financial success. The truth of the matter is, the majority of our population tends to live entirely off their weekly or biweekly paychecks because they never learned proper money management. This is especially true during strained economic times, when people often live beyond their means (their income and savings) by resorting to using borrowed money (credit cards, loans, etc.). The unfortunate reality is, if these people just took the time to learn how to properly manage their money, live within their means, and commit to implementing these important concepts and tools I've been sharing with you (i.e., budgeting and reinvesting in their own assets), then they would ultimately empower themselves to turn their financial lives around and increase their own positive net worth.

Lessons to Help You Grow Your Future Wealth

As I discussed earlier, understanding and maintaining your strategic relationship with money is crucial in helping you establish good savings and spending habits that will foster your responsible money management skills. Despite any pressure you may feel from the media to try to "keep up with the Joneses," or any negative influence you may have absorbed from watching others' relationships with money, if you find that you tend to be especially vulnerable to your *wants* versus your *needs*, then you will definitely need to practice disciplined restraint and keep your emotional spending in check to make sure you always live within your financial means.

To help you remain disciplined toward building a solid financial foundation for creating your desired long-term wealth and success, I hope the following three lessons (tools) will help you rethink, and curb, any sabotaging urges you may get to spend on emotional purchases.

1. <u>**Good Savings Habits**</u> – America, unfortunately, tends to be a culture of consumers and spenders. As of May 2009 (following the 2008 financial crisis), the Bureau of Economic Analysis announced that the average personal savings rates among most Americans rose to 6.9% (after-tax income), which was the highest savings rate in over 15 years, but still only about equal to the average personal savings rate of the last 50 years. We need to be honest with ourselves—Americans are not savers!

I recently met with my 27-year-old trainer at the gym, and before my workout we got on the subject of savings and investing. When I asked her if she was able to save 10% of her monthly income, she told me, "No, I just can't do that." I cannot tell you how many times I have heard someone tell me they "can't do it." So I will tell you the exact same thing I told her: "Of course you can—if you chose to make it a priority." I could quickly tell I pushed a button as she tried to mask her frustration, but I continued, "It is totally doable no matter how much someone makes. It really is just about budgeting." I'm not sure if she took my advice to heart because, as it turned out, she quit a week later to work at a job with a steadier paycheck! One of the main reasons why so many people can't seem to save a minimum of 10% of their monthly income is because either they never learned how to, or they simply don't budget their money.

Most people spend their entire monthly net income without tracking their expenses, so they have no idea how much money they are actually spending on the items they're purchasing. It's not because they can't do it—it's simply bad money management. If they knew of, and followed my advice by creating a monthly spending budget (like I showed you), and they simply added a spending category called *10% savings*, it would help facilitate them to allocate and deposit 10% of their monthly net income into their personal savings account. This is where the "totally doable" part comes in, because they would know exactly where they could reduce their other spending categories (food, entertainment, etc.) by the 10% they would need in order to cover their monthly 10% savings deposit. By seeing it all budgeted out, they would know how much they actually spent on each category because they would be tracking all of their expenses, thereby making it very clear which category item could be juggled to balance that 10% savings now in their budget.

What would happen if these same people were to suddenly lose their jobs or have to take an unexpected pay cut? Don't you think they would have to make some type of financial adjustment? Reduce their overall spending in order to stay within their means? Cut back in certain places to help make ends meet? If you think about it, there really is no difference between income loss forcing one to juggle paying for their various expenses, versus one being disciplined about budgeting and allocating 10% of their net income to go toward savings (then juggling their other expenses accordingly). Either scenario (a shortfall in one's expected net income, or one's own decision to put money aside) requires a commitment to making some type of financial adjustment. That being the case, why wouldn't you just give yourself a good head start and practice good money management early on?

As a young wealth creator, you need to start taking responsibility for your financial future now. Because first of all, no one has—or ever will—care more about your money than you do. Secondly, no one knows what the future holds, so without that crystal ball, you'll need to be well-prepared for the unknown. So what do we already know? We know that the Social Security Retirement Trust Fund is expected to run out by 2034. We also know that no one should really rely on their company or country to bail them out or take care of them in their old age. And how does this pertain to you right now? You, as a young adult, have a major advantage going for you: *time!* This is why, starting now, you must promise yourself that you will commit to depositing at least 10% of your monthly income (allowance, salary, or any other monies that you may receive) into your personal savings account (which you should plan to contribute to until retirement).

Costs increasing due to inflation and taxes are inevitable. Which is why you cannot simply sit on your hands and do nothing, yet still expect your net worth to magically grow. Successful people don't do that! They look for opportunities in which they can invest their money in order to generate passive streams of income (profit). Sitting on the sidelines because you have no savings or money to invest during profitable economic times is like being benched during an exciting sporting event—don't bench yourself and watch everyone else profit while you kick yourself for not having heeded this advice. Think of reading this book as getting in on an early opportunity you can take advantage of. If you incorporate the 10% savings as a built-in expense into your monthly budget *now*, taking the 10% from your net income and depositing it into your savings account on a monthly basis should become a regular, lifelong habit. Consequently, your disciplined savings habits (including investments) will generate passive streams of income, allowing you to always be prepared to pounce on the right future wealth opportunities throughout your life.

> **TIP**: If you would like to learn more about good savings habits, George S. Clason's book, *The Richest Man in Babylon*, has a great message to remind you to start saving as soon as you begin earning income. George uses the art of storytelling to help explain all the benefits one gains from saving money. I have read countless self-improvement, business, and finance books, but I truly believe that this book should be required reading in every high school. (In addition to my own, of course!)

2. Understanding Good Debt Versus Bad Debt – Whenever we hear the term *debt,* we usually associate it with negative stereotypes: "He owes a lot of debt," or "She is way over her head in debt." However, most successful wealth creators actually learn how to manage two different types of debt—good debt and bad debt. So that you can get a better understanding of each, let's examine both types of debt in terms of good money management.

If you find yourself either purchasing or acquiring some product/ service that requires you to borrow money from a lender with interest (additional charges), and this product/service never generates any *probable* passive income (profit) for you in the future, that's *bad debt.*

Here's an example: Suppose you are watching late-night TV, and you see a product being sold on an infomercial and in that moment you emotionally decide that you *must* have this product *now.* The only problem is, this "must have" product does not offer a payment plan, and will cost $500 (which you do not currently have). But wait…you *must have it*! So in the heat of the moment, you come up with an easy (emotional) solution to get what you want. You will simply charge this amazing product (on one of your high-interest credit cards) so that there will be no delay in receiving it. When the product arrives a few days later, you get some instant gratification. Then, about a month later, the credit card bill arrives.

Now let's presume, by the time your first credit card statement arrives, you still do not have the full $500 to pay for your "must have" product. As a result, you simply choose to pay only the $25 minimum amount due. Disappointed you don't have enough, you tell yourself, "It's ok, because worst case, I will just continue to pay the minimum $25 payment each month until the entire $500 credit card balance is paid in full." Except (and this is a big EXCEPT) it's not just the minimum $25 that you are going to owe each month, because that would be considered an interest-free loan. Since you could not pay the *entire* $500 balance in full when you received the first bill, the sad truth is, your adjusted balance will become $560. That's because your minimum $25 monthly payments will not simply be applied against just the $500 principal amount you owe, but against your new monthly adjusted balance of $560 ($500 x 12% [.12] = $60), an increase which includes the credit card's 12% compounding interest charge.

The following month, when your next statement arrives with the increased balance, you are both confused and shocked because instead of your overall balance going down to $475 for this "must have" product, the overall balance due has actually gone up to $535 ($560 - $25 minimum payment), an additional $35 more than your original $500 purchase price. In fact, upon receiving subsequent statements, due to the compounding 12% interest rate on the $500 you initially borrowed, you will see your balance continue to go up (as it will include all accrued interest) until it is paid in full.

Now let's take a moment to calculate just how much your "must have" product will actually cost you over the next six months, while paying only the $25 minimum payment (and continuing to incur the 12% monthly compounding interest against the original $500 you borrowed):

Month	Begin Bal.	12% Int.	Adjusted Bal.	Min. $25	End Bal.
1	$500.00	$60.00	$560.00	$25.00	$535.00
2	$535.00	$64.20	$599.20	$25.00	$574.20
3	$574.20	$68.90	$643.10	$25.00	$618.10
4	$618.10	$74.17	$692.28	$25.00	$667.28
5	$667.28	$80.07	$747.35	$25.00	$722.35
6	$722.35	$86.68	$809.03	$25.00	$784.03

Begin Bal. – new balance due at the beginning of each new billing cycle

12% Int. – the 12% compounded interest that is accrued based upon the new beginning balance due each new billing cycle (e.g., the adjusted balance)

Adjusted Bal. – the 12% interest rate that is added to the beginning balance due each month (e.g., the adjusted monthly balance)

Min. $25 – the $25 minimum payment that is remitted (paid) and subtracted from the adjusted monthly balance

End Bal. – the new balance due after the $25 minimum payment is applied against the monthly adjusted balance each billing cycle

"What? $784.03? Are you kidding me?!" If those alarmed questions just ran through your head—good! That's a healthy reaction. This is why making purchases with credit cards is so detrimental to your financial success. There are way too many adults who have been stuck in the vicious cycle of trying to dig themselves out from under their massive credit card debt while doing their best to stave off bankruptcy. Many of whom have no idea how compounding interest really works. Most credit card companies specify in their lending/borrowing agreements that they have the right to charge you a compounded interest rate on your outstanding credit balance each month until the balance is paid in full—with NO caps (limits). Meaning, they will continue to compound that interest and make money off of their suckers—I mean consumers—until they either get all the borrowed money (plus interest) in full, or you, the consumer, defaults and/or goes bankrupt (your account goes to collections). So what percentage can they charge you? Well, credit card companies will charge you whatever interest rate they state in their fine print—basically you are at their mercy, take it or leave it!

Now let's revisit the six-month chart and work through the calculations. During the first month, since you will only be paying the $25 minimum amount due instead of paying the *full outstanding balance*, upon receiving your payment, the credit card company will charge you the contractual 12% compounded interest rate fee. In doing so (to review), your outstanding adjusted balance due at the end of month one will increase from $500 to $535, which includes the 12% interest rate fee of $60 ($500 x .12), less your $25 minimum payment.

During your second monthly billing cycle, you will see that the credit card company went ahead and charged you another 12% interest rate fee on the current adjusted balance due ($535), bringing your newly adjusted outstanding balance up to $599.20 ($535 x .12 = $64.20). After you go ahead and pay your second monthly minimum payment of $25, your new outstanding adjusted balance becomes $574.20 ($599.20 - $25). Now, after two months, that $500 "must have" product is actually costing you an additional $74.20.

During months three through six, as you continue to pay just the $25 minimum amount due, you will continue to be charged the compounded 12% interest rate fees on your outstanding adjusted monthly balances. So that by the end of the sixth month, your total new outstanding adjusted balance will have increased to $784.03. That's $284.03 more than the $500 you initially borrowed from the credit card company! "But wait a second," you say to yourself, "I have been paying $25 every month over the past six months, paying a total of $150 toward that $500 balance! So why did the outstanding balance due continue to go up?" Answer: Expensive <u>compounding</u> interest fees (*bad debt*).

Despite the fact that you had paid that $150 ($25 per month for the past six months) toward your $500 credit card loan, you ended up being gouged by the 12% compounded interest rate your credit card company charged you. And that "must have" product became increasingly expensive as the months progressed.

Conclusion/Outcome: Rather than the product only costing you $500, after six months of accrued credit card interest, this product is now costing you $784.03. Keep this up, and in a few more months, you will actually owe the credit card company more than if you bought two of those "must have" $500 products. And, keep this in mind: the outstanding adjusted balance on the initial $500 borrowed, will only continue to keep going up until you do what? *Pay your balance in full.*

This scenario could have been avoided had you paid off the entire $560 ($500 + $60 [12% interest] = $560) credit balance due when you received your first statement. What? You thought if you paid the balance in full when that first month's bill arrived, then you'd only owe the credit card company your original $500 (and that they loaned you that money for free)? Therein lies the problem with not having bought that "must have" product outright in the first place. Credit card companies have been known to still charge interest regardless of whether or not you pay the entire balance during the first month. But, as I have shown you, if you do pay your entire balance in full, then each month thereafter you would avoid incurring all of the additional compounded interest fees that you would have had to pay on top of the initial sum of money you borrowed.

Here's the lesson to remember: If you must charge any items on credit, then make sure to pay off all outstanding balances the very next month to avoid getting stuck in the expensive cycle of paying the monthly compounded interest fees (and any additional late fees [if you don't make your payments on time]). If you find that you are unable to pay off all of your outstanding balances within a month, that's a sign that you are probably using credit cards as "extended income," and that you should not be using credit whatsoever (especially not for impulsive emotional purchases).

TIP: The next time you feel the urge to make an emotional purchase, just pause…and wait…until you are able to save up all the money you need to purchase that "must have" item. Remember how our grandparents' and great-grandparents' generations did it—earn, save, and *then* buy.

Here are some suggestions to help you avoid other bad debt scenarios. Although the interest fees on college student loans do not get compounded in exactly the same way as credit cards, the federal government will charge you interest on the money you borrow for college. If you do decide to take out student loans to help you pay for your education, then you are going to be expected to begin repaying those loans back to the government once you graduate. The amount of your monthly student loan repayments will be based upon the total amount borrowed, combined with the educational lender's calculated accrued interest, and will be spread out over a predetermined period of time. You *must* pay your student loan back no matter what—there is no option for you to default by declaring bankruptcy (as is generally permissible with credit card debt). If you do fall behind, you will be charged additional penalties on your outstanding past due balance, which will accrue until you catch up on making your regular loan payments. As such, instead of automatically resorting to applying for interest-bearing student loans to finance your college education, you should really try to do your due diligence first by looking into securing full (or at least, partial) scholarships, gifts, or grants. Another option you might want to consider to avoid taking out a student loan (or at least minimize how much you'd have to borrow), is to find a job that will accommodate your courses/homework schedule. As I mentioned earlier, in my case, I worked for the Indiana University Telefund (raising money for the University), the radio stations, and I taught drum lessons to help pay for my continuing education. Now, I realize this final suggestion might be aiming high, but here it is: Invest a portion of your available money (what is left over after you have covered your expenses) in various stocks, bonds, etc. in order to help you generate passive income to pay for your education.

Lastly, for all of you young professionals, keep in mind that if you finance the purchase of an automobile or house, then you will incur interest fees on the money that you borrow (from a bank or lending firm) as part of your monthly automobile or house pay-ment. Therefore, if you must finance such a big ticket item (because you cannot afford to pay for the item out of your own savings or investment profits), then I strongly suggest that you do your price comparison research ahead of time, and make sure you keep your "FICO" credit score high so that you can lock in the lowest possible interest rate with your lenders. By doing your comparison research and staying on top of paying your bills on time, your good money management habits will allow you to negotiate a lower finance rate with your creditors. As a result, your overall purchase price will be considerably lower.

If successful wealth creators and money managers do end up taking out loans for big ticket items, the money they have saved up in their "reserves," along with maintaining a high FICO score, gives them the latitude to negotiate much more favorable terms on their purchases (lower interest rates). They strategically protect their income and profits (passive income derived from investments) by rarely making poor emotional decisions that could force them to borrow money and incur avoidable costly interest payments (bad debt). That's not to say there aren't exceptions where wealthy people will strategi-cally choose to borrow money on which they will owe interest. In these cases, you can be sure the financial benefits are advantageous enough (e.g., tax write-offs, potential to earn passive income, etc.) to justify making a purchase that requires paying interest on bor-rowed money ("good debt," which I will discuss below). However, most often they strategically choose to hold off on making pur-chases of any scale until they can earn enough passive income to purchase the item entirely upfront. They do so because they never want to waste any of their hard-earned net income paying interest on borrowed money, when they can instead, *earn* interest on their own...and *then*, spend *that* money however they see fit.

It may seem inconsistent with what I have just shared with you, but not all interest should be perceived as bad. For example, when you deposit money into your savings account, you are actually the one loaning the bank *your* money and in return, the bank pays *you* interest on that money (albeit at a *much* lower interest rate than the credit card companies would charge you).

Sometimes it's not always considered bad debt to borrow money from a bank, investor, or even a credit card company. But this is *only the case* if you strategically plan to use the borrowed money to purchase things that will ultimately positively affect your bottom line (profits) in the future. This type of debt is usually called *good debt* because the potentially positive outcome is considered great enough that it outweighs the cost of the interest you pay on the borrowed money. For example, if you borrow money by taking out a mortgage to purchase a house, a duplex, an apartment complex, or commercial real estate property in order to charge others rent for their occupancy, then you are using the money as an investment with the end goal being, to generate more revenue (profits) in the long run (e.g., paying the mortgage off in full to own the property outright, while continuing to collect rent as passive income). Other scenarios that could be considered "good debt" are when people borrow money to start a business, or reinvest in growing their business (inventory, supplies, machinery, advertising, development, etc.). However, let me say right here and now, that I highly recommend that you **never** borrow money to invest in the stock market (even if you try to justify it by thinking you can get a return on that investment). Unlike investing in your own business, not only could you lose money in the stock market, but you will still be obligated to pay back the money that you borrowed, *with interest*.

Your Credit (FICO) Score Can Impact Your Ability to Borrow Money

Your ability to manage your credit obligations (good and bad credit) is determined by a score (yes, grading doesn't stop when you get out of school), which is called your *FICO* score. "FICO" is an acronym for the *Fair Isaac Company* which was named after the company that first created and computed this standardized credit score. Before a bank or lending institution decides to lend you money, they will review your FICO score to help them determine just how trustworthy you will be in terms of managing their loaned money and by evaluating how well you manage and repay your other loans (debt). Mortgage (real estate) lenders actually think of it in terms of being an "investor" in you. Are you a sound investment in their eyes? Will you be good at managing their property (finding responsible/respectful tenants, maintaining the property's upkeep, etc.) until you have repaid the loan in full? Each month, lending institutions and credit card companies report your payment history to three different credit rating agencies: Equifax, Experian, and TransUnion. In turn, these three credit rating agencies supply lenders with your FICO score. Your FICO score can range from 300 (poor) to 850 (excellent). When borrowing money to make major purchases (house, car, boat, etc.), the higher your FICO score, the better "deal" a lending institution may offer by giving you a lower interest rate for the life of the loan. The lower your FICO score (the closer you get to 300), the higher credit risk you become to the lenders, thereby diminishing your chances of being offered any credit whatsoever. While you should stay away from using credit to create *bad debt*, you should always stay on top of maintaining a high FICO score in case you ever need to rely on credit to grow your *good debt*. So stay vigilant about protecting your credit score by paying all due balances on your monthly credit card and loan statements, *by* their stated due date.

> **TIP:** Make sure your payments are mailed (or submitted online) early enough for your creditors to process and credit your account *on,* or *before,* their actual due dates.

So what makes up your FICO score?

- 35% of your score is related to your current, and past, *payment history* (do you pay your bills timely or late?)

- 30% of your score is related to your *outstanding debt* (your total liabilities/how much overall debt you owe)

- 15% of your score is related to your *length of credit history* (how long you have been managing your various credit debts and payments—the longer, the better)

- 10% of your score is related to your *new credit* (how recently and how often you have applied for, or acquired, new credit or loans)

- 10% of your score is related to the various *types of credit* you carry (credit cards, car payments, mortgage [house payment], loans, etc.)

Here are some tips to help you manage your credit or loan payments:

Create a calendar alert or buy yourself a monthly planner or wall calendar so that you can write the full, or minimum amounts due, as well as the due dates owed to each company. This will ensure that you don't miss your monthly payment. For example: $25 due to MasterCard on August 14th.

As I mentioned, it is crucial that you maintain a high FICO score to obtain lower interest rates on borrowed money. So make sure you always get your payments credited to your account by the stated due date. Each month your bill arrives, make sure you pay careful attention to the actual due dates printed on the statement as these dates may fluctuate. Credit card bills are due every 30 days from the billing cycle date—not necessarily the same date each month (based upon their 30-day billing cycle contractual fine print). You need to leave a cushion of time to ensure that your check arrives, and gets posted (credited) to your account before the due date. Do not wait until the last minute to make your payment! Mail your payment *at least seven days before your payment is due*, because you do not want to end up getting penalized for your payment posting late due to the lender's collections department or USPS dropping the ball.

Of course, instead of mailing in your payment, you can pay your bills online. If you do choose this option, your bank's checking account bill pay system usually shows how many days it will take for that particular recipient to receive your payment, so make sure you have set it up to arrive at least two days before your statement's printed due date. Either way you choose to get your payment to your creditor or lender, just make sure it gets there by the due date because if it doesn't, it will very likely result in either late fees, penalties, or even dings to your credit report (FICO score). And if you're curious about potential late payment consequences, it's all there for you to read in your agreement's fine print.

Finally, to help ensure that your credit is monitored and protected from identity theft, I strongly encourage you to sign up for a reputable credit protection service. Most credit protection companies will charge you either a monthly, or an annual fee, to alert you of any positive and/or negative changes that may appear on any of your credit accounts or your credit reports, as well as notifying you of any fraud alerts or changes to your FICO score.

3. Positive Spending Habits – The last wealth creation technique I would like to cover is positive spending habits. Sadly, many older adults have never learned how to (or choose not to) budget and track their income and expenses, and often find themselves in financial chaos because they spend their hard-earned money with the intensity of an addict. This compulsive spending problem is why I believe so many adults between the ages of 40 - 60 are suffering from financial obesity. Just as overeaters don't manage their food intake, many of these financially obese people live *way* beyond their means and don't manage their money. As a result, their financial woes are often magnified by their habitual use of credit cards to extend their income, while they use shopping as a crutch to avoid their negative feelings of unhappiness and low self-esteem. Some "shopaholics" even go so far as to justify their behavior by convincing themselves or others that they are just "doing their part for the economy," or they're adamant that they "need," or "must have" that particular item to make things easier for themselves or their families. Unfortunately, just as with any other type of addiction, once they get what they want (no matter what, or how much it may cost them personally or financially), they still feel emotionally unsatisfied. So they continue to spin in their own vicious cycle of self-sabotage by spending and charging themselves into even deeper debt.

If any of this is ringing true with you, don't be fooled into thinking that just because you are young and may earn more money down the road, this somehow gives you a free pass to be any less focused on how you manage and spend your money now, versus later in life. Trust me when I tell you, your future money problems will definitely not go away once you add some extra zeros to the end of your income (e.g., $50,000 becomes $100,000) unless you learn how to incorporate positive spending habits and good money management into your overall wealth creation strategies. In fact, if you are not careful, those extra zeros at the end of your income may also lead to extra zeros at the end of your overall debt.

I'd like to share one final anecdote to accentuate this point: Don't fool yourself into believing that someone is immune to debt simply because they choose to work in a profession that makes a lot of money. Citing more than $10 million in tax debt, a famous multiple Grammy Award-winning singer had to file for bankruptcy at the age of 72. It was reported that at the time of her bankruptcy filing, she was down to her last $1,000 in cash, and all her worldly possessions (furniture, clothing, etc.) were assessed to be worth only $1,500. When asked why she needed to file for bankruptcy, she claimed that her financial chaos was due to several consecutive years of grossly negligent financial management. Unfortunately, this singer made the serious mistake of trusting her team of professionals (managers, accountants, and lawyers) whom she had paid to handle her financial interests without having any controls in place to make sure they were doing right by her. Her ignorance cost her her life's savings. Do you think this singer would have experienced this same financial ruin if she had just learned how to budget and track her own income and expenses so she could have overseen her own financial wealth?

The good news is, financial obesity is avoidable and reversible if you choose to acknowledge that your bad debt and previous overspending habits are problematic and detrimental to your overall financial success. And if you are also committed to begin making good strategic (not emotional) decisions that promote good savings and positive spending habits. As a future wealth creator, purchasing products or services on credit while not having the cash flow to pay back the borrowed money in a timely manner (while at the same time possibly incurring hundreds, or even thousands, of dollars in interest payments) will *not* help you grow your net worth and achieve the financial success you desire. As you start training yourself to build positive spending habits, you must pay close attention to removing all emotions from the equation so that you always think strategically before you ever open your wallet and reach for your cash or credit cards (or if you're shopping online, hitting that "buy it now" button linked to your credit or PayPal account). And most importantly, never succumb to manipulative sales techniques that try to pressure you into making an emotional purchase. If anyone ever pushes to sell you something (in a store, over the phone, or through advertising) that seems too good to be true, or the next time you feel the impulse to buy something without first doing your research and/or strategically weighing your options—stop! Take a moment to pause...think...and trust your instincts because if you feel any hesitation whatsoever, you can bet that your impulsive "must have" purchase will most likely never benefit you in the long run.

To develop these crucial habits to always live within your financial means, I have designed the following questions to help you make good strategic purchasing decisions while keeping your emotional spending in check.

1. What is the probability that my purchasing decision will lead to a successful outcome, and how will this product or service get me any closer to achieving my overall goal(s)? This would be a good time to step back and honestly ask yourself if purchasing this product or service would really be a good strategic decision, rather than it just being an emotionally-driven purchase to satisfy your need for instant gratification, or to please someone else.

2. How do I hope to ultimately benefit from this purchase? Do not allow yourself to feel guilty or manipulated into making any purchases that you may later regret. If you are not sure how that product or service can immediately benefit you personally and/ or professionally, go ahead and sleep on it—don't rush your deci-sions. Always remember that if something is too good to be true, it usually is.

3. How long do I plan to use this product or service before it becomes obsolete? Is there a predetermined time limit on how long you can utilize this product or service? What is your exit strategy if this purchase does not deliver the results that you had anticipated when you made your intentional decision to purchase it?

4. What additional opportunities will this purchase provide for me? What reaction are you hoping to solicit from others or how will you benefit/gain from purchasing this product or service?

5. What would happen if I chose to wait another two to six months until I could truly afford to make this purchase without having to borrow any money? Would you really miss some important opportunity, or does it make more sense for you to not go into debt by borrowing money (credit or loan) at this time? What consequence(s) would there be if you just gave yourself more time to simply pause and sleep on it?

Just as with all important life decisions, by continuing to ask yourself "why" when choosing to make future purchasing decisions, you will not only be developing new positive spending habits, but you will also be helping ensure that your decisions align with your intentions and desired outcomes.

> **TIP**: As you embark on your new money management and positive spending strategies, my advice is for you to pick someone close to you, whom you trust (parent, relative, mentor, spouse, significant other, etc.), to meet with you on a weekly or monthly basis to help you review your monthly budget and savings plans so that, like a gym buddy/partner, they can help support you to stay motivated, focused, and hold you accountable as you develop your new personal finance habits for success.

Unleash Your Successful Wealth Creator

WEALTH GENERATION MODEL (Improving your net worth)

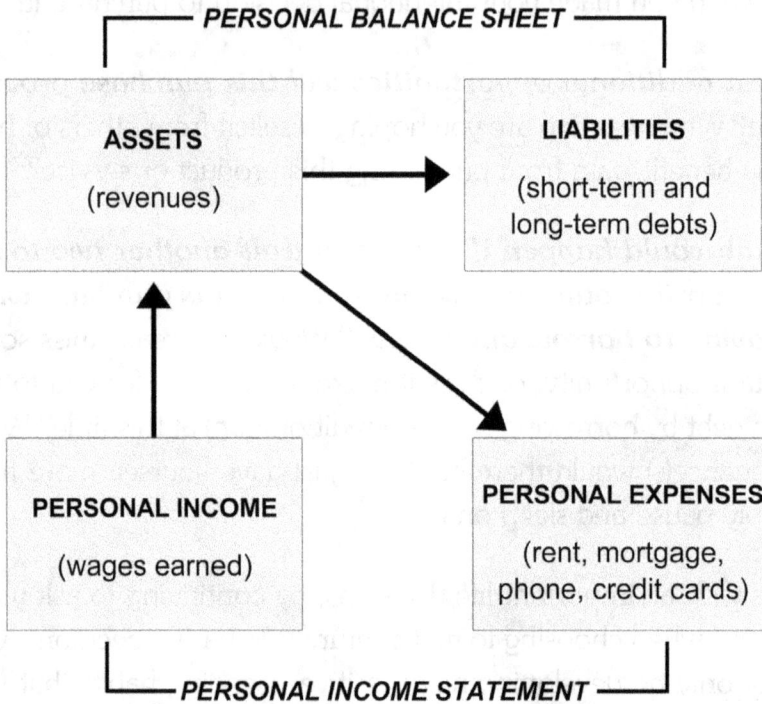

```
┌──────── PERSONAL BALANCE SHEET ────────┐

  ┌─────────────────┐        ┌─────────────────┐
  │     ASSETS      │───────▶│   LIABILITIES   │
  │   (revenues)    │        │  (short-term and│
  │                 │        │  long-term debts)│
  └─────────────────┘        └─────────────────┘
        ▲          ╲
        │           ╲
        │            ▼
  ┌─────────────────┐        ┌─────────────────┐
  │ PERSONAL INCOME │        │PERSONAL EXPENSES│
  │  (wages earned) │        │ (rent, mortgage,│
  │                 │        │ phone, credit cards)│
  └─────────────────┘        └─────────────────┘

  └──── PERSONAL INCOME STATEMENT ────┘
```

As the *Wealth Generation Model* illustrates, your personal income (paychecks, allowances, etc.) should not only be used to pay your bills, but you should strive for allotting at least 20% of your income toward investing in assets (personal savings, stocks, real estate, collectibles, etc.). That way, the potential profits gained from your investments can be used to not only pay for your monthly expenses, but also for any future purchases (houses, cars, etc.).

Below, is a brief breakdown to help you summarize and review some of the financial educational gaps we have discussed:

1. Create a Personal Income Statement so you can begin to budget and track your personal income and your monthly expenses.

Good debt management and positive spending habits will not only help you to reduce your personal liabilities and monthly expenses, but will also help you to increase the amount of personal earned net income you will be able to invest in future assets.

2. *Practice good savings habits* from an early age. This is the foundation on which you will build your net worth. This habit will not only help you to generate more passive income, but if you also continue to make positive strategic decisions (personal and professional) in your life, then you'll be in a much better position to take advantage of all the right opportunities as they arise. You should also start consistently depositing *at least* 10% of your earned net income into a savings account as soon as possible so that you provide yourself with a financial cushion of protection should you ever experience a temporary loss of earned net income.

3. *Create a Personal Balance Sheet* to help you manage your assets and liabilities in order to grow your net worth, financial wealth, and success. Wealthy people invest their earned and saved net income into profit-generating assets, and then use that passive income to cover their liabilities and monthly expenses.

Will You Be Able to Ride Off into the Sunset?

I could not close out this chapter on personal finance without at least touching upon the importance of starting to think about, from an early age, how to plan for retirement. You may think you have a lot of time ahead of you before you need to start planning and worrying about your retirement. But don't kid yourself—in a world of constant change and uncertainty, it is never too early to start.

In fact, a couple of months ago, I was having lunch at one of my favorite hideaways in downtown Los Angeles, and I got into a discussion with two guys in their late 20s about their frustrations regarding their reduced salaries, compared to the salaries earned by their professional predecessors 10 years earlier. Among their frustrations, they talked about the lack of financing available to purchase a starter home, their mistrust of the stock market (and investing in general [other than real estate]), and most importantly, shared their fears that they may be the first generation that will be less well-off than their parents' generation.

Is it any real surprise that today's twenty-somethings are concerned about their retirement options? An article called, "Why Even 20-Somethings are Worried About Retirement," in which the writer, Jennifer Leigh Parker, interviewed a 29-year-old web manager at a design firm in San Francisco who said, "My dad would love to retire at 65, but he's putting it off because of the swings in the aviation business." Later in the article, Parker went on to cite a study by State Street Global Advisors showing that adults in their late 30s and 40s are not nearly as prepared for retirement as the generation that preceded them. Moreover, despite their awareness of this issue, it still is not translating into enough concern to see those adults taking any appropriate action to help change their outcome.

Today's 20-year-olds (the "Millennials" or "Gen Y") have suffered through the economic and financial changes that forced many older adults to delay their plans for retirement (because they had not saved up enough for their futures). Cindy Perman made this observation in her CNBC article entitled, "Gen Y and Retirement: Are Young People Saving?" She went on to write that despite living through these financial hardships and witnessing how financially ill-prepared the older generations have become, according to a retirement survey by the brokerage firm Stocktrade, more than half (55%) of Gen Y (those born between the early 1980s through the early 2000s) have not even started to begin saving for their retirement, and 64% of those surveyed, said they don't even think about it. In her article, Perman cited this claim made by a spokesperson for Scottrade: "Of all the non-retired generations, including Baby Boomers and Gen X, Gen Y is the leader in not saving. We call them Generation Procrastination!"

I must say, I respectfully disagree with this spokesperson. Because if Gen Y's members were really the *leading* procrastinators, then why are so many adults between the ages of 40 to 60 in such financial turmoil? Just like so many younger adults, many of today's middle-aged adults also lack the focus and financial knowledge to help them budget, save, and plan for their retirement as well.

Since it is never too early to kick-start your retirement planning, I would like to share five basic tips to help you begin thinking about saving for your retirement:

1. Start saving a percentage of your monthly income in a personal savings account (preferably at least 10%). As we have been discussing, this money should only be used for emergencies, or for opportunities to generate new passive income streams that can lead to greater profits and revenue. And remember, this is your *savings* account and not an extension of your checking account. Resist the temptation to treat it like an ATM—leave it alone and let it continue to grow.

2. Create and manage a monthly spending budget. Learning to live within your means is crucial to prepare you for your retirement. The money you begin saving and growing for retirement should last you a long time (*how* long is dependant upon your life expectancy). Learning to budget and manage your money, from an early age, will help ensure that you have enough money on which to live throughout all of your retirement years.

3. Begin contributing to your company's 401(k) program, or open a standard or Roth IRA. Not only are these plans tax-deferred, but if invested properly, they will grow over time by compounding your annual rate of return. There are various financial retirement calculators that you can find online and based on your savings, they'll help you determine your desired compounded annual rate of return based upon your current income and age, projected retirement age, and the projected retirement income you hope to live off of. The earlier you start planning, the more opportunity you will give your retirement money to grow over time. Don't let the decades fly by (and ask any elderly person, they DO!) and wake up one day wishing you had been more prepared for retirement. But before you start making any contributions, do your research and weigh all of your options (speak with your company's benefits department or a certified financial planner) so you can decide on the route that best aligns with your retirement goals.

4. *Always live within your means.* Make sure to pay off all of your credit card balances on time, and do not incur any large balances that require you to pay a lot of interest (additional fees) on your purchases. If you cannot afford to pay off your entire credit card balance within a month or two of your purchase, then consider delaying your purchase until you can afford to cover your expenses. As we discussed, it is really important to live within your means and protect your credit score, as your good money management will impact your ability to borrow money in the future.

5. *Take preventive measures.* Eat healthily and exercise regularly so that you can avoid any serious or major medical expenses that can either exhaust your retirement savings, or derail your retirement plans altogether. Ultimately, if you don't have your good health, you are missing out on one of your greatest assets.

> **TIP**: By learning how to become financially literate from an early age, you will establish successful, lifelong, wealth-generating habits to help enable you to retire down the road comfortably, confidently, and with peace of mind.

In the fall of 1986, as a young graduate student at Indiana University, I remembered having a pivotal moment one night with some friends at a local music club when, out of the blue, I loudly proclaimed, "I am going to be a millionaire by the time I am 30 years old!" I can still recall how confident I felt when I made that bold statement, and how determined I was to see this dream (not goal) come to fruition. Shortly following that outburst, despite all the confidence, energy, and passion I had for my so-called dream, as a 23-year-old young adult, I remember feeling helpless and confused when I wondered how in the world I was going to generate that amount of money ($1 million) in just seven short years. Instead of focusing on creating a wealth-building strategy, or seeking out the advice and counsel of others (as we have been discussing in this book), I just proceeded to work hard and thoughtlessly spend the net income I had earned from working my various jobs while attending Indiana University. It didn't even occur to me to save or invest any of that net income in wealth-generating assets. Fast forward three years from then: I was 26 years old, I had just moved to Los Angeles, California to pursue a career in the music industry, and I was just four years away from my million-dollar payoff—right? Wrong! Upon my arrival in Los Angeles, I still did not have a wealth creation model, or a financial mentor. And so, by the age of 31 (one year past my so-called millionaire dream age), I still had no clue about how to generate true wealth. So once again, I find myself compelled to reiterate: Please learn from my mistakes and take these hard-earned lessons I've shared here with you, and run with them to start growing your success today.

Congratulations! With all of the financial information and tools you now possess, you can start taking the appropriate steps toward establishing new ways to enhance your own financial knowledge and confidence to become the great wealth creator you are meant to be! Therefore, your next goal should be to patiently commit whatever time is necessary in order for you to understand and adopt all of the positive financial habits that I have shared here with you. By staying focused, committed, and disciplined, you will be able to work through all of the financial information, tools, guidelines, and Calls to Action provided for you in this chapter. In doing so, you will be setting yourself up to achieve the wealthy financial future you desire.

Call to Action

Over the next three months, complete the following steps and then incorporate them as part of your continual monthly financial planning.

Month 1

Begin tracking all of your daily expenses by date, payee, amount, and expense category in your notebook or handheld device. For example:

DATE	PAYEE	AMOUNT	CATEGORY
8/1/2013	McDonald's	$ 3.25	Food
8/13/2013	Unocal 76	$ 20.00	Gas

Then on a weekly basis, transfer that information to your monthly spending chart. For example:

AUGUST	RENT	FOOD	GAS	ENTERMT	UTIL	MISC
1	$200.00	$3.25				
2			$5.00	$5.00		$5.00
3		$4.50			$20.00	

Additionally, compile all of your current assets and liabilities so you can apply that information to your Personal Balance Sheet. For example:

Assets
    Cash (savings, checking accounts): $
    Investments (stocks, CDs): $
    Collectibles (stamps, baseball cards, jewelry): $
    Retirement accounts (401(k), IRA): $

Liabilities

Home mortgage: $

Car payments: $

Student loans: $

Credit card totals: $

You should also organize your credit cards by interest rates so that you know your potential risk for borrowing against all of your credit cards. For example:

MasterCard #1: 16% annual percentage rate (APR)

Visa #1: 13% APR

MasterCard #2: 12% APR

Visa #2: 11% APR

To calculate your monthly credit risk, multiply your total balance due, by the credit card interest rate (example: $500 x .12).

Month 2

Based upon the monthly spending totals that you tracked and compiled (by category) during your first month, create a monthly spending budget with your budget allocation percentages. For example:

MONTHLY EXPENSES (spending):

	Budget Allocation	Budget Amount
RENT	30%	$ 195.00
FOOD	15%	$ 100.00
GAS	5%	$ 33.00

You should continue to track your monthly expenses as you did during the first month, but manage your spending so that you stay within your monthly budget allocations (example: food $100).

Month 3

Now adjust your monthly budget allocation amounts/percentages to include an expense category called *10% savings*. Then, by reducing or adjusting your other spending categories, you can begin making and tracking your monthly 10% cash deposits into your personal savings account (if you have not already begun doing so).

Continue to save and track your budget on a monthly basis until you decide to make any further adjustments. Your goal will be to stay within your monthly budget, and to make your monthly 10% cash deposits into your personal savings account.

If applicable, update your monthly balance sheet's asset and liability totals, and calculate how long you could live off of your current net worth if you stopped receiving weekly or biweekly earned income.

Step 1:

After you have updated your current assets and liabilities, and have determined your current net worth, add up all of your current monthly expenses so that you can figure out just how much money you would need to have in order to cover them by using only your current net worth in any given month.

Step 2:

1. Divide your monthly expense amount by your current net worth (found on your Personal Balance Sheet) to determine how many months you could live off of your current net worth.

2. In addition to continuing to track and manage your monthly budget and expenses, making your 10% monthly savings deposits, adjusting your monthly asset and liability totals, and calculating your net worth on a quarterly basis (every three months), you should also do the following:

    a. You should look into contributing a portion of your gross (pre-tax) earned income into your company's 401(k), or a standard or Roth IRA, so that you can begin compounding your annual rate of return for retirement as soon as possible.

b. Consider investing in stocks or a company's direct purchase/ investment program (but only if you can afford to risk that money in the stock market) by directly contacting the company's investor relations department or a local brokerage firm. Start researching how you can begin generating passive income so that you can continue to increase your overall net worth.

3. To help you start developing positive spending habits, before you decide to make any new purchasing decisions, I would like you to ask yourself the following five questions (which I introduced earlier in this chapter). For the next few months (until this process becomes second nature), in your separate notebook, write down your answers to the following questions so that you can evaluate how, and why, you strategically came up with your decisions to buy a certain product or to utilize a certain service.

1. What is the probability that my purchasing decision will lead to a successful outcome, and how will this product or service get me any closer to achieving my overall goal(s)?

_____

_____

_____

_____

2. How do I hope to ultimately benefit from this purchase?

_____

_____

_____

_____

3. How long do I plan to use this product or service before it becomes obsolete?

_____

_____

_____

4. What additional opportunities will this purchase provide for me?

_____

_____

_____

5. What would happen if I chose to wait another two to six months until I could truly afford to make this purchase without having to borrow any money?

_____

_____

_____

_____

"Accept responsibility for your life. Know that it is you who will get you where you want to go, no one else."

~ Les Brown (motivational speaker)

9
Epilogue

YOU DID IT! By your commitment and dedication to reading this book, working through all of the Calls to Action, and being brave enough to live up to your true potential, you have taken the important first steps toward learning how to achieve your desired goals for lifelong success. Moreover, your time was well-spent here because, as you've read, my approach in helping demystify success for you made this far from a superficial "just dream and feel good" book. As I have made it abundantly clear, since I had to learn these lessons and insights the hard (and expensive!) way, I was compelled to share these success tools and secrets with you in order to give you the successful jumpstart I wish someone had given to me when I was growing up. Because, unfortunately, they just don't teach this stuff in high school! Thank you for investing in yourself to do what's necessary to attain what you really desire in life by working hard, practicing patience, and staying dedicated to seeing your goals through to completion. I truly hope that by incorporating these guidelines, tips, and tools into your daily habits, you will be aligning yourself to live the life you really want. So always remember to pause—make strategic decisions, plan, and then take action to achieve the successful outcomes you desire.

To help you take immediate action toward achieving your goals, here's a quick recap of the guidelines, concepts, tips, and tools you've learned in this book:

- You now understand the importance of heightening your *awareness* through your journey of self-discovery, which will enhance your ability to spot opportunities and increase your odds for success.

- Despite any negative misinformation you might have unintentionally been told from parents, teachers, or friends, you will no longer allow *fear* to prevent you from pursuing your passions and goals.

- By getting in touch with, and staying true to your own *core values and beliefs*, you will find and grow happiness within yourself. As you build up your self-esteem, while continuing to enhance your authentic personal brand, you will be much more inclined to align with people who share your values and with whom you can build healthy and mutually supportive relationships.

- As you begin to *manage your time* more efficiently, you will become more productive when completing your action steps toward attaining your desired goals, leaving you more free time to pursue your other interests.

- Once you truly begin to *change your thoughts*, your *actions* will follow suit, and you will attract and manifest positive opportunities, which will ultimately change your outcomes in life.

- By aligning your *knowledge, talents, and strengths* with your desired *intentions*, you will learn *why* your actions ultimately drive you to make better *decisions*, which will lead to more *probable* outcomes for success.

- As a true *wealth creator*, you now possess real-world financial knowledge that will help you to create the wealth you desire, while at the same time, it will also help you to avoid the financial pitfalls that have paralyzed and plagued so many of today's adults between the ages of 40 to 60.

I am extremely confident that if you choose to continue utilizing the information in this book over and over (and over!) again, you will soon discover that with each reread, you will not only be reinforcing what you've already learned, but you will also discover new ideas that you can continue to build upon.

For anyone who has truly accomplished something important in their life, they had to realize early on, that success is something that does not come quickly. Success is, rather, something that has to be cultivated through a lot of commitment, perseverance, patience, and hard work. For me, that hard work started with a simple question, "So, how's that life working for you?" There is no better time than NOW for you to take action and begin (or reclaim) cultivating your own success.

Where Do You Begin?

One of the hardest, yet most enlightening, moments in a person's life, is when they finally decide to leave their unhealthy comfort zone and change the things in their life that no longer work. I define this "a-ha moment" as taking complete ownership of your life and your desired outcomes for success.

By analyzing your responses to all the Calls to Action, and the insights that you learned in this book, you will fine-tune your goals so that you can realign them with your *probable* outcomes for success.

Make the commitment *now* to start addressing your fears and to begin creating the life you ultimately desire.

Embrace the "Why?"

For the past couple of years, I have been spreading my message that success is all about never being afraid to ask, "*Why?*"

As I mentioned earlier, most toddlers repeatedly test their parents' patience by constantly asking, "Why? Why? Why?" By the time these young, inquisitive children enter their formative teenage years, they have all but lost their ability to ask *why* because most people today simply live life in a world of *how*. "Just tell me *how* to get the job," or "*How* should I do this to your satisfaction?" There is no creativity in living by the word, "*How*," as it epitomizes following the status quo!

My belief is that young people have simply become afraid to ask "Why?" because they are worried about being perceived as stupid by their elders, peers, or even worse, a parent, teacher, or someone else they look up to. Perhaps one of those people even shamed them into being afraid to ask *why* because they themselves could not answer that "Why?" question. So instead of admitting that they didn't know the answer, and fearing that would make them look silly or stupid, they brushed the inquisitive one off to save face. Most theoretical-thinking young adults are becoming the minority in our society due to the mass suppression of the "Why?" And since questioning the status quo is necessary in order to grow and improve, this detrimental trend desperately needs to change so our society can smoothly progress into the future. <u>You</u> can be that change.

Theoretical thinking allows us to understand not only *how*, but *why*, we do things. It allows us to think creatively to either problem-solve a situation, or improve upon something that has simply "always been done that way." In my humble experience, truly successful people always go the extra mile to figure out the *why* because it provides them with the ammunition to consistently attain their success. Once you understand the *why*, you can improve upon any idea, continue to innovate during changing times, or more importantly, know when to move on from something that no longer works or has become obsolete.

This is why I strongly believe that in order for you to really achieve your success, you will not only need to learn *how* to get good at something, but *why* you should make the effort to do so. I can pretty much guarantee you that any highly successful person you meet will have already figured out not only *what* they wanted to do, but *why* they wanted to do it. By simply committing yourself to embracing the *why*, you will greatly enhance your outcomes for success.

"Successful and unsuccessful people do not vary greatly in their abilities. They vary in their desires to reach their potential." *~ John Maxwell*

T.I.M.E. for Success

Throughout this book, I have provided you with compelling theoretical and practical knowledge to help you demystify and reinforce why it is now T.I.M.E. (Timing, Intentions, Motivation, and Empowerment) for success.

Timing is all about identifying your opportunities. To become successful, you need to continue to enhance your awareness so you can spot opportunities that may directly, or indirectly, align with your chosen path. To ensure that you always take advantage of such opportunities, you need to take the time to really focus on what you want to accomplish in both the short-term and in the long-term. Recognizing your passions, desires, and goals, from an early age, will definitely help align you with your potential opportunities for success.

Intentions help you reinforce *why* you are driven to pursue your passions, desires, and goals (which also reaffirms your ability to spot the opportunities that offer the highest *probable* outcome for success whenever they arise). Again, delving into exploring the *why* empowers you with the confidence and creativity to go beyond simply understanding the *how*. Truly successful people always go the extra mile to figure out *why*, so they can consistently recreate their successes over and over again.

Motivation is the action behind your success. It is the process of aligning your internal passions, desires, and goals with your external resources (mentors, knowledge, financing, etc.) in order to achieve your desired outcomes. Many successful people create their own masterminds and surround themselves with a circle of trusted people who can provide them with advice, support, and sometimes even financial resources to help them achieve their success. When you establish your own circle of trusted advisors, your mastermind should consist of people who will not only serve as excellent role models, but they should also be willing to help bolster your success by serving as sounding boards, sharing their contacts, information, advice, etc.

Empowerment embodies your ability to confidently trust your instincts, and your strategic decision-making abilities, which ensure a higher *probability* that you will achieve your desired outcomes for success. People who have not yet attained their sense of empowerment, frequently allow others to "get inside their heads" and become swayed by their (forecasted and often, unsolicited) negative or unsupportive input. Instead of heeding their own good instincts, they discount themselves by allowing those disapproving opinions to influence them in rethinking their strategic decisions. And unfortunately, at their own expense, they rarely proceed as they had initially intended in an attempt to appease the other person.

"We all have dreams. But in order to make dreams come into reality, it takes an awful lot of determination, dedication, self-discipline, and effort." ~ Jesse Owens

Invest in Yourself

- Manage your fears and emotions.

- Become aware of your core values and beliefs.

- Create your vision, mission, and goals.

- Make strategic decisions, plan, and take action on *probable*, versus possible, outcomes for success.

- Practice good money management. Save at least 10% of your income, manage your spending, and continually invest in your assets to grow your passive income and net worth.

- Revisit your responses to the Calls to Action so that you can immediately begin to effectively accomplish each of your desired outcomes. Review your responses on a regular basis, and revise as needed.

- Reread this book as needed!

Now go use the lessons, secrets, and tools in this book to help you spot your opportunities, reaffirm your intentions, motivate and empower yourself to take action, think and plan strategically, and always make decisions that best align with your core values and goals for personal and financial success!

Again, as you well know by now, I chose to write this book to demystify your success because I really wanted to provide you with the same knowledge I wished someone had shared with *me* back when I was in high school. Now one day when someone asks you, "So, how's that life working for you?" you can confidently smile, and say, "AMAZING!"

NO EXCUSES, just go for it!

I wish you huge success in all your future endeavors and all the best in life.

Appendix

THE FOUR QUADRANTS FOR LIFE BALANCE

1. PHYSICAL

2. EMOTIONAL/
   SPIRITUAL

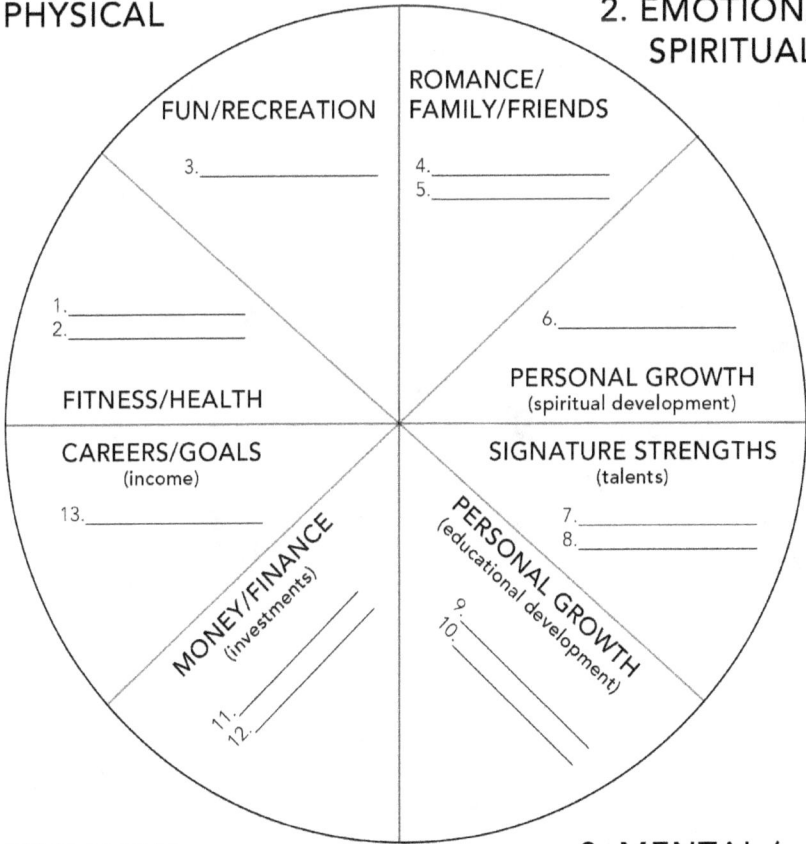

ROMANCE/
FUN/RECREATION   FAMILY/FRIENDS

3._____   4._____
                 5._____

1._____
2._____   6._____

FITNESS/HEALTH   PERSONAL GROWTH
                                 (spiritual development)

CAREERS/GOALS   SIGNATURE STRENGTHS
(income)   (talents)

13._____   7._____
                                 8._____

MONEY/FINANCE   PERSONAL GROWTH
(investments)   (educational development)

11._____   9._____
12._____   10._____

4. FINANCIAL

3. MENTAL/
   EDUCATIONAL

MONTHLY EXPENSES

MONTH	RENT	FOOD	GAS	CAR	TRANSPORTATION	UTILITIES	ENTERMT	CABLE	CREDIT CARDS	TELE OR CELL	MISC
1											
2											
3											
4											
5											
6											
7											
8											
9											
10											
11											
12											
13											
14											
15											
16											
17											
18											
19											
20											
21											
22											
23											
24											
25											
26											
27											
28											
29											
30											
31											
TOTALS											

About the Author

Larry M. Jacobson understands what it takes to inspire today's young adults, as well as adults of all ages, to achieve the success they desire. As an authentic and dynamic speaker, he has spoken at major colleges and universities and has been a featured guest on several radio and podcast programs. A strong advocate for self-improvement, Larry earned both an MBA and doctor of education degree in organizational leadership while he served as an executive for one of the world's largest music and publishing companies. He continues to empower others to pursue solid financial habits and concrete personal goals/plans while inspiring them to grow their own success. He is currently a Professional Options Trader and ProActive Investor (wealth investment) Instructor for Online Trading Academy, and resides in Los Angeles with his wife, Kate.

INVEST IN THESE OTHER INTERNATIONAL BESTSELLERS

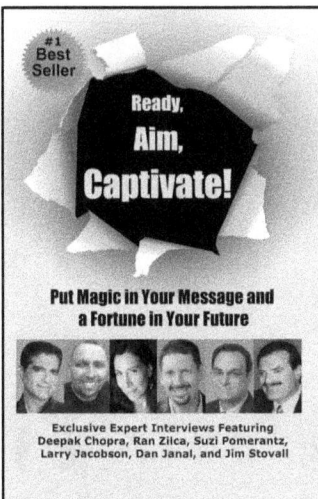

Please visit www.LarryMJacobson.com to learn more about these best-selling titles. You can also sign up on the website to receive the latest information about upcoming events and products, as well as bonus extras.

www.ingramcontent.com/pod-product-compliance
Lightning Source LLC
Chambersburg PA
CBHW070800280326
41934CB00012B/2995